# Sentiment and Self

Portrait of Richard Blechynden
*Courtesy of Gerald Johnson Fox*

*Sentiment and Self*

# Richard Blechynden's Calcutta Diaries, 1791–1822

Peter Robb

OXFORD
UNIVERSITY PRESS

OXFORD
UNIVERSITY PRESS

Oxford University Press is a department of the University of Oxford.
It furthers the University's objective of excellence in research, scholarship,
and education by publishing worldwide. Oxford is a registered trademark of
Oxford University Press in the UK and in certain other countries

Published in India by
Oxford University Press
YMCA Library Building, 1 Jai Singh Road, New Delhi 110 001, India

ISBN-13: 978-0-19-807512-7
ISBN-10: 0-19-807512-X

Typeset in 10/12 Horley Old Style MT Std
By Excellent Laser Typesetters, Pitampura, Delhi 110 034
Printed in India at De Unique, New Delhi 110 018

*For*
*Charlie, Anna, Jenny,*
*Luke, and Timothy*

**Self**   that which in a person is really and intrinsically *he* (1674); an assemblage of characteristics and dispositions which may be conceived as constituting one of various conflicting personalities within a human being (1595).

**Sense**   the perceptive faculty (1585); natural understanding, intelligence, esp. as bearing on action or behaviour; practical soundness of judgement (1684); what is wise or reasonable (1600).

**Sentiment**   sensation, physical feeling (1829); mental attitude (or approval or disapproval etc.); an opinion or view of what is right or agreeable (1639); a thought coloured by or proceeding from emotion (1762).

—From Shorter Oxford English Dictionary (1959)

# Contents

# Preface

The British Library (BL) holds over eighty volumes of diaries and a few other papers left mainly by Richard Blechynden, Calcutta surveyor, architect, and builder. Blechynden's diary has seventy-three volumes. There is a shorter diary by one of his sons, Arthur. The first goal of this and a companion study is to bring Blechynden's diary to attention.

A major connecting theme is the narrative of self through recorded experiences. The setting is early Calcutta (now Kolkata) and hence the establishment of a colonial city and a colonial system. The companion volume, *Sex and Sensibility*, concentrates on stories about concubines (*bibis*). This volume provides rich details of the daily life of Calcutta from the perspective of a European and his household. An important subsidiary theme is the British impact on Indians; the focus is on how Indian experiences affected the British.

An intimate portrait emerges, particularly stories of Indian servants and mixed-race children that mark the construction of a new English identity. It was forged by empire and through experience; from ideas of race and duty and from practices of work, petty administration, and law. As manners conflicted, sense competed with selfishness. Propriety and rules were promoted, with ambition but little success. Indians fell short, in the British assessment, but so did the British themselves. From these deficiencies, there emerged new ideas on norms, regulation, and identity.

The first two chapters' main subjects are values, clashes of culture, and race. Servants bring us to employment and law (Chapters 3 and 4). Blechynden's mixed-race children (Chapters 5 to 7) take us there too, and to education as well as social and cultural assimilation (Chapters 8 and 9). For two sons and (in Chapter 1) a cousin, the main issue was a profession. For the daughters, the corresponding touchstone was a suitable marriage. For all, moral and proper behaviour defined their English identity:

self-framed, not just against 'otherness', but by sentiment—active steps expressive of attraction and repulsion in regard to ethics, culture, and conduct.

## SOURCES AND CONVENTIONS

The Blechynden papers in the British Library are Add. Mss. 45578–663; Richard's diary is Add. Mss. 45581–653. Despite its extent and importance, it has been hardly noticed by historians and is not mentioned in William Matthews, *British Diaries* (Berkeley 1950) or J.S. Batts, *British Manuscript Diaries of the Nineteenth Century* (London 1976). Blechynden's diary will be cited as 'RB', by date of entry only; Arthur's (Add. Mss. 45654–61) as 'AB'. The relevant volumes may be discerned from the shortlists. When a full date is given in the main text, the same reference to the diary will not be included in an endnote. Multiple citations in one note are grouped by date and not subject order in the text. For clarity, quotations have minor modernizations of spelling and punctuation, lest Blechynden's inconsistent or non-existent practice give an impression of hasty or even semi-literate composition—quite false, because quite different from how his contemporaries would have 'read' the text.

I have retained the spelling of Indian and European personal and place names and titles as they appear in the diary, choosing one variant where the diary is inconsistent. More modern transliterations are given in the glossary and the index (which also covers the Notes but only for discussions that include names or subjects mentioned in the main text). My thanks to Aparajita Mukhopadhyay for helping with my transliterations. Richard Blechynden, called 'Blech' by his friends, is referred to as 'Blechynden', and other members of the family by their given names. If possible, I have identified other characters despite the diary's vagueness.

# Acknowledgements

I am glad to acknowledge that the British Academy supported some of the research for this book, mainly in London but also in Calcutta. A further year's research leave from the School of Oriental and African Studies (SOAS) enabled me to bring the project to fruition. Seminar audiences, most notably at the Jawaharlal Nehru and Oxford universities, made constructive contributions on the early drafts of some sections. Editors and referees of the *Indian Economic and Social History Review* provided helpful suggestions on an article marking the first journal outing for my engagement with Blechynden's diary—'Credit, Work and Race in Calcutta in the 1790s: Early Colonialism through a Contemporary European View', *Indian Economic and Social History Review*, vol. 37, no. 1 (2000), pp. 1–25. A few fragments of the present book appeared in Peter Robb, 'Clash of Cultures? An Englishman in Calcutta in the 1790s' (London 1998). Some sections in Chapters 8 and 9 are incorporated or adapted from 'Children, Emotion, Identity and Empire: Views from the Blechynden's Calcutta Diaries (1790–1822)', *Modern Asian Studies*, vol. 40, no. 1 (2006), pp. 175–201 © Cambridge University Press (reproduced with permission).

I am very grateful to Donald Jaques and Gerald Johnson Fox for information on the Blechyndens, and also to Mr Fox for permission to reproduce a miniature portrait of Richard Blechynden for the frontispiece.

I owe a great debt to my wife, Elizabeth, who came eagerly to the British Library to transcribe some of the bulkier materials and sustained me with enthusiasm for what she called a 'soap opera' and an entertainment.

# Introducing Richard Blechynden, 1759–1822[*]

The Blechynden family had held land for generations to the west of Ashford. Thomas Blechynden (1702–1740) had at least two sons, Thomas and Richard, and two daughters, including Jane Harriet (1739–1815). Richard (1732–1775), a sugar broker in London, married Mary Brown. Their son, also Richard Blechynden, our diarist, was fifteen when his father died. Blechynden's uncle, Thomas, was the father of William Marmaduke; his illegitimate son was also called Tom. Richard's aunt, Jane Harriet, married James Theobald, who became Richard's benefactor, his 'second father'. Theobald (died 1802), a Fellow of the Royal Society and the Society of Arts, lived at 16 Great James Street off Theobalds Row (the name is a coincidence), a newly developing area adjacent to the fields north of Grays Inn (see John Rocque's map, 1745). Richard Blechynden and later his children lived there too.

A Kentish boy, Blechynden first attended school at Eltham (now in Greater London) and was educated in mathematics and astronomy by William Wales, celebrated astronomer and master at Christ's Hospital. While serving as a midshipman in 1780, he was taken prisoner when aged twenty, captured by the French and Spanish from a British ship. He found his way back to England from Spain and Portugal via Ireland, wrote an account of his adventures, and bound it up in book form. He was sent to sea again in the East Indiaman *Deptford*, leaving England on 5 April 1781, undertaking a cadet's usual training in navigation and charts, arriving at

* Adapted from Peter Robb, *Sex and Sensibility: Richard Blechynden's Calcutta Diaries, 1791–1822* (New Delhi 2011), where the full references are provided.

## Parts of the Blechynden Family Tree, 1702–1940

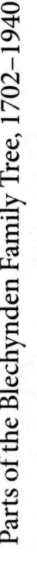

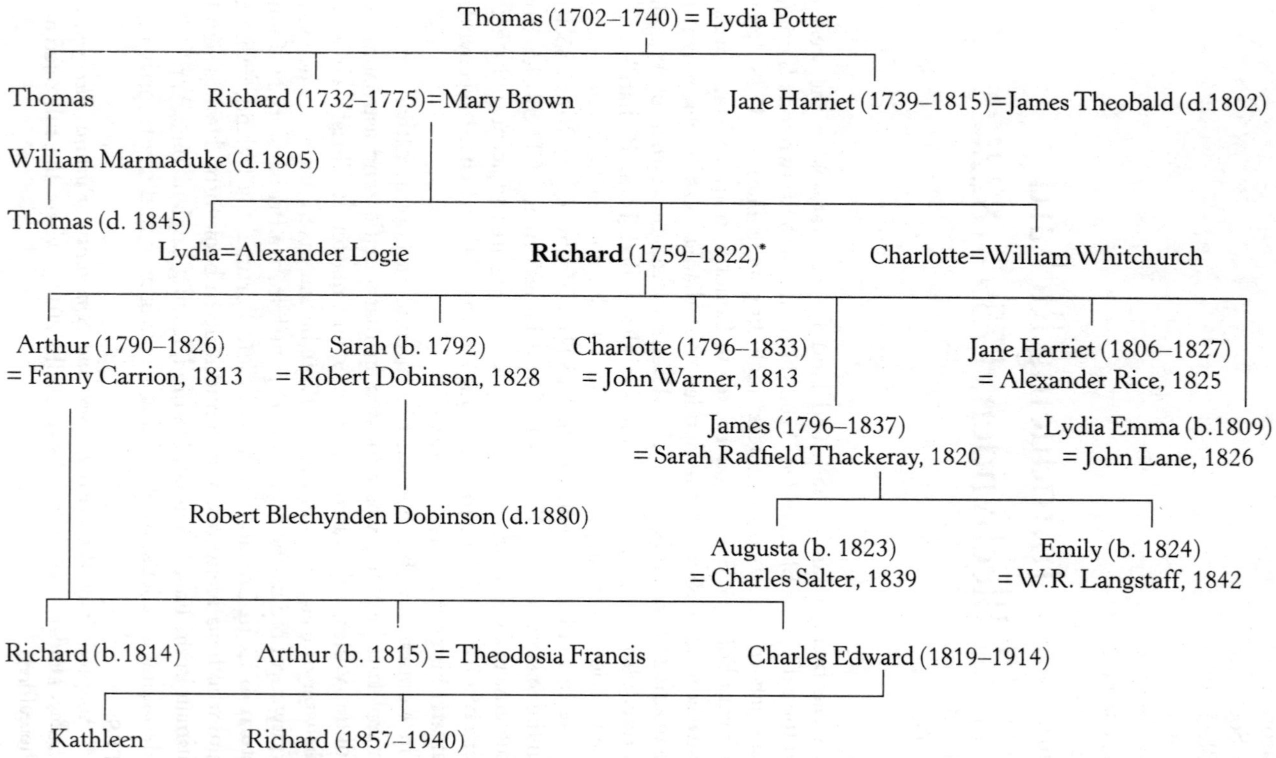

Thomas (1702–1740) = Lydia Potter

Thomas

Richard (1732–1775)=Mary Brown

Jane Harriet (1739–1815)=James Theobald (d.1802)

William Marmaduke (d.1805)

Charlotte=William Whitchurch

Thomas (d. 1845)

Richard (1759–1822)*

Lydia=Alexander Logie

Sarah (b. 1792) = Robert Dobinson, 1828

Charlotte (1796–1833) = John Warner, 1813

Jane Harriet (1806–1827) = Alexander Rice, 1825

James (1796–1837) = Sarah Radfield Thackeray, 1820

Lydia Emma (b.1809) = John Lane, 1826

Augusta (b. 1823) = Charles Salter, 1839

Emily (b. 1824) = W.R. Langstaff, 1842

Arthur (1790–1826) = Fanny Carrion, 1813

Robert Blechynden Dobinson (d.1880)

Charles Edward (1819–1914)

Arthur (b. 1815) = Theodosia Francis

Richard (b.1814)

Kathleen

Richard (1857–1940)

* The diarist; his infant son Sydney (d.1793) is not shown.

Balasore Roads (near the mouth of the Hugli) on 21 May 1782, aged twenty-two. Soon afterwards, he left the ship and made his way to Calcutta.[1]

Blechynden became skilled as a surveyor and architect. He lodged at one stage with Arthur Hesilrige, then a Junior Merchant,[2] and around 1784, found regular employment as unofficial assistant to Calcutta's then surveyor of roads, Edward (Eduardo) Tiretta, a colourful figure (born 1726).[3] Blechynden also worked on his own account, mainly as a civil engineer, architect, and building contractor. He became progressively deaf in one ear from around 1788. By 1791, when he started his diary, he had shares in the *Chronicle* newspaper (for which he wrote until mid-1796).[4] He lived in rented houses in town, and owned a garden or country house and stables north-east of Calcutta, off the Dum Dum (later Belgatchya) road, three or four miles—or about an hour's walk—from Tank Square. By 1806, after renovations, it was a very large, lower-roomed house with plenty of grounds and a tank of excellent water.

In the early 1790s, partly because of wars with the French, demand for houses and improvements was curtailed; the *Chronicle* was struggling; debts were being called in. Blechynden's post with Tiretta disappeared, a casualty to the expenses of Tiretta's recent and (it would prove) sadly brief marriage and also to changes in the city's government. Blechynden only rarely had enough cash (anyway very scarce in Calcutta) to pay his staff and household. However, from July 1797, he worked as Company-appointed assistant to Tiretta, who was permitted to retire in October 1803. Blechynden succeeded him as Superintendent of Roads. The post of Civil Architect was abolished, but later Blechynden's son Arthur was admitted as deputy and (despite gaps) successor to his father. Richard Blechynden remained in his post until his death on 4 February 1822.

Throughout his time in India, Blechynden engaged in public infrastructural improvement, as well as private building contracts and surveying for the Supreme Court and others. He was respected generally not only for his work for Calcutta but for his fairness, and hence much employed with powers of attorney, in mediation, and as a legal executor. He wanted to return to England, but was 'fettered' by his large family. He had two sons, of whom only Arthur would survive infancy, in 1791;[5] and five more illegitimate children by four mothers between 1792 and 1809.[6]

## NOTES

1.  Blechynden was born on 15 May 1759: Richard Blechynden's Diaries (RB hereafter), 15 May 1793; Journal (1781). His sister Lydia had been in

xviii Introducing Richard Blechynden

Calcutta, but married, set out for England, and was lost at sea: Stephen Taylor, *The Caliban Shore: The Fate of the* Grosvenor *Castaways* (London 2004), pp. 10–11. William Wales FRS, of Christ Church Newgate and the mathematical school of Christ's Hospital, served as astronomer on Captain Cook's second voyage. Other personal details: indiafamily.bl.uk; *List of Civil Servants in Bengal Establishment*, O/1/1-20, Oriental and India Office Collections (OIOC), and other lists, British Library (BL).

2.   Sir Arthur Hesilrige (Hazlerigg in *Burke's Peerage*), appointed Junior Merchant in 1773, then unemployed without allowances, was later a district magistrate.

3.   A portrait of Tiretta may be seen in James Gilray's etching 'The Bengal Levee' (9 November 1792) in the National Portrait Gallery, London.

4.   The *Chronicle* also operated a jobbing printing press. On printers: Nikhil Sarkar, 'Printing and the Spirit of Calcutta' in Sukanta Chaudhuri (ed.), *Calcutta: The Living City* (New Delhi 1990), p. 129, and Graham Shaw, *Printing in Calcutta in 1800* (London 1981); Shaw, *Bibliography*; Tapti Roy, 'Disciplining the Printed Text: Colonial and Nationalist Surveillance of Bengali Literature' in Partha Chatterjee (ed.), *Texts of Power: Emerging Disciplines in Colonial Bengal* (Calcutta 1996), p. 31.

5.   Two sons: RB, 9 November 1792. A daughter was born on 21 November 1792. A later reference (see Chapter 5) implies that another child died before the diary was begun.

6.   For further family information, see http://www.blechynden.co.uk.

# PART I
*Sensibility and Sense: Blechynden's Calcutta*

# 1

# Making Sense
## An Englishman and Calcutta

We do not look in great cities for our best morality.
—Jane Austen, *Mansfield Park*[1]

## CALCUTTA VALUES

Our view of Calcutta in this period comes from a few sources often repeated. For the 1790s, *the* street map is that of Aaron Upjohn.[2] It was castigated in great detail by Blechynden for its inaccuracies and want of proper survey.[3] Among literary sources, contemporary evidence has been passed down, often with exactly the same quotations, through James Long and other nineteenth-century writers to more recent volumes commemorating Calcutta's 300 years. The Company's newly won city, like modern nations, has been presented with a definite and continuous history. Uncertainty is evident, appropriately, with regard to its origins before European settlement; and it needed its claims to glamour. As Blechynden's son Arthur recalled, though the air outside the town was refreshing and sweet, inside it the 'low, sandy, swampy soil' made for 'nasty smells', implying an unhealthy environment in the ideas of the day. Calcutta's palaces and public buildings, intended at this period to impress Europeans more than Indians, were at once grandiose and ersatz: neoclassical but compromised by local conditions in design and materials.

For the early Europeans, a picture is painted of a lavish lifestyle, an elaborate hierarchical social round, and remarkably short hours of office work. Alexander Macrabie, Sheriff of Calcutta and brother-in-law of Philip Francis, is repeatedly quoted for his shamefaced tally of their servants in 1775: a total of 110 for four men 'chumming'—that is, sharing

Francis's house. These were among the very greatest of the Company's men in Calcutta, but they are taken to typify the conditions of European life. Blechynden thought that the average number per household, living or working under the same roof, would have been about twenty-five. At a time of moderate or at least improving prosperity, he himself employed around thirty-five directly, some involved in his professional life and one supported to run a charity school. Servants worked long hours but most were not resident.[4]

The British community in Calcutta is also portrayed as being largely middle-class exiles, even in the most comprehensive modern account.[5] Despite the numbers of servants employed, this is partly misleading. First, unlike the Company grandees, many Europeans made their homes more or less permanently in India, in practice if not by intention or commitment. Secondly, though poorer Europeans are seldom mentioned, they certainly existed in large numbers. Military personnel of all ranks provided by far the majority of the European residents of India, but in addition, as a study of the records of the sheriffs of Calcutta revealed: 'at the close of the eighteenth and the beginning of the nineteenth centuries British trades-men and mechanics carried on a large business and worked at their trades in Calcutta. Of coopers there were many, shoemakers were to be met with by the score. Tailors, carpenters, coach and shipbuilders were very much in evidence...' In the Park Street cemetery, there lie (beside highly placed Company servants and officers, rich merchants and professionals, and their families) a cattle breeder, silversmith, printer, livery stable keeper, tide waiter, cooper, undertaker, postmaster, schoolmistress, and master. Blechynden was once petitioned by a European wanting work on the roads. The implication is that different social layers existed even among the relatively small number of Europeans. Blechynden inhabited one of these: of upper-middle rank, in Calcutta terms. He socialized mainly with merchants, petty officials, lawyers, clerks, and military or marine officers. Moreover, among his friends who were permanent Calcutta residents, many were Anglo-Indian, meaning India-born and often of mixed race. He also had social contacts with elite Indians. At all levels, there was more and earlier exchange between Europeans and Indians than is sometimes thought.[6]

Blechynden would have probably have disagreed with Voltaire, who said that men differ in their customs and not their essence, but agreed with Burke that 'no discoveries are to be made in morality'.[7] He did not think Burke's 'great principles of government' were well represented in the Company or Calcutta, though aspects of 'modern' government and society were apparent. A curious feature of contemporary attitudes (Blechynden's included) was the ability to distinguish in moral terms between overt conduct and conduct that was ostensibly hidden but universally known. The East India Company turned a blind eye to rule violations, petty and vast, except when transgression was formally and officially brought to its attention, a very serious step for anyone to take.

Similarly, just about every man kept a concubine (or bibi) and many married men had mistresses, but no one officially acknowledged these relationships—European men and unmarried women openly met together in private, but never on formal occasions, and only the 'unprincipled' brought their liaisons into public view. For example, when Wellesley's French mistress was too openly paraded, Blechynden thought it 'a bad example particularly in a *married man*—and the Governor General & whose Countess is so soon expected out'.[8] Blechynden also informed one married lady, who asked if he had sent his children to England, that he had sent his nephew and niece, for he was a bachelor; this gave the lady enormous amusement. The contrast with other, frank conversations was marked: Blechynden blushed at his friend Mme Deverinne's graphic account of her piles and menstrual cycle, but was quite content to have a long conversation with her about bibis. Another married woman, the second Mrs Samuel Jones, wife of the chief clerk at the Post Office, joked about Blechynden's having 'roved from flower to flower'.[9] This behaviour should not be called hypocrisy; it was adherence to a particular code.

It implied a relatively unordered world, nonetheless. There were many attempts, even in early Calcutta as in Europe, to discipline space and conduct, arising from ideas about the proper character of cities and society, and also from practical needs—to keep the roads clear of encroachments; to reduce disease or crime; to avoid fire and arson (fires were very frequent in the grass huts of early Calcutta); to manage the exchanges and conflicts of interest between people in a place at once crowded and new. The measures were often unsuccessful, but the efforts helped construct public norms and expectations in the interests of residents, traders, and travellers.[10]

At a personal level, similarly, while experiencing confusion and dislocation, Blechynden sought an ordered inward view of himself and probity in his dealings with others. His personal ideals were closely related to reputation, and also to conscience and pride, to standards of conduct as of architecture, and to a spirit of scientific inquiry. He had used the cliché 'all the riches of the East',[11] but constantly told himself that he sought integrity before wealth. Already, at twenty, when taken prisoner in 1780, he nearly came to blows with a Spanish captain who admitted putting profit before honour.[12] Later, in Calcutta, after quarrelling with the auctioneer William Dring, he wrote: 'I earned my Bread ... in honesty. I also wished to earn it with honour.'[13]

The values Blechynden sought were sharpened by the heightened and constant threat of untimely death,[14] as was evident, for example, in the thoughts of pride, propriety, and posterity that shaped his reaction to the demise of Sir William Jones in 1794, at the age of forty-eight. He went to Jones's garden house on hearing of the death and found the body with 'a fine placid smile upon his Countenance' but (to his astonishment) lying in the dark in an upstairs room quite unattended. Blechynden called for candles and a servant to keep watch, partly for fear of rats, but also out of a sense of what was proper for the man. Blechynden's attitude to Jones rested on his idea of him as someone who would long be revered. But he also wrote: 'As his lamented death lay uppermost in my mind I could not help regretting the little attention that appeared to have been paid to this great man.' He was aghast that no autopsy was carried out 'to ascertain the precise cause of a death on which all Europe would fix their weeping eyes'. Indeed, the *Dictionary of National Biography* claimed Jones died from depression and overwork in the absence of his wife, when it seems from Blechynden's report that he suffered from an abdominal tumour, for which Jones had sought no treatment, telling his doctors that as it had appeared of its own accord, he expected it to go away likewise.

Blechynden had thought it important to inquire into 'every particular of this uncommon Genius', assuming that in death his nature would be revealed, as if Jones had been a protagonist in a Renaissance tragedy.[15] Blechynden also described the pomp of the funeral procession and, later, visited the tomb. Its inscription reads: 'Here lies the mortal part of a man, who feared God, but not death, and maintained independence but sought not riches: who thought none below him but the base and unjust; none above him but the wise and virtuous.' Blechynden could endorse such a model of values and rightful conduct. Such a 'really great and good man', he wrote, 'snatched away'—'whilst the wicked and ignorant are permitted, not only to walk this planet, but to commit their depredations upon it'.[16]

Honour also implied lineage, education, and class: it 'became gentlemen of ... high rank and station'. But, in Calcutta, society was not firmly established and men of doubtful background could rise (as arguably also in contemporary England, though to a lesser degree). That great man, Robert Downie of Downie & Maitland and the Ganges Insurance Company, had come to India as a carpenter's boy on the *William Pitt*. One of Blechynden's former boarders, William Roper (of the Bombay Marine), became the butt of hearty jokes when it was learnt from a newcomer that his father was a hairdresser at Penrith. Another friend, the marine officer Proctor, 'chumming' with Roper, had a secret nickname for him when he gave himself airs: he then became 'Nunez', after a barber in Alain René Le Sage's romance *The Adventures of Gil Blas* (1715–35), translated by Smollett (1749). Proctor soon quarrelled with Roper and decided not to live with him any longer.[17] Blechynden and his fellows had some merriment also at the expense of Hubert Cornish, because his father was alleged to have been a mace-bearer in Exeter. He was short, plump, and haughty, but also assistant and brother-in-law to the Governor-General (Sir John Shore), wielding considerable, if at first unofficial, power. Blechynden held Shore to be honourable but was furious with Cornish over Calcutta surveying appointments in 1794. From a rude response to a letter, he suspected Cornish of having supported Aaron Upjohn, the bassoon player turned engraver and map-maker, 'a pushing unblushing fellow', with whom Blechynden was in dispute over debts.[18]

The fortuities of Calcutta complicated matters. Samuel Jones was 'kidnapped' to become a private soldier, rose to sergeant, was employed in various military offices, was discharged and appointed as a clerk in Calcutta, and then moved to the Post Office. However, when he did not acknowledge as a relation by marriage the tavern-keeper Lewis, who supplied him with excellent dinners, Blechynden thought that 'natural enough when their respective situations are considered'. On the other hand, Jones regaled him with stories of his courtship of his first wife, Miss Giffen. She was also pursued by the auctioneer William Dring, who sought the support of Richard Brittridge, an engraver, promising him a share in his business if he succeeded, but adding that he would first have to give up his own so that Dring could 'countenance him as a gentleman' and permit him to join his firm. This did not match Blechynden's thinking. 'To hear this with a grave face exceeds all power of farce,' he wrote. 'An auctioneer to conceive himself superior in rank or consideration or public utility to an engraver!' Dring's suit failed; he quarrelled with Brittridge, who did not get his partnership. He went to produce indigo up-country.[19]

Status certainly followed from one's occupation as well as one's origins. In the circumstances of India, conduct made the man, and public approval counted. Morality sometimes even seems to have been more professional than personal, perhaps because regular structures and practices of commerce and public office were not yet established. Minute rules of social conduct palliated a world in which there was still no definite public procedure for establishing jobs, salaries, contracts, or recruitment. Hence

Blechynden prided himself on his professional skills and placed architecture above other possible pursuits. For example, he was invited to take over the management of a stables and horse-riding ménage because (he was flatteringly informed) he was renowned as the best horseman in India; but he declined. He loved horses, kept many, and broke them in himself, but could not see himself, an architect, running a riding school.[20] In his own sphere, he frequently mocked those who were 'uninformed', according to his own standards, and bemoaned clients' reluctance to take 'proper' advice. He studied his manuals of architecture and engineering, lending out his copies and offering his advice, laughing at ignorance, insisting on order and proportion, and was saddened when clients were reluctant to spend a little extra in order to beautify the city in which they lived. Poring over Chambers's *Civil Architecture*,[21] he made his own contribution to the Palladian splendours of the city of palaces. For Blechynden, as for Palladio, the architect's mix of proportion and utility was designed to contribute to civilization and to social harmony and improvement, which were also the goals of science and of regulation.[22]

Such professionalism did not carry everything before it. Wellesley's grandiose Government House was not entrusted to the Civil Architect Tiretta, whose plan was uninspiring in the Governor-General's opinion, but to a virtually untried but immensely self-confident, ambitious, and unscrupulous young engineer, Captain Wyatt. A few years later, another engineer, Colonel John Garstin, was commissioned to build Calcutta's Town Hall, and did so (in Blechynden's judgement) with a mixture of arrogance, poor design, miscalculation, and bad execution. When part of the portico fell down, several critics were overjoyed. Blechynden reflected that 'overbearing conduct' did not make one liked. Only fellow military engineers were called in to investigate at first, and Garstin blamed the poor soil. Blechynden told the chief engineer, Colonel Alexander Kyd, that there was nothing wrong with the soil, or at least it was equally bad everywhere in Calcutta. Blechynden was later called on to make a report himself and draw up plans for the Town Hall, and rather regretted speaking out. At the very same time, however, Garstin was sneering, in front of Kyd, about untrained 'engineers'. The occasion was a plan for a salt *gola* (warehouse) at Howrah prepared by Kyd's son, James, that James calculated would cost Rs 45,000 as opposed to Garstin's estimate of Rs 172,000. James demonstrated that his calculations were correct, but it took his father a whole day to convince Garstin.[23]

Paradoxically, the 'amateur' pursuit of knowledge was another important aspect of prestige, as seen with William Jones; professionals might not always carry the day. Blechynden, for example, regarded doctors as experts and called one in extremis for himself, family, or servants; but he also doubted their skills, refused their treatments, and objected to their cost. He kept up a keen personal interest in medicine, confidently treating people and animals, providing his own medical treatments, and carefully recording dosage and outcomes in a spirit of inquiry. In this, he was not so far from his Indian patients—or his professional clients—as he imagined.

Blechynden's guiding principles were experiment (or experience) and science, whether in his profession or in his enthusiasms. He undertook architecture and building in the same spirit as he calculated longitude (very up-to-date), took astronomical readings, and corrected people's timepieces. In that same spirit, he added a complete set of Buffon's *Natural History* to his library. He kept a meteorological diary intended for the Royal Society. Others of similar bent existed in town: he appealed to them for copies when white ants ate parts of his own record. Similarly, Henry Trail kept a meteorological diary at Calcutta in 1784 and Thomas Pearse made observations with barometer, thermometer, and hygrometer, and of wind direction and rainfall, between 1785 and 1788. Pearse set his watch by his astronomical clock to determine the hour of Warren Hastings's famous duel with Philip Francis, whose watch was half an hour ahead.[24]

Keenly interested in astronomical and surveying instruments—John Hodgson, Surveyor-General of India, bought 'a very good plane table' from Blechynden's effects after his death in 1822—Blechynden was often asked to demonstrate techniques and to resolve scientific disputes. When his friend, the mariner John Wales, told him that sound travelled at the same rate regardless of atmospheric conditions (whether hot, dry, windy, and so on), Blechynden doubted it and immediately proposed an experiment, reasoning that if it were true, it would provide a expeditious and accurate way of measuring distance, given that a baseline could differ every time it was taken, as the chain stretched or was affected by grit or heat—for which reason he preferred to use trigonometry. Science was also to be served under Blechynden's will, written in 1808: he asked that, even if the executors had to pay for it from his effects, there should be an autopsy to ascertain the cause of his death and also, if possible, of his deafness—'the better to Cure or relieve others Suffering under similar symptoms'.[25] What all this suggests is that professionalism would become the yardstick, by superior method, consistency, and prestige.

Technological certainties and personal status, duty, and propriety, each reinforced the others. Behind them lay national pride, which they helped define. Blechynden, a friend of many Frenchmen, considered them 'monsters in human shape' for the murder of the 'inoffensive Louis' and became even more savagely critical after the execution of Marie Antoinette—though he was able to 'manage' one of them, Le Breen, 'who tho' a furious democrat can talk very pleasantly if people will a little humour his frenzy'. He was unrelenting against any British disloyalty and indiscipline. Suspecting a ship's officers had incited their men to mutiny 'at being sent away without being able to sell their Investments', he sneered: 'This is Patriotism'; they 'deserve no indulgence'; if he were Governor, he would 'break the Captain of the ship'. When 'our own Countrymen' disobey their orders, he asked, what would be the effect on the Company's sepoys? He criticized the illuminations in 1793 celebrating the end of the Anglo-Mysore war of 1789–92, thinking 'the natives (if not the European powers here) must think we were cursedly frightened during the War that we express so great a Joy at Victory over a Barbarian & his undisciplined Rabble'. He kept away, not liking such 'dissipation & frivolity' but concerned for British prestige.[26]

Hence the Britons' supposedly superior virtue and orderliness were used to justify their mastery over others. Blechynden shows how this idea was internalized by an ordinary Englishman and how such men helped create it. Motivations at a personal level provide no justification of colonialism nor assess its underlying purposes and effects. But they do present self-image and 'duty' as necessary elements in any explanation of what occurred.[27]

## EUROPEAN FRIENDS

Blechynden's diary is replete with what amount to chronicles of friendship. It cites dinners and visits and conversations on a daily basis. It assiduously records mutual obligations, loans, charitable lottery purchases, and donations to debtors in prison. It mentions exchanges of gifts and the sharing of lodgings, garden produce, and other belongings—lending horses; sending out crockery or furniture; and bathing and fishing in each other's tanks. Blechynden, for example, was given a horse and a puppy; he gave a friend a colt; he received about 160 plants (cauliflower, horseradish, and so on) from another.[28]

Why should this have been so? Does this practice merely reveal a commonplace of human society or does it have features peculiar to Calcutta? It does seem that these relationships had particular importance in Calcutta at a time of political and commercial adventurism. To judge from Blechynden, friendship was strongly emphasized as part of the expatriate's self-image. Accordingly, it was accompanied by a definite etiquette, ritual, and even bureaucracy. Blechynden could be pedantic about the niceties of conduct: he was, for instance, scathing that Hayes should have declined to dine because he had not had a *written* invitation and yet had sought to introduce his wife to Blechynden for the first time 'in a public Race Ground', before Blechynden had paid the couple a visit or even congratulated them on their marriage.[29] Blechynden's not infrequent fallings-out invariably related to some perceived slight or inconsiderate treatment, over social trivia as well as serious matters such as debt and payment for services.

Hence, though he was himself choosy in his acquaintance and regarded as touchy and even irascible at times, ready to break with someone irrevocably over a slight or disservice, he was also uneasy about possible consequences whenever he saw others in disagreement. A good example, showing the lengths to which friends would go to smooth out difficulties, is provided by an argument between the merchant W. Collins and Barnett, a ship's captain, in November 1795. Collins had Blechynden woken in the night to tell him that he and Barnett had agreed to meet in a duel. The animosity had begun when Collins made out a bill for coolie hire, amounting to only fifteen rupees; Barnett had run his pen through one item, for two rupees, that he said was not his. Collins regarded himself as insulted because Barnett had defaced the bill instead of speaking to him about it. At the time, Barnett was living gratis with Collins and his business partner, Callendar. Since this incident, Collins believed, Barnett had been ridiculing him and showing him marked dislike. Collins spoke to Callendar, who agreed that Barnett should be asked to seek other accommodation. So, on his return home, Collins was surprised to find the other two men sitting together. Barnett got up and went away when Collins arrived; Collins said that he thought that Barnett was leaving that day and hoped it would be soon; Barnett overheard; more words ensued; the challenge was issued and accepted. Blechynden, whom Collins wanted as his second, apart from having no desire to be accessory to murder, was determined to prevent this outcome even if he had to dissuade the antagonists as they faced each other. But Collins was just as adamant: things had gone too far.

The next day, Collins arrived with letters from Callendar and another acquaintance, Munro, presumably Barnett's second, both of them urging peace. Blechynden went to Munro to urge him to mediate and saw Barnett, who said that Collins had accused him of 'fattening upon him & Callendar' and struck him with his stick. Blechynden and Munro suggested that both parties write out their grievances for them and they would deliver 'a written opinion'. This was agreed. Collins's list started long before with 'little trifling matters—not passing the bottle to him at table & such like nonsense'. Barnett confined himself to the previous evening's argument. Blechynden and Munro drafted separate responses and then combined them into one. Blechynden attributed the quarrel to 'trifles brooded over', but said that as he could not attribute blame, there should be 'mutual forbearance and forgiveness'. He also pointed out the danger, if the quarrel had a 'fatal Issue', to the 'Mercantile Interest of Callendar & Collins'. This last was toned down by Munro, who feared that it might look as if Collins had set him on to say it. They settled on a call for 'liberal mutual forgiveness' and 'absolute silence for the future on what has passed under forfeiture of the esteem of Friends'.

When Collins read the joint letter, he was silent but Blechynden 'could see by his Countenance that he was pleased with the Contents'. Barnett was not satisfied and wanted an apology for the blow. Blechynden gave him a lecture. Collins could not make an apology as the quarrel originated with Barnett, however trivially. Moreover, Barnett was in Collins's house and so, if he had taken offence, the more spirited response would have been to leave it. Did he intend to be on terms of intimacy with Collins once again? He did. In that case, how could he want him to humble himself? In any case, he had agreed to abide by his and Munro's arbitration. No doubt Collins *was* sorry he had struck him, as he was in his own house and Barnett unarmed. Barnett replied by saying that it would be enough if Collins would say just that, as a 'plaister to his sore'. Blechynden quibbled about the words: Collins should say he was sorry that he did not recollect Barnett was unarmed. Barnett accepted this; the arbitrator passed the message; Collins agreed. Munro and Barnett were summoned into the hall. Blechynden brought Collins upstairs. He walked up and offered his hand, saying, 'Capt^n Barnett I am sorry that I had no sufficient command over my anger, to reflect when I struck you with my stick that you had none in your hand.' Barnett shook hands.

Blechynden said that he hoped they 'mutually forgot the Business without any nasty mental reservation'. They said they did. Collins went away. Blechynden added to Barnett that Collins had spoken first and offered his hand first, in his own house, and so he hoped that if they dined at home that day, he would ask Collins to drink some wine. Barnett said he would. Blechynden rushed after Collins, who turned out to be planning not to dine at home. Blechynden persuaded him to send an excuse and remain so that Barnett would not think the reconciliation insincere. Collins agreed and no doubt the wine was duly offered. Four days later,

Blechynden was able to check for himself by dining with Collins. Five days after that, Collins, Callendar, Munro, and Barnett had a 'very merry' dinner together at Blechynden's gardens.[30] In all this, no doubt the possibility of death by duelling was a consideration. But the elements are also distinctive: the earnest rallying of friends, the quasi-judicial formality, the written arbitration, the role played by rituals and by shared meals, and the concern felt for commercial interests. Together, I suggest, they illustrate the importance placed on friendship for sustaining Europeans in colonial Calcutta.[31]

Blechynden recorded many shared acts of comradeship as well as the subtle rules and expectations governing them. He also cited many cases of irritation and forbearance. Friends did not just help each other, therefore; they put up with a great deal of inconvenience to support the conventions of acquaintanceship. Feelings *were* involved and departures frequently gave rise to expressions of regret. Blechynden was greatly upset—in tears—at Tiretta's final departure, for example, after he had been staying with Blechynden for some time. Blechynden slipped away from a farewell dinner held by Mme Deverinne by climbing over a balustrade on the terrace to avoid the distress of the final goodbyes among friends. At dinner next day with his daughter and Blechynden, Tiretta confessed that he had done exactly the same, after merely squeezing his hostess's hand and saying 'adieu'. Blechynden sent them off to the ghat (landing place), kissing the child and saying nothing; they 'affected cheerfulness'. Blechynden's then bibi, Isabella, was in tears upstairs.[32]

Intervention of all kinds in each other's affairs was symptomatic of a general intimacy and transparency among friends, characterizing European life in Calcutta. Are there special features, then, in these friendships? It seems that they mattered particularly because of the Europeans' relatively small numbers, their attitudes, their socializing, and their mixing of domestic and working environments. The last of these begins to explain the powerful interventions by friends (and enemies) in personal and supposedly private matters as well as the part friendship played more generally in political and economic life. Self-interest encouraged and defined the bonding among Calcutta's Europeans. Money was the key.

In this period, as is well known, influence and patronage were encountered at every turn. In Calcutta, friends also provided funds for those who were short and they guaranteed loans for traders and would-be partners in commercial ventures. Friends employed and secured work for each other. Friendship, as much as law or official intervention, regulated personal and even public finances. If a loan were not being repaid, for example, negotiations among friends were likely to provide a more secure and cheaper remedy than suing or imprisoning the offending party.[33]

Behind everything lay a legal framework that could lead to litigation and imprisonment. I do not underestimate the importance of these sanctions. Potentially, arrest was very serious. Blechynden had a brief imprisonment in 1791 that filled him with shame. His sometime friend and host Arthur Hesilrige lost his post with the Company when he was imprisoned for debt.[34] Many others had to hide or were imprisoned for long periods and so were unable to conduct any business and had to rely on the charity of friends. But the legal and technical underpinnings, though real, were often ineffectual or corrupt in practice. Defining them does not go very far towards showing how financial arrangements worked on a daily basis.

Half a dozen small examples will illustrate the connection of money and friendship. First, transfers at a distance and liabilities were managed in part through personal association, including kinship. Blechynden managed his costs in England commercially through agency houses that could draw on London, but frequently evoked the claims of friendship to secure such deals when funds were short. The brother of Callendar, of the merchants Collins & Callendar, was seeking his fortune in Penang and drew very many bills upon his brother in Calcutta, who determined to pay no more. One of the bills, however, came into the hands of the merchant Alexander Aberdein, and so Callendar agreed to pay him as soon as his brother returned. The latter's voyage proved unsuccessful, however, and when he reached Calcutta, he was unable to pay. Aberdein then issued a writ against Callendar on the basis of his earlier promise, even though the bill was for Rs 1,500 and the legal costs would be Rs 240. The money was paid.

Secondly, the system envisaged support across communities, one expression of which was the frequent recourse to private lotteries. Mrs Gardner advertised tickets at Rs 100 each for a lottery to raise money to support her and two orphan children. Blechynden was 'frightened' at the cost, but then thought that 'great as the sum is', it was only proper he should sign up. He had had a building job from Gardner in 1789, though he lost money on it because of a sudden rise in the cost of *chunam* (plaster). Also, Mrs Gardner had often dined at his garden house. Moreover, given his 'miserable situation', there was no knowing when his own three 'helpless children' might be in need of charity. When the time came to pay, he borrowed the money from his neighbour and then friend T.P. Doncaster, gave him the ticket, and received a receipt, thinking that if he was lucky (usually he was not), the prize would cover all his debts to Doncaster and still return him a balance.[35]

Thirdly, even regular official appointment and a long-established business did not guarantee access to liquid funds. When Edward Tiretta was
seeking to send his late wife's sister (Josephine de Carrion) to be educated
in England, he found himself unable to furnish the cash needed to support
her there. For four or five months, the advocate Robert Ledlie had owed
him Rs 1,500 due 'on demand', but Tiretta could not obtain the money.
He also had two of the Company's eight per cent certificates but no
one would accept them for cash. Hearing this, Blechynden stressed how
disagreeable it would be for the child to arrive in England without any
funds, even though her proposed guardian would 'cheerfully provide every
thing'. He suggested Tiretta give his Company certificates to an agency
house in return for bills in London, or, as a last resort, he (Blechynden)
would give him a draft for £100 even though he was already in debt
in England.[36]

For want of liquidity, personal bonds were widely negotiated, sometimes drawing people outside the networks of trust in which the bonds
had originated.[37] On 4 January 1793, Nathaniel Rees bought one of
Blechynden's that he had been unable to redeem from its original holder,
one Harrypersaud. In return, Rees gave Harrypersaud his own bond, payable in June 1794, for Rs 2,000, at ten per cent interest. He had then passed
fifty rupees in cash to Fuckerchund, Harrypersaud's *gomashtah* (agent),
and received Harrypersaud's receipt for Rs 640 as if that amount had been
paid in cash. In other words, Rees had purchased Blechynden's bond at a
discount, for all these sums together fell short of its principal and interest. The discount was probably the greater in that Rees demanded a false
receipt to augment the amount he ostensibly had paid in cash, and could be
expected to produce that receipt to reduce his liability when his own bond
fell due. Harrypersaud was presumably cutting his losses by transferring
the debt to someone he thought more likely to pay. For Blechynden, the
only way to stave off Rees seemed to be to issue a bill of equity, which
would cost twelve gold mohurs plus twenty more for the attorney; but he
could not afford it and so eventually he removed the threat by paying yet
others to whom Rees owed money and receiving Rees's bonds to the same
amount as his own.[38]

In such ways, liabilities would be drawn back into the circles of friends.
Similarly, the merchant D.E. Vialars, of the agency house Vialars &
Co., demanded payment of a bond of Blechynden's for Rs 21,600, itself
apparently part of an arrangement with a third party. Vialars had received
a court judgement in which the lawyer had wrongly entered Rs 21,000.
Blechynden thought the interest charged usurious—Vialars had taken

advantage of his distress—and others urged him not to agree to change the Confession of Judgement; but he was 'very averse to that' for fear that it would damage his reputation if he did not pay in full. Vialars agreed to a compromise, but soon demanded payment. Blechynden then 'drained his friends dry', taking out a series of other loans, so as to meet the demand. The start of the process was Rs 2,000 from William Dring, to be repaid in a year at ten per cent; Rs 2,000 from another business client, Gavin Hamilton (of Hamilton & Aberdein), at two months; and Rs 1,000 from French & Aberdein. Vialar's lawyer (Thomas Boileau) refused this part payment of Rs 5,000 and eventually Blechynden raised the rest of money. In extremis, he also frightened the printer William Cooper, by a hint of legal action, into beginning to repay what *he* owed him.[39]

Similarly, complex arrangements involving bonds and mortgages were generally needed to secure capital for new enterprises or buildings. The retired Company servant William Pawson owed Blechynden Rs 2,900 in respect of work Blechynden had carried out, building a livery stables, a business venture of Pawson's with his daughter's husband or partner, Soubise.[40] During these works, Blechynden became a very frequent guest at Pawson's table and Pawson at his. For many years, Blechynden remained Pawson's advisor and friend. At his death, Blechynden did not press Pawson's daughter for rent owed to him. In 1795, Blechynden held Pawson's bond at twelve months, some of it money advanced by Blechynden himself to pay for the works. When Pawson's finances deteriorated further and Blechynden was also in sore need of cash, he received an offer from Robert Downie to buy Pawson's bond for Rs 2,500, less Rs 150 advanced to Blechynden by Downie against a bond from Soubise. As an important merchant and the manager or guarantor of private accounts, Downie often had the funds to become the spider in such webs of debt: his firm of Downie & Maitland was (among other things) a major rice importer and did not depend only on the more episodic long-distance trade.

Downie's plan was that Pawson's bond, which did not fall due for months, would be rolled up into a mortgage of Rs 9,000 (on the stables) that Downie said he would obtain for Pawson from 'a friend'. Blechynden complained that he then stood to lose Rs 400 plus the interest owing on the bond, and so offered to split the difference with Downie, selling him Pawson's bond (with all the interest) for Rs 2,700, less Soubise's Rs 150, which debt would be passed on to Blechynden. The counter offer was neither acknowledged nor accepted. A little later, Downie sent Blechynden a few rupees, the interest due on another Rs 200 owed to Blechynden by Soubise. Downie said that he had deducted the amount from Pawson's account. Blechynden asked what was going on and then found that the mortgage, which Downie rather shamefacedly admitted had been completed without including Blechynden's bond, was not with 'a friend' but with the partnership of Downie & Maitland. Blechynden was annoyed not to have been paid, even at a discount, as he was being besieged for money every day by a 'gang' who had got wind of the possible windfall.

Clearly, the need for trust between the parties to agreements did not rule out sharp practice. Later it transpired that the mortgage on the stables was at twelve per cent and made up of Rs 3,000 owed to Downie, Rs 2,000 to the engineer Kyd (at only eight per cent interest, Downie pocketing the difference), Rs 1,000 to a Portuguese, and the remainder, according to Pawson, to Blechynden. It very much seemed that Downie was claiming interest on money he had not advanced. Blechynden advised Pawson to ask for a full statement of the account. What was more, Downie had tricked Pawson out of his share in the *Chronicle* newspaper by telling him that he had a buyer who could not wait and that the price was good, and when Pawson hesitated, demanding repayment of the money he had lent him to buy the share. The purchaser turned out to be himself, motivated by the expectation of a dividend. Blechynden, a major shareholder in the press, resolved to ensure at a meeting of the *Chronicle* proprietors that Pawson received the income he was due up to the date of sale.

The likelihood of such behaviour made picking creditors even more like picking friends. Not long after Downie's opportunism came to light, Doncaster—hearing of Blechynden's distress—tried to persuade him to accept a loan of Rs 3,000 at forty days, saying that he had no need of the money as he was going to Chittagong (where he would engage in a fraudulent salt venture that later led him to litigation and ruin). Blechynden said that there was no way he could repay such a loan, but he could transfer Pawson's bond to Doncaster and take Rs 2,500 for it. Doncaster would not hear of this, arguing that in refusing a loan, Blechynden showed that he had no friendship for him. For his part, Blechynden, trying to be careful in his choice of creditors, was determined not to place himself under an obligation to Doncaster. But he had Doncaster's note for the money and Doncaster would not take it back. Therefore Blechynden sent him Pawson's bond and eventually received a receipt.

Finally, a whole variety of pressures often had to be exerted to secure repayment, as debtors were frequently insolvent. Pawson's stables were not a great financial success: in August 1796, a riding master having been appointed, there were only two scholars and six horses in the riding school. Already in February, Blechynden had inquired about the profits, striving to find ways of being repaid. In June, Pawson offered a late and part payment of the bond which Doncaster said he would have recommended Blechynden not to accept, except that he was himself a party to the agreement. Blechynden then hid behind Doncaster in various subterfuges designed to force Pawson to repay the remaining debt: he ranged between contravening the expectations of courtesy and appealing to Pawson's better nature, on one hand sending the bond with a servant without a covering note or pretending that Doncaster was about to go to law, and on the other reporting that Doncaster was going home to England so that Blechynden was sorely distressed to find the means of repaying him. Pawson, with Downie's support, then asked for yet more time, saying he had set up a lottery in which he had sold 125 tickets and so hoped soon to be able to repay the debt. Hitherto Blechynden had been annoyed when he thought Pawson, now further indebted to others, was contemplating the lottery to purchase an annuity for his daughter rather than to repay his creditors.[41] The pressures and subterfuges employed to secure the repayment of debts also often played on the personal sense of obligation.

These examples are very different, relating to the difficulty of obtaining cash, remittances at a distance, indirect liability, bonds, and lotteries; but they have features in common. They tell us that behind the forms of negotiable paper (bonds, bills, drafts, or lottery tickets) lay assumptions relating to kinship, acquaintance, solidarity, reputation, and honour. Because bonds were readily consigned to others, debtors could acquire a new, unexpected creditor in respect of an existing debt, potentially breaking down the ties of trust. But they could also meet obligations through complex layers of new or renewed and reciprocal loans that were, as much as anything, expressions of friendship or at least business partnership. The instruments covered by these examples included ways of raising capital for business ventures; but also, they were juggled incessantly in order to meet ordinary expenses at times when income was irregular. In this period, moreover, they were very generally used to cope with short-term crises. A hard-pressed man with reliable, solvent friends could generally stave off ruin.

Many of the values, solidarities, and exclusions operated also between Europeans and Indians. But among Europeans, friendship went further, beyond the solidarities of exile or of fear. Friendly gestures underwrote not only the social but also the economic and political systems. Personal enmity decided much in the same spheres. As far as money is concerned, the role of friendship was crucial. Its observance was not just a truism of human relations or even eighteenth-century thinking but a necessary weapon in a difficult environment. It was for this reason that friendships were carefully expanded, through formal introductions only, creating networks that provided their adherents with work, credit, accommodation, and hospitality. Blechynden's diary repeatedly shows how important a part various public interventions played in private and even intimate aspects of life; equally, it shows how social relations helped create and protect credit and venture capital. This convergence was not accidental. It suggests that a nascent gentlemanly order existed among migrant Europeans of diverse origins in late eighteenth-century Calcutta, at the height of what Cain and Hopkins characterize differently as 'old colonial'.[42]

## AN INDIAN–EUROPEAN ENTANGLEMENT

Here is a story introducing interactions to which we turn in the next two chapters. It concerns a married Brahman woman called Gourt Money, Blechynden's country neighbour Doncaster, and the two men's households. It illustrates several aspects of the relationships between Europeans and Indians, arguably in the most significant and formative sites of their interaction: mores and the household. Taking up important themes of this book, it shows the active roles of Indian servants and also the changing role of law (especially through the special status accorded to marriage, at least in Blechynden's eyes). Finally, it illustrates how social relations among Europeans developed to reinforce changing ideas of proper conduct, not least through the reaction to transgressions.

Doncaster, a speculative businessman, had been staying for several months in Blechynden's garden house while his own house at Belle Couchée was being refurbished, having also reoccupied it after letting it to Charles Key Bruce, later editor and proprietor of the *Mirror* press.[43] In June 1797, the justice of the peace, Matthew Louis, reported that Doncaster was disguising himself in Bengali clothes at night and 'going into Black-men's houses', and that a complaint had been lodged against him with the justices. Louis was trying to put a stop to the legal process.

Blechynden went to his garden house and said nothing to Doncaster for a while, though noticing that the top of his head was shaved. Eventually, he raised the subject. Doncaster 'laughed or rather pretended it' and asked if Blechynden had not heard of it from his *sircar* (steward). He had told him nothing, said Blechynden. They went in to dinner and Doncaster said that it was 'a business of some months' standing'. His own sircar, Netaije, had informed him in January that a certain Brahman made a practice of letting his wife out to anyone who would pay well. But the woman objected to going to Doncaster and so he went to her in disguise. He made an arrangement with the husband, kept a *mehanah* (a small palankeen) and a team of bearers for her, and a *chaukidar* (watchman) at the Brahman's house. Latterly, the woman had become tired of being 'made into a common prostitute', as (he said) she put it, and so she was staying in a little bungalow Doncaster had in his grounds. The husband wanted her back and had applied to the justices.

Blechynden told Doncaster frankly that this narrative 'bordered on the marvellous' and he did not expect the justices to believe it, especially with a Brahman involved. Doncaster insisted that it was true and that the woman had quarrelled with her husband because he had taken another wife. Blechynden pointed out that Doncaster was committing adultery, even if the husband was a monster. The law would not be an idle spectator, he added; Doncaster must take the consequences if he insisted on retaining the woman.

Next day, Nilmunny Ghose, invariably called Lilloo, one of Blechynden's sircars, said that the Brahman had been with Ramnarain Misser (no doubt a vakil, or pleader), who was preparing a petition for him to the Supreme Court. Blechynden warned Doncaster and urged him to either pay off the husband and keep the woman, or dismiss the woman and still give a present to the husband. As another option, he could send her to the justices to complain against her husband for putting her into prostitution and to demand a separation from him. Doncaster was worried but would not do anything. He claimed to have no partiality for the woman, who was not young. Blechynden could not understand his motives. Lilloo reported that the Brahman was going to petition Bruce, Blechynden, and Barber & Palmer. Blechynden asked if it was true that he had let his wife go out to Doncaster. Lilloo thought so. Then (said Blechynden) Lilloo should warn the Brahman 'not to present any of his filthy petitions or even to show his face'.

Lilloo reported that the 'pimping sircar', Netaije, now 'cohabits' with the woman at night in Doncaster's bungalow whilst Doncaster slept in the house; even worse, Netaije 'had the impudence to sleep' upon one of Blechynden's hall couches. Blechynden had been angry at how soiled it was and now found it was 'from his dirty hide!' 'Only let me catch him doing it—or hear that he has done so again,' Blechynden wrote. The dhobi (washerman), Ramohan, agreed that Netaije slept almost every night with this woman of Doncaster's. She had left her husband on the sircar's account and now the two of them were making Doncaster 'the Cat's paw to pay the piper' (the mix of metaphors being Blechynden's). Doncaster returned with

Netaije, whom Blechynden accused of sleeping on the couch. He denied it faintly, but Blechynden called in the malis (gardeners), who silenced him. Blechynden complained of this 'insult' to Doncaster, who had listened to the exchange and, with an odd look, promised that it would not happen again. Blechynden said he would make sure it did not. He ordered the couch covers and pillowcases to be washed and the couch bedding put away.

The following weekend, Blechynden spent some time putting his garden house to rights. He made a point of asking the malis if they had actually seen the sircar asleep on the couch and they both asserted that they had, for he had been there every night. They said that when Blechynden was in town, the woman would come and go into Doncaster's room. Netaije would wait, lying on the couch. When the woman came out, she would lie there with him. When Blechynden was at the gardens, the woman would be brought to Doncaster's bungalow. Netaije again would replace Doncaster and stay with her all night. Mary Wade, the bibi of James Wade, a pilot with the Company's Marine and Blechynden's neighbour in town, had more detail to add. By her account, Doncaster had given gold bangles to the Brahman woman, and her brother, or someone claiming to be her brother, was demanding money from him. When Doncaster, tiring of this, ordered that the man should be kept out of his property, the woman had become very angry and threatened to give the man her bangles instead. The 'crowning of the whole is—that Doncaster caught Netaije & her *Rem et Rei*—on which she fell on her knees promising that nothing of the kind should happen again—and he at last not only forgave her but actually has taken Netaije into his service again!' Blechynden had no idea how Mrs Wade came by this story, but he enjoyed it very much and shared it with others.

He did wonder what Doncaster's other servants thought, and had his answer a few days later. One of them, Govindram, told him that he believed his master a 'little crack'd'. He was going about the house without shoes or stockings, wearing only a banyan (undershirt) and waistcoat, a Bengali gold chain round his neck, and pantaloons with their legs turned up over his thighs. Govindram's father Neederam was in disgrace with Doncaster because he had remonstrated with him about keeping a woman who was, he said, 'a common prostitute'. Blechynden said that he had heard in Calcutta of Netaije's offence and retention—and Govindram confirmed this, adding only that, laughably, Netaije was now forbidden to go near the bungalow. A couple of months later, Blechynden met Govindram again, over his cow, which had strayed into the garden. He said that Neederam, who had served Doncaster for eighteen or twenty years, had been dismissed for his remarks. Blechynden thought that such a faithful servant should have been superannuated upon a pension. Neederam went to Dacca to seek work.

At the end of August, Netaije himself turned up at Blechynden's gate, making 'very humble salaam'. Blechynden told Lilloo to turn him out, but Lilloo begged that he might be admitted as he had 'something very particular to communicate'. When he came in, he brought with him the Brahman husband, who said his name was Jaggermohun Banargee. His wife was called Gourt Money. He wanted Blechynden to give him a chit for an attorney so that he could complain to the Supreme Court. Blechynden said that he would not do this for anyone, let alone for 'such a fellow as him who had stood pimp to his own wife'. The husband said that that was not true. In his version of events, he had been employed by Doncaster to superintend repairs to his cutter. While he was away, Doncaster had gone to his house in disguise and stolen his wife. Blechynden told him Doncaster's different story and (he wrote) 'reprimanded him so severely with his loss of cast & the great disgrace he has brought upon all Bramins that he burst into tears and seized my feet'. Blechynden persisted in refusing to help and warned Jaggermohun not to go to the law, because his own hands were not clean. He spoke in English, with his writer Gopey Naut Doss translating—he wanted witnesses in case the man really did go to court.

Later, he upset Jaggermohun again by reminding him that he had given his wife to a man who ate cow's flesh. But the Brahman rallied and again asked for Blechynden's help. He wanted his wife back. Surely, said Blechynden, she was contaminated? Jaggermohun said that the father of his other wife had taken her away and all his relations had left him; even inferior castes would not associate with him. He needed his first wife for company. Blechynden said that he must want revenge and would kill her. Jaggermohun insisted that he was fond of her and she of him. If only she could hear his voice, she would return to him. Blechynden said that she gave 'curious proof' of her affection and he had better not have her back, or she might poison his food.

Taking advantage of Netaije's presence, Blechynden also complained to him again about his couch. He denied responsibility. He said that he sat there a couple of times waiting for Doncaster, but it was the woman's 'greasy hide' had soiled it, 'Doncaster & she having carnal knowledge of each other thereon *in his presence!*' 'They all stared,' recalled Blechynden, 'but I blushed at the idea of his being an European—& we made him repeat it that there might be no mistake.' Netaije said that Doncaster had seen Gourt by accident one day and had lusted after her. He promised Netaije Rs 1,000 to secure her for him; the temptation was too much for Netaije.

He had not yet had the money, however, he complained. Blechynden said that he had forfeited it by having relations with her himself.

Rival ideas about marriage were evoked in these exchanges. Propriety was also an issue: Blechynden was appalled at the extent to which Doncaster had 'violated the rights of hospitality'. As if 'bawdy' and 'Braminical adultery' were not enough, it appeared Gourt Money was not Doncaster's only partner. He was 'perpetually having whores' to the house. One night, Netaije had been bringing a girl for him from Calcutta and when she saw the guards at Saum Bazar bridge, she knew that they were leaving the limits of the town and would not go on, calling out to the sepoys. Netaije had told them that he was taking her to Blechynden, the name they knew, rather than Doncaster, and they let her pass. Blechynden pointed out that this and having the Brahman woman in his house put him in danger from the Supreme Court and even of being deported from Calcutta. Netaije stared and attempted an apology. Finally, Blechynden ended the discussion, his 'train of thinking' very much changed.[44]

What does this sorry tale tell us, finally, about European friendships? Dealing with servant's interests or grievances could threaten friendly relations between European men.[45] In this case, a breach between the two neighbours, Doncaster and Blechynden, was occasioned by the amorous servant Netaije. A couple of days after Blechynden reprimanded him, in front of Doncaster, for allegedly sleeping with Gourt Money on one of Blechynden's couches, Blechynden received a chit from Doncaster to thank him for the accommodation and to say that he was leaving the house and returning to his own. Blechynden knew Doncaster's house was far from finished, its new plaster still wet, and so replied that he could not understand this note except as meaning that Doncaster had taken offence at his reproving 'a dirty Bengally', and if he did not find Doncaster still at his house, he would conclude he wished to drop his acquaintance.[46]

After a delay of two days, Doncaster replied that he was not being capricious, as Blechynden had suggested, and the 'occurrence of Sunday'— which he had never intended to mention again had Blechynden not done so—had not 'solely influenced him'; rather, he referred to Blechynden's response. Doncaster had not imagined his servants' faults would be a fit matter for Blechynden to investigate, he wrote, or that he should have thought it necessary to do so, considering Doncaster's evident desire for the 'good order and decency' of the house. He had already investigated Netaije's conduct himself and had severely reprimanded the man over his sleeping on the hall couch. (In the later conversation with Blechynden, Netaije denied this, saying that Doncaster had only told him not to speak to Blechynden on the matter.) A mali, angrily brought in by Blechynden and eagerly believed (said Doncaster) could not possibly have been an eyewitness and would not have known anything except for Doncaster's reprimand. Finding the couches stripped had convinced Doncaster that he could not just ignore the matter or put it down to Blechynden's ill health. However, he had not left with the intention of dropping their acquaintance—'a very cold term' for the footing on which they had been—but rather because it was necessary to do so if they were to continue their good relations. A 'curious farrago of contradiction', thought Blechynden. He would not reply. He did show the letter to another former house guest, Grant, and they had a good laugh, Grant saying that the surest way of living in friendship is to keep apart.[47]

The next time Blechynden was at the gardens after the argument, Doncaster's man had arrived and started laying the cloth for breakfast, saying that his master had told him to do so. Hitherto, food had been brought from Doncaster's kitchen: breakfast might typically be boiled rice, salt fish, bread and butter, and tea. Blechynden stopped the man and sent him back with his compliments to Doncaster, adding that if he chose to breakfast with Blechynden, he would be glad of his company, but his own breakfast was coming from Calcutta. After this, relations with Doncaster were not restored. When Blechynden was urged by friends to ignore his neighbour's note, he replied that he did not like to have his 'feelings put in competition with those of his [Doncaster's] pimp'.

Doncaster made overtures again a few days later, reminding Blechynden that he had offered to lend him money to pay for his children's passage to England, but Blechynden replied with thanks that he had raised the money needed. He saw the intention, he thought, which was try to come back to Blechynden's because he was 'cursedly cramped for room' where he was. Blechynden bore him no ill will, he claimed, except to 'abominate hypocrisy'. A couple of days later, Doncaster called on Blechynden in passing, but received a cool welcome, and the next day did so again, awkwardly, after hovering a while at the gate. Blechynden, already dubious about financial involvement with Doncaster, now had no immediate need of his preferred financial aid. He was concerned at the nature of his commercial ventures: he could not trust a man, he thought, whose concerns over an Indian servant (and a series of Indian women) seemed to have been placed above his regard for a European gentleman.

Later, Doncaster was imprisoned on charges relating to salt dealings and, despairing of release, sent for Gourt Money again. She had been amusing herself with Govindram, the bearer, which Blechynden supposed was natural enough, as they were both Hindu and Doncaster was very ugly; but also ungrateful, as Doncaster had spent a lot on her. Some months before, Blechynden was told a gardener had been keeping another man's wife in a lower room at his garden house. Discovered by the husband, the couple had decamped to Doncaster's grounds. Blechynden remarked drily that it was indeed 'a proper place for an adulterer'. More seriously, attempts to define and preserve propriety within his own household had been shaping his relations with friends and servants. Here we glimpse some examples of the rules of law and conduct framing English norms and aspirations, and also of the exchanges promoting Indian understandings of or dissent from European ways.[48]

## THOMAS BLECHYNDEN (C. 1801–20 MAY 1845)

Related to friendship was Blechynden's strong family sense, also derived from his own experience. According to Laurence Stone, there is evidence, at least in higher social groups, of strong ties between siblings, especially brothers and sisters from the eighteenth century. Blechynden, an orphan, repeatedly protested his affection and gratitude to his aunt and uncle in England, the Theobalds, who supported him as a child and to whom he wrote often. He very frequently lamented the fate of his dear sister lost in the wreck of the *Grosvenor*. He assumed his relatives would care for his children in England as a duty, not only in return for the remittances he sent them. On her death, he wrote sadly of his aunt, a second mother to his sisters and himself as well as to his children. Arthur was taken in by her in Great James Street, near Gray's Inn. His aunt, Charlotte Whitchurch of Bramley in Hampshire, taught him English (he said).[49]

In turn, Blechynden took responsibility for Tom, the illegitimate son of Blechynden's cousin Marmaduke, left to grow up in Calcutta when his father returned to England. Tom's story shows how ties and responsibilities were strongly located within families, particularly around concepts of obligation and gratitude that were important to Blechynden and that he expected and welcomed in others. Tom came into Blechynden's household as a result of an involved series of events. Blechynden was intimately involved from the start, long before Tom came into his care. The story began when Tom's father, Marmaduke, returned to Calcutta from Bombay, possibly 'heart sick' and certainly in for an unpleasant surprise. While he was away, his mistress, Tom's mother Sally Everell, had moved in with a ship's captain, Richard Aungier.[50] Marmaduke had travelled back with a Captain Joliffe, working on his ship as second mate. On his arrival in Calcutta in October 1803, he was discovered by Blechynden unexpectedly in Bow Bazar. A previous visit had left the cousins estranged. Marmaduke shied away and his cousin was inclined to do likewise, but thought better of it. It was too cruel to cut him and so Blechynden spoke to him.

Blechynden was pained not to invite Marmaduke home to breakfast but believed from experience that if once he got him into his house, he would never get him out again. Marmaduke was looking for the lodgings of his previous captain, Phipps, who had also been an open admirer of Sally Everell. Blechynden pointed out the place. Marmaduke dashed in to ask about Sally. Later, he wrote to Blechynden that he was 'sensible of his past follies' and they should not be at variance, especially given the 'mean character' of the man who was the instigator of their differences. Admitting that he had been the 'aggressor', he asked for forgiveness. He claimed that he wanted neither money nor accommodation, and indeed it soon emerged that he was staying in Serampore to keep away from a creditor, a man also known to Sally, called Spencer, to whom Marmaduke owed Rs 640 for accommodation at Cape Town.

Blechynden inevitably allowed himself to be drawn in. He could not allow Marmaduke to go to the dogs, however 'unsteady and weak a character' he was. Blechynden was also already thinking about the environment in which Tom, still a baby, was being brought up. About this time, Blechynden had witnessed at the Police Office a case brought before the justices concerning Phipps's servant or midshipman, Joseph. He wished to leave Phipps, but Phipps wanted him to return with him to England. Some surprise was expressed in court when it appeared that someone so young was frequenting bawdy houses. Blechynden sent a note to the justice, Macklew, saying that the occasion of the boy's corruption had been Phipps's using him as his pimp (in pursuit of Sally and others).

There followed a social call to Blechynden by Richard Aungier, presenting himself as a friend of Marmaduke's. Blechynden said he had given 'singular proof' of friendship, which evoked no reaction. Aungier claimed that he had taken on Sally only because she was not provided for and that he was trying to get Spencer to accept Rs 200 in settlement of Marmaduke's debt. Blechynden remarked only that people ought to honour their debts when they could and that the real need was to get the boy, Tom, from Sally. Aungier said that it would be a great punishment of the mother to deprive her of her child and that he was willing to provide for him. (There was also Tom's sister, who was in England, but Aungier knew nothing of her.) Blechynden replied that he did not choose that a child who shared his name should be dependent on a stranger.

It did not take Marmaduke long to begin claiming his cousin's support. Snatching at a reminder that Blechynden had once been willing to advance Rs 11,000 to buy a share in a ship, provided Marmaduke had the command, he asked Blechynden first to do so now, at Rs 7,000, and then to lend him Rs 10,000 to buy a share for himself. Trade was 'dull' and ships were for sale relatively cheaply. Blechynden, taken aback, decided that it would be better after all for Marmaduke to gain more experience as a first mate before he took on a command. In the meantime, he advanced him fifty rupees and, as the threat from Spencer had been removed, made him move from a tavern into his house. He took to staying home to be company for Marmaduke as he was low-spirited, and ended up paying some of his debts, which were far more extensive than admitted, including a settlement of Rs 100 for the Rs 136 owed to a European tailor, Moffat—all for clothes for Sally, to Blechynden's irritation—as well as a debt of over Rs 200 to Aungier that Blechynden felt had to be discharged in the circumstances.[51]

Marmaduke's focus was on Sally. Tearful and frantic, he talked of giving her 'a pat on the head' and taking her away in a palankeen. Blechynden told him that he was well shot of her, but Marmaduke took no notice and unexpectedly put his plan into effect. There was a fracas in which he was seized by a constable, who was also injured. Marmaduke was brought before the magistrate, Thoroton, and ordered to provide two separate securities of Rs 1,000 and his own recognizance of Rs 5,000 for a violent assault on 'Sarah Ellis' and Aungier's servants. Blechynden provided one security and asked Tiretta for the other, and explained to Thoroton that Marmaduke had brought Sally out, had had two children by her, and had not abandoned her; her ill conduct had made him half crazy. Thoroton said that he had been too violent for the justices to ignore his conduct. It had also been decided that the 'stupid constable' (Hodge) had overreacted in the fracas and would have to be discharged. Blechynden, like Thoroton, regarded this as compounding rather than mitigating Marmaduke's fault. Marmaduke then became determined to get a passage home and wanted the magistrates to order Sally to leave Calcutta so that she would be forced to accompany him.

True to his cousin's wishes, Marmaduke next took legal action to get custody of his children. Blechynden wrote the deposition for him, appealing to Sir John Royds, as he was said always to favour the petitioner. The initial response was that Marmaduke must first ask for the child to be given up, which he did, sending a copy of the petition and certificates from a Rev. Wringham (presumably to prove paternity). The bearer was refused admittance to Aungier's house and when this was reported to Royds, he agreed to a hearing. Sally was very alarmed and appealed to Phipps for help, fearful that she would be ordered to give up her child, now fourteen months old, because he was a boy.

When the case came before Sir John, Sally of course was neither present nor consulted, though Blechynden's men—Gopey, Davy Persaud Naug, and Rammohun Chatterjee—all attended. Aungier was represented by Blechynden's old enemy William Townsend Jones, who sought to blacken Marmaduke's character by referring to his being bound over for violent behaviour. Marmaduke responded that he had not brought out Sally to prostitute herself and had been trying to save her from perdition. Aungier represented Marmaduke as a 'vagabond' and claimed that Blechynden had told him as much. As the squabble developed, Royds told them to be silent and adjourned the hearing to consult Blechynden, who was rather annoyed at having been drawn in. He explained to a surprised Sir John that Marmaduke was not a vagrant, but had been chief mate of an Indiaman and had had nearly thirty years at sea, and though not employed just now, was looking for a post: he could find one at any moment. Blechynden also criticized Aungier, and Royds said that he certainly did not care for the company he kept, presumably referring to W.T. Jones. Would Blechynden bind himself to maintain the boy for life, asked Sir John. Blechynden replied that he would of course support Tom if Marmaduke died, but otherwise could hardly make such a commitment to another man's illegitimate child. At this, Royds decided that he would not interfere, given that the boy was so young. Much later, Blechynden was told that Sally had been willing to swear the child was not Marmaduke's rather than risk losing him and had been relieved that she had not needed to perjure herself.[52]

Losing this battle—to Aungier rather than Sally—Marmaduke soon decided to take up a place found for him, calling in favours, as third mate on the *United Kingdom* under Captain Richardson. It became available because the fourth mate was unwilling to sit the examination allowing him to be promoted. Marmaduke was then shaken by news that Aungier and Sally were arguing: she had threatened to go back to Marmaduke, and Aungier had had to go 'down on his hands and knees to her'. Blechynden urged his cousin to take no notice. But next day, Richardson called to tell Marmaduke to report to the ship and confirmed that Sally and Aungier had been married. Marmaduke went to the United Kingdom, carrying fifty rupees and some cold meat as a gift from his cousin. It was on this voyage that he took Blechynden's children, Charlotte and James, to England.[53]

Not long after her marriage, Sally was treated for a flux and not expected to live. She died on 5 May 1803, creating speculation about who would look after her two-year-old son—Blechynden or Aungier. At first, it was the latter. However, early in 1805, after Aungier had gone to sea and no word had been had from him, it was said that there was scarcely any hope he was still alive, unless (as was possible) he had gone to America. Tom had been placed with a Mrs Anne Mountain, a hairdresser's wife, and at first 'tenderly treated'. But now that his stepfather was feared lost, he was far from comfortable—or so Blechynden was told by Reddell, an associate of Aungier. Would Blechynden give Tom protection? Blechynden was torn, as he saw it, between the call of humanity and justice to his own children: if he took responsibility for Tom, it would be for ever. Many sentiments divided his heart. He put off giving Reddell any answer and asked a ship's captain, Sharp, if he would be able to get the boy back to England. Sharp said that it would be impossible and argued that Blechynden should have nothing to do with him. He received the same advice from Aungier's own cousin, recently arrived from Europe. Blechynden wrote back to Reddell and said that any interference from him would be premature, if not improper; but he would write to Tom's father, Marmaduke.[54]

In September 1805, news came that Marmaduke too had died. Blechynden immediately expressed concern about his cousin's children, including his daughter in England, and sent to find out how Tom was placed and whether Aungier had left funds for his support. Again, reports of his treatment at Mrs Mountain's were not reassuring. Tom had been found wandering along the river and then had been harshly received and locked up when returned. Cassinaut made inquiries, however, and said that Tom was treated the same as Mrs Mountain's own daughter and Blechynden would do well to leave him where he was. Downie agreed, giving Mrs Mountain a good character. For his part, Blechynden was not eager to take on Tom.

Family feeling prevailed, however. Blechynden could not 'in conscience refuse a fostering hand'. Further inquiries confirmed that Aungier's ship had surely been lost. A letter from its first mate had complained that it was too low in the water and two pumps had to be kept going constantly. No further letter had been received; there would surely have been some communication if the ship had reached America. It was recommended that Blechynden put Tom in the Free School and, when he was old enough, to have him train as a pilot, which Blechynden thought a good idea, though 'the boy's liking to it' would first have to be ascertained. A few weeks later, Anne Mountain contacted him and he decided that Tom would have to come to him. Mrs Mountain said that Aungier had left a will in the boy's favour and she would not mind maintaining him, but could not do so. She had a shop to run and he was a great plague to her. He was constantly getting into mischief and breaking valuable goods, including a twelve-rupee container of rose water that he then mopped up with new silk stockings. Aged about four, he could drink as much madeira as she did and had recently become quite 'outrageous' after drinking some raw brandy. Her husband endorsed her report. Despite these unflattering testimonials, Blechynden promised he would make 'some family arrangements' and then take Tom home.

Mrs Mountain asked them to wait a few days until Tom's clothes were back from the wash. He was not ready when Blechynden sent his palankeen but came the same afternoon, with Mr Mountain and a note: notwithstanding the trouble and vexation he had caused—and a piece of mischief the night before had given her the courage to let him go—Mrs Mountain was grieved to part with him; she trusted he would be better provided for; and if Blechynden were agreeable, he might spend one or two Sundays a month with her. He had been furnished with six morning and two evening dresses, four nightshirts, two pinafores, two pairs of boots and one of shoes, a couple of hats, a cot with mattress and pillow, a curtain, sheet, pillowcase, and counterpane, a powder box and puff, a hairbrush, a small-toothed and a pocket comb, a book, a sword, and a gun.[55]

He had some medical problems that Blechynden had checked out.[56] He needed to 'unlearn' many things. 'Damned' seemed his favourite adjective, and though he had been sent to a school, he had not learnt to say his prayers. Blechynden's bibi Isabella took him in hand, not yet having children of her own. Tom provided her with companionship and quickly adjusted to his new life. Their first outing was to take Isabella's mother home after dinner. They went on quite long walks together, getting their feet wet while visiting the Seebpore bund, for example, where Blechynden was working. One Sunday, the Mountains' palankeen arrived for Tom at 11 AM instead of 4 PM, the usual time. Isabella refused to let him go as she would be left alone. As the palankeen did not return at 4 PM, she took Tom with her on her afternoon ride and dropped him at the gate. The durwan picked him up and he started to cry very loudly, something he had also done on previous visits. Mrs Mountain came out, seemed angry, and called him a spoilt child. Hearing this, Blechynden decided that the visits should stop.

In 1808, Tom turned seven and was sent to Pritchard's school 'over the way' at Blechynden's expense, at two rupees per month for reading, to be raised to three rupees once he was able to write. Some time after his eighth birthday, he transferred to Mr Maclean's school. Great things were not expected. A few days later, the palankeen went to bring him home and came back without him, as he was in disgrace for having hurt another boy. He stayed at Maclean's another eighteen months, however, until he was sent back to Pritchard's, who agreed to board and educate him for thirty-two rupees. Maclean was asked to send his bed, chest, and clothes (and a bill). The new school was pleasantly situated and Pritchard a 'well informed young man', though Arthur Blechynden, in a typical remark, thought his wife evidently a 'country educated lady as her manners fully shewed'. He told Pritchard something of Tom's character so that he might 'correct his morals', said to have been injured in Maclean's care.

Later, Tom also was sent to England, returning in October 1818. He had been refused a cadetship by the Directors, which Blechynden thought ungenerous, given his father had served the Company for thirty-one years. He resolved to help Tom if he could, reflecting that he might be grateful, as a poor orphan, at a time when some of his own children were proving 'undutiful'. After this, Tom assisted Blechynden in his work, preparing pens, riding out with him on his duties, and attending him at a property arbitration; but he seemed to be lacking in energy and even competence. One pleasant, cool day, they went on a survey, after which Tom complained of fatigue. Surveying, he announced, was even worse than snipe shooting. Blechynden thought it abominable that a lad of eighteen or nineteen had less stamina than a man nearing sixty—who had found the whole experience delightful and had returned home in high spirits. It was 'mere laziness' in Tom. He never volunteered to help, nor asked a single question. He would not even look through the telescope of the theodolite out of curiosity. He kept having to sit down and, when sent to check the measurements the peons were making, walked at a snail's pace. As a consequence, Blechynden exclaimed: 'What I shall do with him the Lord alone knows!' Even at home, when there was copying to be done, Tom would be found wandering about with his hands in his pockets instead of offering to help.

Blechynden began to test him: for example, getting him to multiply 125.6 by 108.6 and trying him in Latin (which Tom claimed to know) and French. Blechynden decided a great deal of money had been thrown away on Tom's education, which was 'very little to the credit of Mr March's tuition' (in England). A little later, Blechynden asked Tom to show him the square root of 288, which he could not. On examining him more closely, Blechynden found that he knew little of the 'higher parts of arithmetic and nothing of trigonometry'. He concluded that except for the 'enlargement of his ideas by visiting England he might as well have remained in this country'. He repeated: he had 'thrown away a great deal of money on him'. Eventually, Tom found a place as an assistant in the Accountant-General's office.[57]

Blechynden's impatience should not conceal the main fact: Tom remained in his care. Blechynden's acceptance of this duty, without support, speaks to a sense of familial responsibility that was not only common, it was unavoidable. Another example will remind us of how this worked. It relates to Colonel Robert Kyd, founder of the Calcutta Botanical Garden, and his relative and heir Alexander. It exemplifies the expectations, in a world based on patronage, of the duties of relations and the part to be played by connection. A cousin of Robert Kyd's was a navy captain in East India service. His son, Sandy, or Alexander, had arrived in Calcutta in 1772 without employment but with a letter of introduction to Robert Kyd. But Robert decided (he wrote to his cousin in Fifeshire) that Sandy should be sent back on the first ship, because in the changing circumstances of India, there was no choice but that he should enter the army, which should be after he had qualified as an engineer and artillery officer, and above all (using all the influence his father could bring to bear), once he had gained an ensign's commission. To achieve this, Robert provided Sandy with money sufficient to cover his expenses for two years and also introduced him to friends who, 'in case of any accident happening to myself, will receive and provide for him in a manner next to what he would have expected from myself'. Before taking it upon himself to devise this 'startling' plan, Robert consulted his friends, who supported his judgement. The plan worked. Alexander had a successful career as an army engineer and was appointed Surveyor-General as well as to other high posts. He retained a keen sense of his debt. After his cousin's death in 1793, he commissioned a memorial to be designed and built by Richard Blechynden, incorporating an imported urn by Thomas Banks, the neoclassical sculptor.

The code of conduct here is very plain, as also when Alexander Kyd helped Blechynden during his greatest financial crisis, and Blechynden marvelled at his 'innate generosity', doing so much for someone who was 'no relation': 'What claims have I on Major Kyd,' he wrote, '...that should entitle me to put my hand in his purse?' In fact there *were* claims, related to kinship, friendship, and nationality (in that order), heightened by the exigencies of Calcutta life at this time. Duty to kin was the last word, as well as a guiding principle of Marmaduke's and then Tom's troubled relations with their cousin, Richard Blechynden. Loyalty was both strong and necessary for a European in Calcutta.[58]

# 2

# A Pernicious Race?

I cannot but conclude the bulk of your natives to be the most pernicious race
of little odious vermin that nature ever suffered to crawl upon the surface of
the earth.
—King of Brobdingnag, in Jonathan Swift, *Gulliver's Travels* (1726)[1]

## THE WHITE AND BLACK TOWNS

We now come to consider British attitudes to Calcutta and its Indian
inhabitants. In that context, the king of Brobdingnag's verdict on Gulliver's
description of his own land and customs is a two-edged sword.

It is said the settlement of Calcutta grew rapidly and was 'built without
order'; and yet also had become a 'city of palaces' by the late eighteenth
century. 'Built without order' is from Alexander Hamilton's *New Account
of the East Indies* (1727); but he too noted the segregation of Indian and
European inhabitants. Calcutta always contained two separate, segregated
entities: Indians inland and Europeans on the riverside. The town
showed seaborne outsiders a superficially European face. It needed to be
*represented* as ordered, and regulation of a kind was in place from early in
the eighteenth century. Thus there were great houses, business premises,
and modern amenities for the Europeans, and grass and mud huts for the
Indians—with exceptions among the Bengali elite. Pradip Sinha, one of
Calcutta's leading historians, called the divide a 'cleavage in ... [the] urban
fabric'. The result on the European side was 'Forever England', the title of
one study, or, as another put it, 'a half familiar background' increasingly
withdrawn from Indian society.[2]

Fear of contamination by 'black inhabitants of the lower orders' is
repeatedly reported by historians, as in Banerjee's felicitously entitled
*The Parlour and the Streets*, citing two ordinances from 1818 and 1821

against native foot passengers crossing the Esplanade and against coolies and workmen making a thoroughfare of the Walk between the hours of 5.00 and 8.00 morning and evening. Swati Chattopadhyay, by contrast, has asserted that the description of a divided city rests 'on scant evidence', both architecturally and in terms of the buildings' uses and occupants. She identifies instead a 'hybrid colonial culture' that Europeans were reluctant to recognize: their camouflage was to over-define the 'black' and 'white' towns.[3] Let us explore these issues further.

Too much should not be made of it, but—forty years after Plassey—there were certainly occasional panics at the Europeans' precarious situation amidst throngs of possibly hostile Indians, especially at a time of European war. In April 1799, for example, rumours spread that the Muslims were in league to 'cut us all off on the 5th of June next during the Mohurram'; the family of the Dacca nawabs was implicated. Some of this was the usual demonizing of the French. Blechynden thought they were probably to blame and should all be deported. One Beaumais had been sent out of the country in January. Blechynden commented that there would be no peace with any of the country (Indian) powers until every 'intriguing Frenchman' had been excluded. When the French general Perrow offered to place all his money in the Company's treasury so that he could remain under surety for good behaviour, Blechynden was concerned that the Company would be tempted. More immediately relevant, a French armourer and cutler, Pierre Augier, had been caught in Calcutta with 600 new gunlocks that he had tried to pass off as scraps of old iron.

Among Muslims, letters had been intercepted and arrests made in Murshidabad: three, at least two men of rank, were sent down to Calcutta under guard. A militia had been formed among the Europeans in 1798 and now its drilling took on new significance. Blechynden hoped that their preparations would 'prove to Blackey that this is not the season to put their intentions in execution'. Orders were given to keep weapons away from Frenchmen, even during cleaning, and also to store them in bedchambers, ready for a call to arms. That year's celebration of Muharram was later banned in the city. Just before it, some Calcutta residents were still anxious, though perhaps by then they were thought a trifle ridiculous by others: Downie told Blechynden that he had seen 'little [Thomas] Raban [an attorney] ... busy agreeing' with a Sikh to provide a guard of fifty men for his garden house. A committee was appointed (Barlow, Harrington, and Blaquiere)[4] to consider the defenceless state of the town and 'put it into some state of security'. They called in Blechynden to see to the deepening of the Maratha ditch and extending various walls. He advised a deep entrenchment and bank across the main road near the burial ground in Park Street as well as various other temporary ditches. He was then informed that it was no longer necessary, because the news of the defeat of Tipu Sultan had reached Bengal from Mysore—notably, the British already thought of 'India' or least 'Muslims' as a single entity and loyalty. Blechynden was asked instead to work up a plan on the best way of securing the town permanently—for example, against thieves. Dacoity—robbery by armed gangs—remained an occasional problem even within Calcutta. He devised a scheme for enclosing the town.[5]

Meanwhile, in April, rumours and events had been increasing anxiety. True, the merchant and shipbuilder Jonathan Gillett was less alarmist than most. He was assaulted one night, in the midst of the panic, by his *consomah* (house steward), *hookabadar* (hookah bearer), and *mater* (male sweeper), but he merely knocked them downstairs and 'contented himself with turning them out of his service'; they had been drunk and unarmed. By contrast, one Graham acquiesced when his munshi (interpreter, secretary) strongly urged him, out of friendship, to leave Calcutta and retire to his own house and remain there quietly—'something very important is going forward,' mused Blechynden. He heard a Captain de Lemain had his throat cut at Benares by his hookabadar, who first drugged him by putting opiates in the hookah—a lesson, thought Blechynden, on the need for 'vigilance over these villainous people'. An acquaintance walking at night was shoved into a drain by a 'stout Musselman with a talwar [sabre] who called him a "firingy banchute"'[6]—ergo, there is 'certainly a very heavy storm brewing'. Another's durwan (doorkeeper) was seen flourishing a sabre outside the Free School and shouting that the British had lived there long enough and would all be killed; he was arrested and set to beat *surky* (plaster). Blechynden wondered, '[H]ow many warnings do Government want?' Muslims were said to be drilling in secret every night outside Calcutta—'all very fine'. There were fifty or sixty at a time, according to another report, vowing to kill the Europeans. Five *hackerries* (carts) laden with arms were seized by a constable—bayonets, swords, muskets, and pistols, some of them French: 'we have been lulled into too much security,' commented Blechynden.

Communications with Indians at all levels continued as normal, but at the same time, Blechynden thought the threat real: 'we are always unarmed and surrounded by a host of servants.' He would be on his guard. He cast about 200 musket and pistol balls, and decided to keep a pair of loaded pistols under his pillow. In newspapers and at dinner tables, similar precautions were advised. Blechynden inspected his own household. He found his durwan with a rusty-looking talwar that he said belonged to his brother, left with him to be cleaned. Drawing the sword, Blechynden found it sharp and well-oiled, and so confiscated it. This decided him on a full inventory. Currim, his peon and *sekilgar* (armourer and knife grinder), first claimed that all their weapons had been taken by the *chaukidar*s, evidently in a round-up of the houses. He had recently sold a pistol to Nusser Ullah, a Muslim dealer in petty articles in Mulcha Bazar. Under pressure, he admitted that he still had an old sword belonging to a deceased chaukidar and another belonging to Wales's sice (groom), which he was to clean and sharpen in return for eight annas. Then he admitted that he had a dagger belonging to Blechynden's hookabadar, Panchew, who had sworn Currim to secrecy. Blechynden quizzed Panchew, who denied having any weapon in the house—he was not a peon (guard) or a chaukidar, he said—but finally he too acknowledged that he had given the dagger to Currim to clean. He had denied this as he thought Blechynden would be angry at his employing Currim, he said; but it was an old weapon from 1781, when he had been in service during Chait Singh's rebellion; he had four children; and so on—becoming, as Blechynden put it, 'mighty submissive'. Currim then confessed to having a sabre belonging to Ramzanny, the *dhye* (maid), given to him for mending. She explained that it belonged to her son, who was (said Blechynden) 'quite a boy' and had gone to sea with Powell, Blechynden's friend. In all, Currim produced twelve weapons of various kinds. Blechynden locked them in a clothes press.[7]

Nonetheless, despite this instance and the numerous arms possessed by servants and apparently maintained by Blechynden's sekilgar, the *rarity* rather than the existence of such scares might be remarked on, given what Blechynden claimed to be a ratio of one European to every 18,000 Indians in Calcutta. The divide between Europeans and Indians was not generally based on fear and hostility. More important to separateness were colonial definition and enumeration, alongside modern means of communication and organization, which changed the scale and nature of felt identities in India as elsewhere. Out of these apparently objective and universalizing tendencies, there developed labels such as 'India(n)', 'Hindu', and 'Muslim'. This is an argument about contexts and consequences, not suggesting that categorizations (even those such as 'manly' Rajputs or 'effeminate, clever' Bengalis) were invented without any input from observation or indigenous stereotypes: there is evidence of ancient and broad pre-colonial identities as well. But the British developed an essentialized shorthand as the major mode for understanding the people they ruled, and changed the categories' character and function.

This supports the view that though there was no permanent stand-off between hostile camps, there *were* categorizations of space and people dividing early Calcutta. In particular, questions of employment, social relations, and law spilled over into issues of race. The contemporary analysis of human society implied steady movement from wild to tame, from barbarian to advanced. As European experience grew more complex, one response was to incorporate all chronologically and geographically remote civilizations into a single universal scheme that still flattered Europeans. Another was to identify a civilized and temperate middle zone, already familiar from Ptolemy and Arab geographers, with regions that did *not* lie between the tropics. David Hume blamed the weather. As a man of the Enlightenment and a Scot, he found a virtue in hardship: the need for clothing and warm housing led ultimately to property, government, and civility. The focus became supposedly intrinsic characteristics (or race) and a narrative of causation (or science). Thus, it has been argued, the social map was 'filled with colour'. During the eighteenth century, even Englishmen realized that there could be a barbarian within—the heretic, the poor, and the proletarian—and a civilized outside as great cultures and histories were encountered. How could this be finessed? Egypt, Athens, Rome, the new Jerusalem, the Indo-European region, and the supposedly non-African Zimbabwe were all found European identities or connections. A choice of markers also became useful: dress, customs, and treatment of women; skills and abilities; art and architecture; law and polities; and finally skin colour and physiognomy. When colonial experience, especially in India and the Far East, showed that favoured attributes were attainable by others, it was necessary to concentrate on the intrinsic and the physical.[8]

C.A. Bayly has written: 'What began to change in the last twenty years of the eighteenth century was that the notion of "native depravity" became generalized to [apply to] all Indians.'[9] In this familiar view of racism emerging, race relations in Calcutta are usually assumed to have been more relaxed in the eighteenth than in the nineteenth century—James Long popularized this idea and many have taken it up. The arrival of greater numbers of Englishwomen is usually blamed for the deterioration. On Blechynden's evidence, the scarcity of European ladies in earlier days has been exaggerated; but changes are certainly apparent in sexual conduct. Two main issues here are the alleged hardening of the distance between British rulers and Indian subjects after the first quarter of the nineteenth century and the alleged shallowness of Western contact with and impact upon the bulk of India's people.

Much change may be attributed to the increase of bourgeois and Christian sentiment generally among the British officials, officers, professionals, and merchants who served in India under the Crown, as well as to laws reflecting these attitudes. It is related also to the greater salience and organization of racist thought and to eugenics. The second issue—lack of contact—is reflected, among other things, in the argument that British rule was wholly coercive, except from the perspective of a few collaborators who gained privileges and legal rights, standing upon the thin crust of colonial 'improvement'. It is claimed that the common people of India—amongst whom one would number servants and concubines—hardly participated in the enclaves of colonial civility and law, but instead kept to their own traditions of belief, practice, power, and protest. There is an obvious contradiction between the two positions, one noting and the other denying or minimizing cross-cultural influence. We will explore this briefly before turning to some case studies. More generally, Blechynden's diary enables us to reassess the agreed trajectory of change. It displays racial attitudes aplenty and does not suggest tolerance that would later give way to prejudice. It enables us to understand more clearly what was happening.[10]

## RACE, WORK, AND CHARACTER

As already discussed, many practices and attitudes among all types of people excluded 'outsiders' in eighteenth-century Calcutta. Friendship, kinship, and nationality defined much that bound people together. Patronage and influence persisted as a delicate game of hints and favours. At the same time, these subjective ties and processes were increasingly mixed with calls for objective efficiency, honesty, and professionalism.[11] In that context, the application of order not only subordinated and oppressed but also elevated and liberated Indians. The rules assumed European superiority, but gave Indians opportunities. A mixture of attitudes by Europeans to India facilitated equally mixed reactions by Indians to Europe. Here one finds Indian agency. Blechynden was contemptuous of what he called 'Blackey's' skills—in medicine, for example, and in building. When Blechynden's servants were very ill or did not improve under his treatment, he blamed their recourse to Bengali doctors—another metaphor for colonial attitudes. Considering 'a Black Mans Estimate' for a verandah, he found it cheaper than his own, but very defective as to foundations and other specifications, 'setting Architecture at defiance'. Called in to see if he would finish a building, Blechynden replied 'very candidly' that he did not 'finish other people's Work and much less a Black-mans'. (However, to oblige this client, he would do so, 'thinking within myself', he wrote, 'that it might lead to something better'.) In addition to racial arrogance, all this suggests competition.

Blechynden used Indian workers and foremen as well as Indian materials, and he thought about Indian weather and conditions. When he lamented the standards of the Indian builders, he also feared them as rivals. In 1793, he refused to provide full plans for a new warehouse and dwelling, suspecting that the client would merely 'send for all the black Mistry's [sic; meaning contractors, artisans] in Calcutta to try who would do it cheaper'.[12] He refused to provide another client with a 'particular estimate' showing details of work and materials for fear that it would be passed on to one Chand Mistri, who he had seen waiting for him to leave the client's premises. In 1795, he heard that his former employer and partner William Dring had contracted with Chand to build new warehouses and stables. Later he remarked that his lack of money and work was not surprising 'in a Country where people are mean enough to get plans and Estimates from a man then employ a native to bungle them and injure his fame'. He was particularly incensed that Dring had earned his money 'in an easy way' by 'opening the Mouth and crying out', yet begrudged payment for 'the exertion of Talents cultivated at great expence'. He took satisfaction in inspecting Chand's work and predicting that the arches would collapse unless strengthened.[13]

But Indian builders had soon learnt the style expected of them, the architectural gestures that impressed employers. It is hard not to conclude that Blechynden despised them because they were undercutting him. In a similar spirit, in 1813, one British petitioner to the Company complained at its employment of Indian shipbuilders 'to the actual injury and positive loss of this nation'. In 1824, Bishop Heber would write of seeing, on his approach to Calcutta, not only many boldly crewed and seaworthy vessels in styles he described as Maldivian, Bengali, and Chittagong, but also many others, 'which implied a gradual adoption of European habits, being brigs and sloops, very clumsily and injudiciously rigged, but still improvements on the old Indian ships'.[14]

Blechynden tried to compete on quality. One client, Davidson, had taken an estimate from an Indian contractor and found it came within Rs 1,500 of Blechynden's, which 'was not a sufficient saving to counterbalance the different qualities of … work'. Blechynden also had no hesitation in appealing indirectly to his employers' patriotism. A discussion took place on European competitors for building the stables for William Pawson.

Blechynden generalized this as a preference, all things being equal, for a European over a Chinese shop. Pawson said that he would choose the Chinese. Blechynden argued: 'Providence has wisely emplanted this Partiality in us—for we prefer our Parents' and relatives, then friends, then Countrymen.' He also thought his countrymen more deserving because they had larger wants, including a passage home.[15]

The usual picture is of Europeans destroying Indian livelihoods, and public posts did increase for Europeans from the 1790s. But Europeans did not benefit similarly in most trades or all professions. One obvious job was that of the writer (East India Company clerk), which Indians would do for one-third the cost of Europeans: educated Indians and, above all, Eurasians came to dominate the profession. A *Chronicle* printer, William Cooper, lost his post in 1795 and was replaced by an Indian or Eurasian who 'did very well & therefore could save the expence of a European to the office'.[16] Blechynden feared the Indian contractors *because they could do what he did*, but were less restricted than he was as to costs and clients. Truly, this was a colonial dilemma. It implies that racial slurs had a pragmatic element, relating to competition rather than dogma.

That is not the end of the matter, however, because broader racial stereotypes persisted at the level of supposed moral character as well as alleged professional capability. Here too Blechynden provides many examples. In 1791, he was appalled at the lack of reaction among spectators when a boat full of passengers overturned on the river Hugli. It 'required a great deal of persuasion and threats', he wrote, to get any response from people who were 'setting very quiet in their Boats & smoking their Hubble-Bubble' on the excuse that the passengers would drown before they could be reached. Most were saved by nearer rescuers. 'This apathy with respect to dissolution,' he decided, 'arises from their Idea that death is a state of perpetual Idleness — and is constitutional with them.' He cited an alleged Indian proverb: 'it is better to stand than to walk', 'better to sit down than to stand', 'better to lay down than to sit', 'much better to sleep than to lay down, but Death is the best of all.' Already Indians were being defined by fatalism, as also by incompetence, ingenious dishonesty, and inflexibility. Blechynden enjoyed an anecdote about a nawab who suspected that his servants were stealing food from his favourite elephant. He found that the elephant had been trained to give a portion of his food to his keeper and then to each of the overseers in succession. The more supervisors the nawab appointed, the thinner the animal became. Blechynden blamed his own troubles with servants on their inferior quality, claiming that only one, Gofarrah, matched up to servants in England (which he had left so young)—not only, it seems, in reliability but also in readiness to take on a range of different jobs.[17]

A related criticism of Indians was that they lacked charity even within their own kin groups, let alone more generally. Europeans set themselves up deliberately as the contrary example, which had the additional benefit of garnering prestige in their own eyes. An example of this occurred at Blechynden's charity school, where he saw a sick man in the sun, apparently dead. He sent to inquire after him and found that he was alive, but complaining he was given only dal to eat. Blechynden sent for the Brahman schoolmaster of the school and threatened to dismiss him unless he gave the man good, well-boiled rice. The Brahman complained that the man had a voracious appetite. Blechynden said he should curb the excess but still give him enough nourishment, in small quantities and at frequent intervals. Later, he went to check and found the man apparently recovered, sleeping under a shed. The man died, however, and as he was Hindu, Blechynden ordered him carried to the river. The Brahman said that some of the man's caste wanted three rupees for a feast and intended to bury him. That puzzled Blechynden but the Brahman claimed that some Hindus did bury their dead. Blechynden thought the relatives deserved to be flogged, for they neglected the man while he was alive and then wanted money for a funeral feast. In the end, he was prevailed upon to provide a rupee, which was what it would have cost to have the body carried to the river and burned. About this time, Blechynden mentioned casually that he had also maintained a poor Muslim man for six or seven months, until he too died. Blechynden was appalled to hear that his body had not been buried but was devoured by jackals.[18]

A similar incident, at a time when he was preoccupied with personal distress, reiterated this aspect of Blechynden's attitudes to Indians and Indian customs. He was exercised by a report that a man had been left to die on his land, at the gardens. His mali wanted to 'throw him' somewhere else. Blechynden was shocked at the inhumanity of this and went to see for himself. The man was in fact sitting on the road in the sun, with violent dysentery. Blechynden ordered the gardeners to bring his small tent for the man and told them to keep him warm, and sent for a member of his family—he was said to belong to one Andiram Das and to have been removed so as not defile his house by dying in it. A woman appeared and Blechynden 'reproved her for her brutality'. He had his servants boil water, pour it over toasted bread, and get the man to drink it when it was almost cold. He also ordered a strong congee (rice water) with wine in it. Checking over some days, he found that the woman had run off in the night, that the man was improving, and then that he had died—for want of 'proper attendance', Blechynden supposed, because he thought the treatment would cure him, once he started to feel better. Andiram Das refused to take the body and Blechynden had bearers carry it to Andiram's house. Andiram pleaded with them to take it to the river, as he really had not the money to do so himself.

A few weeks later, Blechynden allowed himself to be persuaded not to kill a bullock that had been rampaging on his property, fighting his deer, eating his cabbages, and so on. He did this 'at the solicitations of the natives' because they told him that it belonged to a poor widow and also because he was aware 'how careful they are of the lives of Bullocks &c.' No sooner was it out of his compound, however, than he discovered it belonged to Andiram. He was very angry, for had he known this, he wrote, he 'certainly would have killed it by way of punishing him for his inhumanity...—and letting him know that Europeans set a higher value upon the life of a fellow Creature than a Bullock tho' he does not'.[19]

## ENCOUNTERS WITH DIVERSITY

The tone, then, was impatient with and intolerant of Indians. It is unknown why Blechynden employed a Brahman schoolmaster and supported the charity school, on his own land near his garden house, but it had a secular rather than a Brahmanical curriculum.

Blechynden once came across a fakir who had suspended himself by the heels from a be-flagged A-frame. He was said to intend to remain in that position, taking only a little milk, until the next full moon; he had already been there four days. Blechynden suspected that he was cheating by resting on the ground under the covers, but anyway: 'God did not bless us with bodily strength and wisdom to prostitute both in this manner but to use [them] to the benefit of ourselves and our fellow creatures'— a month's hard labour would have been 'a more acceptable Service to God and Man'. The fakir was still there after another four days, calling out to Allah. Blechynden told him that he was going to have to 'ferritt him out' after another three or four days, as his people were about to repair the road.[20]

On other customs, he expressed himself more strongly, if convention-ally for an Englishman of his day. He refused even to visit a 'Takoor Bharry' (*thakurbari*, house for an idol) unaccountably being built for a Hindu by his neighbour, Doncaster. Blechynden called it 'Pagan idolatry' and himself 'a Christian (though a very unworthy one)'. He also 'secretly rejoiced' on hearing of the death of the wife of Andiram, one of his contractors, because she was thus saved from burning on her husband's funeral pyre when he should die. Many years before, he had seen that 'cruel ceremony' and, in late 1799, took care to keep well away when encountering a large crowd come to witness another. In 1801, while on the river, seeing one more impending sacrifice and once again great crowds attending, he was approached by a Brahman who begged him not to land as it would interrupt the ceremonies. He said that he had no intention of landing, and then for good measure told the man what he thought: sati was 'atrocious and deliberate Murder'. Blechynden saw the face of the woman—coarse and homely, apparently poor—and believed she showed every symptom of horror and fear. His feelings upset, he instructed his people to ply their oars to get them away, until at a distance of about a hundred yards, he came across several Hindus bathing, 'who thought the scene of too little consequence to merit their going to see it'. The very next day, by contrast, he stopped to watch a Hindu cremation, in a spirit of inquiry, reflecting on the elaborate arrangements secured at the cost of just one rupee.[21]

At best, it seems, when it came to Indian identity and mores, Blechynden would affect indifference, accept the status quo, or remain ambivalent. One day, he returned home to the gardens and found the terrace in front of his bearers' house dug up, with a great fire and two cauldrons of rice and curry. He was told that the sice to his horse Padre was to be circumcised. In the morning, the sice had asked permission to go home. Blechynden was astonished: at the impudence of 'making such a tamassah' (spectacle) on his premises, at finding the sice was Gowallah by caste when he had thought him Muslim, and at the 'folly of the man who is near 40 and has children'. The man himself seemed stupefied by some drug and so Blechynden gave the company at large the benefit of his opinion. The ceremony was only ordained by Muhammad, he said, 'from a principle of cleanliness (and a very necessary one with such a slovenly race as the Mousalmans) but could not be intended as a visible token of religious profession since it is performed on a part that ought never to be seen'. As the sice 'had been a Hindoo so many years', he thought it 'better he should continue so'. At any event, the ceremony would not be performed on his premises and any servant of his who attended it would be dismissed with loss of wages. He had the gate locked. When he checked, he found that only one sice was absent—not one of his but one engaged for a friend's horse. Blechynden kept the gates closed until about eleven o'clock the next morning, when he let everyone out and gave the keys back to the durwan.[22]

Already, then, in the late eighteenth century, the Europeans' encounters with diversity did not imply involvement or sympathy, often quite the reverse. Social environment, upbringing, and education were regarded as *explanations* of Indian inferiority and European superiority. Culture bore the main burden, but in addition dishonesty, fatalism, and indolence were being associated with skin colour. That such prejudices were already general among Blechynden's fellows is suggested by many casual instances, such as his son James being admired for being so fair-skinned when his mother was 'black'. There was the curious case of a bibi who appeared pale-skinned (if blotchy) in 1800 but had been as dark as her brothers in 1788; presumably she had been using skin whitener.[23] For his part, Blechynden was concerned for his public reputation when he worked for and dined with Pawson and his black son-in-law, Julius Soubise. When Pawson asked if black people did not marry white women in England, Blechynden answered yes to soothe him; the old man appeared to him quite crazy. Soubise, celebrated in his day, was an African West Indian brought up in England; he already had a 'Coffree' daughter.

At one dinner, Soubise's wife (if such she was, for a legal marriage was doubted), her 'Bosom ornamented with a Portrait of Soubise!', was asked by 'a beast' of a guest if she wanted children like those of another European present. She took offence and said she could not have one 'so fair' by her husband—though Blechynden noted she had had (possibly by another father, he suspected) a daughter 'as fair as alabaster' who had died. Another dinner *chez* Soubise was with a 'curious collection' of mixed races, and at yet another, 'the Company were 2 black Women, 1 Black Man and 1 European'. On yet another occasion, calling to see about whitewashing a house occupied by Pawson, Blechynden was struck by the diversity of the children in his family—'some black some white some brown'.[24] It seems Blechynden noticed skin colour more than he expressed any prejudice about it.

But prejuduce there was. When Soubise led Pawson into debt, Blechynden tried to persuade the old man to extricate himself from the relationship, bring his daughter home, and provide her with an annuity. Pawson said that she would never leave Soubise. Blechynden claimed that the couple were not married: he had checked with (the Portuguese) Padre Goevans. Pawson was eventually convinced of this, but then doubted that Soubise would live more than a year or two: his health was 'much broken and he has not a leg to stand upon'. Blechynden asked what then induced his daughter to stay with him: 'it could not be his Colour—or the Company he brought home', or money. It could not be love if he was 'without a leg to stand on'. Only infatuation, said Pawson.[25]

There were many layers of misconception and arrogance. For a start, culture was tacitly assumed to be inborn, in an Englishman and (we saw) a 'Gowallah' or a Muslim. However, balancing contempt for customs or capacity with an everyday acceptance of difference (as with skin colour), we also find accommodations. Blechynden threatened to kill cattle that strayed on to his land; but, he admitted, could not bring himself to do so on account of people's feelings. When a Brahmani bull broke branches off his large trees and rooted up his plants from China, he set the dogs to frighten it (they 'only barked') and attempted to cut off its horns; but, though he was 'almost determined' to kill it, which seemed highly to delight the Muslims, he spared its life 'in compliance with the prejudices of the Hindoos'.

In the end, the impression of outright European bigotry and isolation is qualified on at least four grounds. First, at a social level as well as in business, there were certainly exchanges between Europeans and Indians. The Post Office clerk, Samuel Jones, illustrated the inevitable interdependence. He was rescued from drowning by a washerman and (at his request) settled three rupees a month on him for life, apparently not calculating how this open-ended commitment contrasted with the lump sum he had first offered. Everyone was amused by the blunder, but clearly did not consider a reward out of the ordinary.[26] Social connections also occurred. Blechynden attended a dinner, for example, in Clive Street with 'the Moguls'—Khan Sahib, Meer Sahib (Abul Kasim), and others (not all of whom joined in the meal with the Europeans). He responded to pressure over the 'heavy disappointment' that would be felt when friends tried to cry off, being unwell. He participated on his own terms, disparaging the 'indifferent nautch', but praising the 'excellent beef, saddle of mutton, roast goose, potatoes, french beans, asparagus &c.' and the fine claret that was served. He partook of some 'pelow' out of politeness ('compliment'), and found he 'might as well have put a spoonful of all-spice into the mouth'; but was interested to hear 365 distinctive flavours of pilau could be prepared, so that in one simple dish there could be variety.

Later, Abul Kasim made social calls on Blechynden; on one evening visit with Khan Sahib, he sang Persian songs. Blechynden invited Mirza Jalil and Khan Sahib to his garden house. Abul Kasim was given a puppy on one visit. On another, he ate and drank everything that was on the table; shared a hookah with Blechynden (despite the great fuss made 'about cast' by lower-class Muslims); partnered him at billiards against John Dowling (of the Accountant-General's office) and William Farrer, a ship's officer;

played chess with Dowling; and discussed the propriety of printing the Qu'ran. (He was strongly against it—'God's name should only be written by proper persons, and in clean chambers'.)[27] Again, in 1816 and 1817, Rammohan Roy was among the Blechynden family's new acquaintances. Rammohan visited the garden house (enjoying a dispute with Blechynden about Napoleon) and received gifts (of roses on one occasion) and return visits, when Blechynden somewhat impatiently inspected Rammohan's false horizon, his orrery, and his swing.[28]

Secondly, the stereotypes were already contested by Indians, as they would be at the height of racial theorizing. Blechynden was once in conversation with Gopi Krishna, nephew of the celebrated Maharaja Nabakrishna ('Knobkissen' in the diary), the wealthy Kayastha ally, revenue collector, moneylender, and Persian teacher of Warren Hastings. Blechynden repeated a saying of Sir William Jones 'that a Black man was any time to be found who would swear [some falsehood] as an Evidence even to the greatest Crimes for only 4 Annas'—presumably one of the earlier examples of this perennial accusation. Gopi responded by referring to one of his former European employees, the officer of an Indiaman, who had told him how he 'swore to a false manifest—and when ... asked how he could do so, ... said "he did not kiss the Book he only kissed the Thumb"'.[29]

More generally, from their standpoint of superiority, Europeans complained of 'the impudence of the natives of all classes in Calcutta'. Agreeing, Blechynden commented that 'by these means we shall lose the country'. Europeans and their values were contested fundamentally, despite casual acceptance by Abul Kasim and many others. Blechynden, trying unsuccessfully to prevent a formal application to the justices of the peace, once spent hours investigating a furious complaint by Tiretta's hookabadar Buxoo against a man who had been claiming that Buxoo ate of Tiretta's food and thereby had lost caste. The man (in a relationship with a woman whom Buxoo's father kept after the death of Buxoo's mother) was organizing a social boycott, warning everyone not to eat, drink, or smoke with Buxoo, who insisted the accusation was untrue.[30]

Thirdly, curiosity reduced the barriers. Even in a would-be universalist age, the Western scientific imagination was not always engaged by the particularities of India: practical men could pass by curiosities without comment or uncomprehendingly, while more earnest inquirers often focused on the abstract or rarified and on what high-class informants could tell them—William Jones and the pundits, for example. On the other hand, it is striking how men whose lives were necessarily practical, material, and focused on Western standards and ideas—administrators, merchants, engineers, and architects such as Blechynden—attended the Asiatic Society's regular meetings to hear reports and papers.[31] Though Blechynden was surprised to see the younger Joseph Barretto at a meeting, not realizing 'black Portuguese' were admitted,[32] the Society's professed compass and the focus of European inquiry were nonetheless universal.

The idea of a sharp division between Europe and India obscures this aspect of the Enlightenment—famously expressed about India, for example, by Samuel Johnson to Warren Hastings in 1774, a letter full of the 'wish for information' and 'intelligence', urging the Governor to 'inquire', 'examine', and 'survey'; and also to 'trace', and to 'know', and to inform. Blechynden thought himself well enough informed about 'Hindu mythology' to be able to instruct his Brahman sircar Rammohun Chatterjee, whose knowledge was 'very superficial indeed', rather than the other way round, in two long conversations in 1801. The spirit of inquiry was practical as well as philosophical, as the Asiatic Society also demonstrated. While walking one day to rest his palankeen bearers, Blechynden noticed Indians making twine and saw that 'the boy who turned the spindle to which the flax was fastened, moved his hands alternately up and down'. Intrigued, he went over to examine the process and found it 'very simple & very ingenious'. A string of flax was laid across the higher of two small rollers and each end was wound a few times in the same direction round the lower one. The twine was then twisted by pulling on the ends alternately with the right and left hand, as if drawing a bucket from a well; the lower roller always rotated the same way. Blechynden was 'much pleased by this piece of ingenuity'.[33]

Finally, Europeans were never immune to India and were impeded by it—often literally. Indian practices and festivals quickly developed in Calcutta. All down the river, Blechynden noted in October 1791, came hundreds of boats 'parading about with the Goddess Durga and the Shores lined with the people ..., covered with them so that we could scarcely pass'. In June 1795, he witnessed 'the Rutt Poojah when the Wooden Pagodas are dragged about the streets and they and the immense concourse of people who accompany them entirely stop the way'. Next month, Calcutta was also 'full of noise' for Muharram.[34]

European involvement was helped because, though some visitors and place-holders bemoaned a supposed contrast with the order and sophistication of Europe, India in the late eighteenth century was not really so strange to Europeans as it might seem in an industrialized or post-industrial age—not as to the gap between rich and poor, privileged and downtrodden, nor in everyday routines of food and drink, treatment of household servants, dangers of disease, difficulties of travel, haphazard and unsanitary conditions of housing, fear of fire, violence of some neighbourhoods, uncertainties of income, or irregularity of justice and government. Sentiment in practice derived from such experiences as well as from general codes and values or from imagining European moral and intellectual superority.

Blechynden was deeply involved with India and Indians through his concubines and servants, and they with him, in his private life and at work; he was a member, not just an observer, of a broader community. As we shall see, little distance separated some Indians and some Europeans: in particular, employer–employee and household relations were inevitably close, if not necessarily cordial. The 'Boys from the Charity School with their Bramins at their head' came to ask Blechynden for the loan of his tents, for example, so that they could celebrate their holiday. He was brought a present of a pair of slippers by his contractor and agent Davy Persaud Naug on the occasion of Davy's brother's marriage; he had not had such a thing, Blechynden recalled, 'since the days of poor Ramsundar Banargee', one of Davy's predecessors. Later, Blechynden was supposedly famous for his racial impartiality. Towards the end of his life, it was remarked in court as he was giving evidence that 'if there is a man in the Country to whom it is perfectly indifferent in his decisions whether the Parties are Europeans or Natives that man is Mr Blechynden'.[35] Certainly, his derogative asides seem more to reflect his times than his convictions, and his relationships with non-Europeans suggested care as well as disdain. Amid prejudice and despite much intermingling, there was of course a divide, as desired on both sides; but in practice, it was less complete than is often supposed.

What changed, then, between the period covered by Blechynden's diary (say 1790 to 1820) and the following decades? The widely perceived deterioration in Indo–British relations may be related to enthusiasm and evangelism in a context of ignorance. Tolerant and curious Europeans, lovers of India, and their opposites existed in every generation. But as is well known, after the early nineteenth century, the tone of much British public discourse became harsher and if not more arrogant than in the past, then more dismissive of alternative cultures and histories. It is the tone not of Warren Hastings or William Jones, encountered in the last chapter, but of James Mill's *History of British India* (1818). Repeated and violent diatribes against Indian character and abilities accompanied the 'pious clause' permitting Christian missionary activities in Company territories. They also followed the broader ambitions for regularity and reform adopted when a one-time trading company focused on government, lost its monopoly, and was increasingly subordinated to the British Crown.

By contrast, Blechynden was seldom savage, more often pragmatic, for all his casual condemnations and certainty of European and British superiority. He was generally principled, even priggish, but not doctrinaire; he espoused and practised reason and endeavour rather than faith. In this respect also, the diary reflects a transition and offers a lesson.[36] The exceptions and shared experiences transcending the harshness of Indo British relations were not limited to a particular period and seem to contradict some of the usual conclusions. The image of the white and black cities that never met implies that one was an enclave of modern privilege and the other a morass of poverty or a sump of tradition. Or at least it presents Europeans bringing modernity and Indians accepting or rejecting it. But both simultaneously had to come to terms with the complex environment in which they found themselves—that is, with a changing world, and with the place, and with the past. Indians of all classes played a part in the development of Calcutta and the city was a conduit for ideas and practices.

Peter Marshall claimed that there was a sense of 'race' but not 'racism' in the British sense of exclusiveness in Calcutta at this time; he thought Western ideas were accessible to Indians—through architecture, furniture, theatre, books, and newspapers—though brought in or developed for European use and prestige. Others, anxious to stress non-European agency, have argued for locally reformulated, even alternate, modernizations. They stretch definitions and credulity if taken to mean a decoupling of developments from one another, but otherwise rightly emphasize the porousness of trends and the interpenetration of ideas.[37] Indians certainly experienced Calcutta's demarcations and disciplines and used its bye-laws and facilities. They were often excluded but never exempt. Indians too made the city. The acceptance, for example, that they would observe their own holy days was not just a communal distinction; it also helped shape the city's year.[38]

# 3

# Your Obedient Servant?

The child when purchased is fed and clothed by its master, and when it gets to sufficient age to be of any help, is given a small monthly allowance as well.

— Officiating Magistrate of Tirhut, 20 September 1868[1]

## WORKING LAW

If sensibility did not exclude Indians, sense commonly affected them. In particular, the regulation of labour and employment shaped Calcutta lives. The general lot of servants shows the character of Blechynden's household. Master–servant relations were important points of contact between Europeans and Indians. The closeness of such relations is relevant to an assessment of colonial impact. Finally, Europeans' experience with Indian servants helped form their attitudes to Indians and to themselves (or vice versa). Contrasting representations dominate Blechynden's account: just, reasonable Europeans and venal, unreliable Indians. They prevail amid examples of European violence and corruption and of Indian rationality and loyalty. Stereotypes *are* born of experience, but only after interpretation.

By the late eighteenth century, many of the slaves and servants of European Calcutta were Indo-Portuguese[2] and even more were local or up-country Hindus and Muslims. Master–servant relationships were complex, but more formal interventions were being introduced, partly because of the shortage of building workers and servants. The Company itself regularly lost workers to private contractors and made special efforts to recruit (in particular) bricklayers from outlying districts, occasionally requisitioning forced labour, for example, for work on Fort William in 1778. Some of Blechynden's later public projects employed prison labour. Peter Marshall thinks demand forced wages up, but not sufficiently to attract large numbers from agriculture. He further reports that 7,000 bearers in 1766 were said to have left Bihar and Orissa, with their 'presidents' and 'councils', to work in Calcutta. In 1779, the town magistrate was 'so concerned about stories of illegal meeting' and 'the insolence of these people serving whom they please and refusing whom they please' that he ordered their leaders to be chastized. In 1759, wages had been fixed for servants employed in Calcutta (whether by Europeans or not) and in 1774, master-and-servant legislation was applied.[3] The regulations were designed to restrict wages and discipline workers, but allowed redress for ill-treatment—that is, they also imposed some restrictions on employers.

New factors were thereby introduced into the conditions of work in India, but it is not easy to explain just what changed and when. For a start, employment in precolonial India is hard to summarize. The question of slavery makes this plain. In practice, productive, agrestic, and household slaves could be overlapping categories; slaves and forced labourers were not wholly distinct from hired workers. Girls 'given' in marriage also formed an ambiguous category. However, slaves *were*, in most senses, someone's property. Boys and girls could be born to slavery and children sold into it, not least by their own parents and relatives. Infants were cheaper to buy than adults; if they survived, they appreciated in value.

Blechynden encountered one such purchased child in the household of the merchant, Robert Downie. He had thought him Downie's son by a concubine, but was told that the boy, as fair-skinned as any European, had been brought to his house by an elderly 'Portuguese' woman who offered him for sale at three gold *mohur*s. The woman said this was a discount because a Muslim bibi was willing to pay five, but the woman would rather Downie had him. She said that the child had been born to her daughter, a 'half-cast' married at Chandernagore to a Frenchman who had gone to sea and abandoned her; she had literally died of hunger. The grandmother had brought up the boy but could no longer afford to maintain him; she needed money to pay her own debts. Downie agreed to take the boy rather than reporting the woman to the magistrates, to Blechynden's disgust. Blechynden also doubted the story. Hearing that the woman spoke English after several trips to England as an ayah (maid) accompanying children, he concluded the child was probably her own 'bye blow made on board ship'. He agreed that it was now right that Downie should care for the boy, 'for charity's sake', and educate him.

In India, as this example suggests, being 'owned' had not made slaves wholly distinct, in terms of family, caste, or religion, from society at large. On the one hand, though menial and demeaning tasks were undertaken by slaves, which guaranteed them low ritual status, their standing could be improved by changes of role. Favoured slaves could become notional kin: women slaves be the mothers of lords; male slaves could be adopted and inherit land. Slave boys could gain high status as the personal attendants of rajas and, as in well-known historical cases, slaves (and 'untouchables') could become rulers and ministers of state. On the other hand, significant portions of many people's labour was unpaid, in line with various forms of socio-economic obligation; and most men and any woman could *become* enslaved in adverse circumstances and lose status.[4]

Compounding these ambiguities, hired workers were typically acquired by means of complex layers of subcontracting, held together by advance payments, traditional obligations, or paper contracts. This mattered in Calcutta, when Europeans sought Indian workers. Both official regulation and an operative labour market were inhibited by the prevalence of 'leaders' or contractors who recruited and organized labour. There was thereby a mismatch between new laws and the ways work was conducted and managed. The laws did not fully comprehend the manner of employment. They did not apply to slaves. Moreover, in practice, as will be seen at length in the next chapter, the law was often a mockery and workers could suffer under several layers of potential oppression—from their own 'leaders' and from the arbitrary 'justice' of employers and officials.

Nonetheless, slavery was being redefined as work without wages and labour relations were being presented as a matter of contract. Tasks and workers were being regulated, in a mix of inherited and imposed forms. Meanwhile, employers had many complaints. For manual and skilled labour, as demand often exceeded supply and payment was often in advance, the workers did not need to be reliable and nor did their supervisors, the intermediaries and gangmasters who supplied labour to employers. Within households, a wider set of factors also applied; but many of the same failings of labour were evident in household servants, though they were more directly employed by Europeans. Law provided a vocabulary to define and some weapons to challenge workers' recalcitrance. Contracts were general. Absconding was punishable at law. Regulations were designed to restrict wages as well as to discipline workers.[5]

Household servants tended to be paid in arrears but personal palankeen bearers were commonly given advances, for which they or someone else would offer security. A guarantee of good behaviour and honesty was essential for some positions of trust and generally an advantage for employers, though no formal sanction ever worked perfectly. When Blechynden's palankeen bearers ran off one day, he was particularly inconvenienced because Tiretta's head bearer, who had stood security, was also absent with his employer. For others, providing security was too much of a burden. One servant, Hafiz, was sent to James Kyd (son of the engineer), who wanted to employ the man as he had served his father. He came back to Blechynden, however, saying that Kyd wanted him to provide security, which he could not do as he had lost all his property in a fire. Receiving five rupees from Blechynden was better, he said, than having many mohurs if his brother had to provide security. On the other hand, informal sanctions were also available. In 1800, Blechynden's then *sekilgar* Keenoo, supposedly absent through illness, was seized in Bowaneepore, in the south of Calcutta, by another Englishman's peons. He escaped when others came to his rescue, but the peons secured Blechynden's silver badge that Keenoo had been wearing.[6]

Both law, very imperfectly, and labour shortages implied limits on how badly some workers might be treated. The law could enforce the payment of wages owing. Social pressure also might be felt by employers. Blechynden took his responsibilities seriously even when, for want of funds, he had to resist the clamour for money from his own people. He spelt out his attitude when his cousin Marmaduke Blechynden stayed with him in 1797 and 1798 and seemed not to be paying his servants. Richard Blechynden inquired about this and when his cousin said that he had paid all he intended to pay, asked to see a list of names with the times served and the rates allowed. He said that *he* would pay rather than that Marmaduke 'should go away with such a stigma upon his character & blot upon our mutual name'. Marmaduke raised his fist to his cousin's face and said that he would knock any servant down who said he had not paid him. Blechynden gently pushed the fist aside and commented that 'knocking down was not the way of paying debts'. Marmaduke said that he would take their affidavits and if any were unpaid when he returned to Calcutta, he would remit his bill to his uncle Theobald for payment. When Marmaduke moved out of Blechynden's house, he abandoned a bed (which he said that he would leave for the children) and a palankeen. Blechynden decided to sell both to cover his costs as Marmaduke's servants were pestering him for money.

On his next and final departure for England, Marmaduke brought his servant Hans to Blechynden; it was impossible to misunderstand him, apparently, and so Blechynden gave Hans two gold mohurs. Marmaduke then passed on Hans's comment that 'if it was something more it would be more agreeable'. Blechynden said that he had to give what he could afford. Blechynden also interrupted Marmaduke a few days later as he was beating his *chattahwallah* (a servant who carried an umbrella), who had asked for his wages. Marmaduke said that he had just paid him a month's wages and Blechynden commented that there might still be some more owing. He then said that he would give Marmaduke money to pay all his servants rather than having them unpaid as before. He did so and also gave Marmaduke another Rs 100 as mess money for his journey. Blechynden was then irritated even as his cousin was leaving to be accosted by the chattahwallah and by Marmaduke's washerwoman, complaining that they had not been paid. Marmaduke was already in the boat that would carry him to his ship, but Blechynden beckoned it back to shore and said to Marmaduke that in his hurry, he seemed to have forgotten to pay the servants. Blechynden sent them to the boat and Marmaduke put his hands in his pockets and gave them something; evidently it did not satisfy them.[7]

## HIS LOYAL SERVANTS

At the end of the eighteenth century, Blechynden listed his thirty-five servants as 'Rantanoo the Brahman Master of my Charity School, Gopey my writer, Lilloo & Jaggernaut Sircars, Hurry my draughtsman, 1 consomah [house steward], 1 ketmutgar [valet or serving man], 1 hookabadar, 1 durwan, 2 peons, 3 sices, 3 grasscutters, 3 mollies [malis], 1 dooria [dog keeper], 1 washerman, 1 taylor, & 8 bearers, 3 women servants for children and Bebee & a matrany'. Leaving aside the Brahman schoolmaster, these people managed two houses, the gardens, horses and other animals, and those many aspects of Blechynden's professional life that he paid for directly. Their tasks varied: in the absence of kitchen staff, *dhyes* were responsible for feeding older children; a sirdar bearer or *ketmutgar*[8] might organize food for Blechynden and guests, while serving as a valet. Some, like Currim, the peon who also acted as armourer, seem to have been able to gain paid employment from others, as the palankeen bearers could at weekends. The tailor seems to have been paid for piecework. Once, in February 1799—an intriguing snippet of domestic life—Blechynden had to borrow seven rupees from his bibi so as to give the tailor an advance payment for the epaulets he was copying for Blechynden's militia jacket.[9]

Master, guests, bibis, servants, and children constituted the household, and important aspects of its character were determined by the ways in which servants were treated. In Blechynden's case, master–servant relations were a mixture of indulgence, sentiment, and censure on all sides. It is possible to discern patterns and also ideas about servants and their treatment.

Blechynden admitted that he did not like change in his household and so held on longer than some to servants who proved unsatisfactory, for example, disappearing and reappearing without warning. In 1797, at Lilloo's suggestion, Blechynden even re-engaged a servant who had run away in 1791. In 1798, he took back another, Hingun, when the manservant Deenoo was ill. He also urged Sam Jones to take back one of *his* servants, who had appealed to Blechynden for help; Jones agreed to do so, while complaining that the servant cheated him.[10]

Long-term connections were not unusual. Blechynden's draughtsman, Hurry, was employed over many years, though sometimes ill at inconvenient moments. The contractor and agent, Davy Persaud Naug, was a permanent feature. The *sircars*, especially Lilloo (Nilmunny Ghose), Jaggernaut Dey, and Cassinaut Ganguly, served for many years at a time, despite disputes and doubts over their probity. The writer, Gopey Naut Doss, was in post in the 1790s, though ostensibly working for the *Chronicle*, transferred to Blechynden personally in 1792 and, despite the occasional recalcitrance, was with him still in the 1820s. In 1805, too, as Tiretta was leaving India, Blechynden took Tiretta's *consomah*, Gopaul, into his own service.

For the employee, continuity of employment could be important, especially in hard times, as new domestic staff always seemed to be available despite the shortages of skilled workers. Once a coolie made a salaam to Blechynden in the street and he recognized a former servant of his one-time housemate Arthur Hesilrige. He stopped to speak to the man and found that some time before, he had been turned away by Hesilrige (himself shortly to be imprisoned for debt). Being long out of service, the man had had to turn labourer. This was 'a negative virtue at least', reflected Blechynden, 'since he prefers labour to thieving'.[11]

For the employer, long-term connections were both charitable and self-interested. When Blechynden's old bearer came seeking work, he told him that he had none available, but rather than pay him a pension of two rupees a month, he would give him four and have him about the house to do 'any little thing'; he agreed. When Cassinaut suggested the sircar Tilluck be allowed three or four rupees a month as maintenance until there was work for him, Blechynden replied that he should hire him—thinking that he might as well pay a little more and find something for him to do. Cassinaut argued that Tilluck had an opportunity to work at Balasore, but he was 'clever' and so it would be worth Blechynden's while to hold on to him.[12]

In Blechynden's theory, employees acquired rights as friends did. He thought the Company should continue Tiretta in an office in which he had provided 'very long & very honourable services' and that he himself should not be superseded after 'irreproachable' work.[13] When cuts were made in Company establishments at the end of 1792, all but four of the 'classies' (surveyor's assistants) lost their jobs. 'This is Œconomy with a vengeance,' wrote Blechynden, 'Instead of retrenching where it would admit—they lop off necessary men who only earn 5Rs. a month.' Now 'all manner of nuisance may be thrown in the roads', he continued. He decided to retain one assistant, Golaum Hossein, at his own expense because he had been with him so long. When informed of this, 'the great fool burst out a crying'. Tiretta offered instead to keep him as one of those on the payroll while allowing him to work for Blechynden as before. Later Blechynden 'wrote a Character' for him as he was 'going home ill—he has been with me since 15th July 1784—Gave him a printed copy of the works of Hafiz as he can read—he shed tears at leaving me—& I felt all day as if I had received some bad news'.

Years later, Golaum returned and told Blechynden of his adventures: he had been captured by the French; been a prisoner in France; met a French rear admiral (Padet) who sent his regards to Tiretta and Blechynden; travelled to Denmark; and now, having returned to Calcutta, wanted his old job back. Looking at him and his grey hair, Blechynden reminded him of the time that he had not wanted to get wet when they were both wading through a *jheel* (lake) after snipe. Golaum, stuffing Blechynden's watch in his turban because he was the taller, had expressed the opinion that snipe shooting was 'very foolish'—Blechynden always gave away the birds he shot and did not eat them—and that Golaum's beard would go grey from following Blechynden in the sun through mud. Now, Blechynden said, he had not a grey hair on his head and he had shot snipe every season, while Golaum's hair was quite white. Golaum conceded that, having bathed that morning, he could see at a glance [in the glass?] that it was not snipe shooting that made the hair go grey.[14]

Blechynden himself was susceptible to pressure and would support his employees in various ways. One of his sircars pestered him to allow his *budgerow* (river barge) to be put out to a lottery. He eventually agreed. He let the sircar have it at the price he valued it (seventy-two rupees) and then bought one of the twenty-four tickets himself for three rupees. The vessel was won by the *mangee* (the boat's master) in his wife's name. Blechynden also gave Andiram Mistry, one of his painting contractors, two ponies from the gardens for his children to ride. Later, he sent a chit on Andiram's behalf to the magistrates after hearing that he had been confined. He gave Gofarrah, head sice, a children's pony that he had been unable to sell.

Gofarrah offered to buy it for eight rupees but, wrote Blechynden, as 'he is a good servant I gave it him on condition that he only sold it to any one who intended to let a child ride it, as I would not have it put to hard labour'.[15]

Blechynden was cautious in his professional work, partly out of consideration for employees, just as he would sometimes get down and walk to rest his palankeen bearers. Once the magistrate W.C. Blaquiere asked Blechynden to call for what turned out to be a trivial reason and his bearers said that they were incapable of going any further in the heat. He could fully understand their objection but pretended that he was writing to Blaquiere to complain of them; in fact, he wrote to complain of the weather. Blaquiere replied that tomorrow would do. Such consideration was not necessarily repaid: four days later, the same bearers were drunk and fell down, throwing out Blechynden and breaking the palankeen.[16]

In 1800, a workman died after an accident, the only death in Blechynden's eighteen years of construction work to that date. The man fell from the bamboo scaffolding he was erecting at the Court House. Blechynden had just warned the foreman (*mistri*), Sultan, that it was not safe and he ought to take proper precautions; Sultan had replied that these were *his* people, hinting that Blechynden should not interfere. Blechynden had just time to reply that Sultan's people were just as likely to fall as anyone's when the sircar Cassinaut came *walking* up to say that someone had fallen about thirty feet while erecting scaffolding on another side of the building. Blechynden rushed to him—his name was Fudjoo and he was a bricklayer— and found his wrist broken and his head cut, and gauged at once that he was dying from his injuries. Blechynden stopped the work for the day and inquired after the man's family—he had children and an aged father who had only just heard of the death of another son in Murshidabad.

After the man died, John Shoolbred, the doctor in charge of the Native Hospital, opened up the body, 'of course', and found broken ribs and perforated lungs: the man had bled to death internally. Next day, a relation of Fudjoo came for charity. Blechynden told Sultan that as he was one of *his* people, *he* should provide for his family. Sultan said he had given four rupees, which Blechynden replied was not enough. Sultan pleaded that he was a poor man. Blechynden asked Sultan how much he would offer for each rupee Blechynden would pay. At last Sultan said four annas. Blechynden paid over twenty-four rupees in those proportions for the man's family, but then decided it was not enough. He added another eighteen from himself and a further eight extracted from Sultan, making fifty in all. Cassinaut said that this was so great a sum that people would rob the family and it would be better to pay it in monthly instalments; but Blechynden replied that if he did that, he would never be able to stop. Instead, he gave the money to one man, in the presence of another relative, and said that it was all their property but, for safety, they would receive it in instalments. He took back most of the money, gave the man a signed receipt for fifty rupees, and then debited it for twelve rupees. This included eight rupees the family wanted for the funeral feast, which was all they had asked for, regarding the death (they said) as a consequence of the man's profession and of fate.[17]

## HOUSEHOLD INTIMACIES

An important theme is the general closeness of domestic life. With numerous servants, direct involvement was not always possible. Blechynden did not appoint to minor positions himself and was not necessarily even aware of servants' names, as with a new *dooria* in 1798. More characteristically, however, he noticed when the dooria's brother replaced him temporarily: the new man reported as 'lost' a little dog given by Tiretta, Blechynden stopped his wages, and the dog reappeared.[18] Similarly, his horse Bucephalus cast a shoe one Monday and it had not been replaced by Wednesday. Blechynden dismissed the sice on the spot.

More revealing was the expectation of shared sentiment among Blechynden and his servants when Bucephalus died. First, the horse's sice, by then Harroo, came in crying and told Blechynden, who also felt very sad, thinking back sixteen years to 1783, when he bought the horse as 'a wild unbridled colt', paying Rs 800. He told Harroo to prepare a grave and got Lilloo to go for coolies in Calcutta. Two other coolies, three sices, and two malis dragged the body along the terrace. Then the dooria had the impudence to refuse to touch it and so he was dismissed at once. The malis were Hindus, noted Blechynden, yet none of them objected. Blechynden met Lilloo while returning to town; he had been unable to secure coolies there. Finally, Blechynden's old Brahman sircar, Andiram Gongallie, called to express his condolences, saying that he had shed tears when he heard of the death. Blechynden expected that he was seeking employment, as it was rumoured that he had dismissed Lilloo; but merely recalled to Andiram that about ten years before, he had told him that his (Blechynden's) father's soul was in that horse and when it died, the soul would go into a cow, and after that to Paradise: his motive, Andiram admitted, had been to discourage Blechynden from ever selling the horse.[19]

Day by day, most striking are the number and range of contacts between master and servants. Tiretta's boy Thomas, for example, was the constant companion of Blechynden's early-morning rides, on his own pony. Sometimes Blechynden went just 'to please' Thomas, even when unwell. He also let Thomas go by himself with the dogs (in 1795), as it was 'really a great Bore the strolling over the Plain without meeting any thing to chaice'. In addition to his own pony, Thomas often had the use of the horse of Blechynden's seafaring friend John Wales (in the owner's absence), even when Blechynden mildly objected. Once he borrowed it to attend the funeral of 'Baudel's mother', an old woman from Tiretta's house (servant or slave). This loan was permitted even though Thomas and another (Captain Moss's boy Cato) had just allowed one of Blechynden's deer to escape—it had been recaptured 'with infinite trouble'. Thomas was exhorted only to walk Wales's horse, as the weather was hot. He was also allowed to bring Blechynden's son Arthur, then five years old, out to the garden house in a buggy, 'at his own desire'; and on another occasion to present him with 'a pair of Hindustani slippers...brought from Murshidabad'. Refusal of the gift, wrote Blechynden, 'would have hurt the poor boy who shew'd an attention even in this little matter'.

But Thomas was Tiretta's household slave, the frequency of Thomas's attendance upon Blechynden marking the closeness between the two households. In 1796, Tiretta, by now an elderly widower, complained that he spent Rs 550 each month before expending anything on himself: house rent, sircars, writers, his young sister-in-law Josephine (her clothes and schooling), bearers, servants, sices and coachmen, dhye, ayahs, slave girls, and so on. They were all 'ungrateful'. This same day, he had ordered Thomas's mother Reta to leave his employ for shouting at him following an argument with another servant over the treatment of Tiretta's baby daughter. When Blechynden left that evening, he called Thomas to follow him and told him of the 'insolence of his Mother—and the probable consequence to them all'. He said Thomas should tell his mother to go upstairs before Tiretta had had time to turn all her 'trumpery' out of the house. She should beg his pardon, acknowledge her fault, and explain that she was only acting out of good motives towards the child, and of course she should have appealed to Tiretta instead of making a noise, and so on. Thomas went home armed with this speech for his mother to deliver. It seems to have worked, as mother and son remained in Tiretta's employ.[20]

Intimacy is suggested also by what happened during servants' illnesses and death. One evening in April 1797, Reta told Blechynden that her son very much wanted to see him. Blechynden promised to call and, early on the second morning after the request, found Thomas in a little upper-roomed house opposite the east end of the justices' office. He was 'much reduced'. He had a lung infection and was spitting blood; his voice was very faint.

Blechynden thought, from the 'clearness of his eye', that he would not last three days, perhaps not even one. It will be, he thought, 'a great pity'. He was 'a fine handsome well-made active lad': 'what little dependance we should place', he thought, 'upon youth & a promise of [living] many years'. Later that day, Tiretta told him that Thomas had died at 1 PM; he spoke of it (Blechynden was pained to remark) with as much indifference as if Thomas 'had been a dog', though he had been born and bred in Tiretta's house. Reta later considered Blechynden a bad omen and a threat because he had predicted her son's death.[21]

A common way in which Blechynden showed concern for servants was by ministering to them for their minor or even more serious ailments. One day, his manservant Emaundee showed him a cut just above his forehead made, he said, by a drunken European because he would not direct him to a brothel. Blechynden doubted this story, thinking that the servant might have got into a quarrel when attending a brothel himself; but checked him out nonetheless. Emaundee had no sickness in his stomach and no pain, his head and eyes were clear, and his pulse was strong: so, Blechynden supposed, 'all will end well'. Next day, he went to see one of his gardeners, Keenoo, who was feverish and had been constipated for a week. He gave him some medicine and raspberry jam and ordered him a footbath. Checking on him next day, he found him much better and told him to 'live low and keep quiet'. On another occasion, the sice to Blechynden's horse Johnny became very ill and stopped eating (which was 'always their way', said Blechynden). He went to him and found him very hot, with a furry tongue, and very dejected. Blechynden gave him medicine and ordered that he too be given a footbath. He checked him again that night, asking after his bowel motions, and next day sent more medicine. Two days later, the man had only a gentle perspiration, his pulse was sixty-four, and his eyes were very clear. He said he was not in the least better, however, and Blechynden had to speak sharply to him before he could 'rouze him from his dread'. He had no cinchona bark available to combat any remaining fever, however, and so gave him a glass of madeira that he kept stirring with a spoon to make it seem like medicine. This 'performed wonders'. The sice was perfectly well two days later.[22]

When Gofarrah, Blechynden's head groom, was reported to be ill, Blechynden sent for him to come into the house and found that he had a cold—he had had no bowel motion, his tongue was dry and rough, his eyes red and not moist, but his pulse hard and full. He prescribed 'Covinda jelly' and other medicines and told him to keep warm. He had probably caught a fever from getting wet in the rain while perspiring strongly, he suggested. Blechynden then went out to dinner at Tiretta's, ordered his buggy to collect him, and going downstairs, found Gofarrah holding the horse. He was wearing a jacket made out of an old coat of Blechynden's but his legs and feet were bare. Blechynden sent him home immediately and ordered that a footbath be prepared for him. A few days later, he was quite well.[23]

A retired groom, Rumjohnny, was ill with diarrhoea. Blechynden took off his 'shoes and stockings and wade[d] thro' a wet ditch to see him' and administered medicine, with many warnings against Bengali doctors. Rumjohnny wanted to take leave and go to Murshidabad to recover, which Blechynden thought too dangerous. He insisted Rumjohnny stay in Calcutta. Blechynden was anxious, though Rumjohnny was 'no use' to him, 'nor had been for many years'. His wages, he assured him, 'should go on the same as if he was able to attend to his Duty'. Earlier he had been paid a kind of pension of five gold mohurs, which Blechynden put about was only one, lest Rumjohnny be robbed and murdered. He had promised to maintain him as long as he lived, reflecting that he did 'not want to see him die like a Dog without any assistance'. Years later, after Rumjohnny's death, his son Ghwee also died. Blechynden gave Gofarrah money to bury him as near his late father as possible. At a timber yard later, Blechynden watched the people come to take the body away.[24]

He treated his writer Gopey for an eye infection in 1795, and also a peon's abcess the year before; in 1800, he removed an injured toenail from one of his bearers after he struck his foot on a stone, dressed the wound with ointment, and sent the man home. In the wet weather of June and July 1801, he ministered to the successive fevers of a dhye, durwan, and the manservant Deenoo. He had to let the much improved durwan go home for two days, well covered, to be tended by his family because he claimed that as a 'Gwaller', he could not take anything from the bearers, who were 'Mutchmas', or from the other servants, who were Muslims.[25] Blechynden was indignant when Deenoo, now apparently well, told him about a durwan famed for curing headaches and asked if he could go to him. Blechynden said that Deenoo could go to him next time for all his treatment if that was what he wanted. Similarly, many years later, when Rogonaut Mali came to greet him, was unable to stand, and was going home looking very ill, Blechynden merely gave him six rupees, though 'inwardly agitated' as he was an old servant. By contrast, in July 1805, Gopey was 'pestering' him for medicine (which he supplied).[26]

Occasionally (and in more prosperous times), Blechynden went to the expense of calling in a European doctor for a servant. A Dr White was summoned to treat Gopey when he was very ill; a sice who was kicked in the head by a horse was sent to James Hare, Blechynden's own doctor.[27] Meanwhile, perhaps after such experiences, the richer servants would consult European doctors on their own initiative. When Davy Naug was ill with a cold and fever, Blechynden went to visit him at Gopey's request. He found Davy was being given an opium pill each morning by his doctor, one McCowan, who lived in the Fort. Davy was so drugged that he could hardly speak. Blechynden recommended that he consult another doctor and suggested his own, at this time MacWhister. Davy agreed, but McCowan continued to call and reported that the patient was improving and would do so more quickly if his people would stop feeding him. Blechynden decided that it was a matter of great delicacy to interfere between doctors and that he had better leave matters alone and let McCowan take the credit if Davy was really getting better.

Blechynden was perhaps not typical in his private ministrations to the sick and wounded; medicine was one of his amateur interests. But he did believe his medical treatments were part of an employer's duty. His personal staff were entitled even to the use of his own space if necessary. When his sice Punjabee was very ill, Blechynden dosed him with laudanum and spirit of lavender and then moved him into a bed in the lower hall of his own house. Punjabee stayed there for four days until, feeling better, he insisted on moving his cot back into the stables so as to be near his horse. In return, Blechynden believed that the care he provided entitled him to good service. One day, when his palankeen bearers were too slow getting ready, he berated them for their ingratitude and threatened that he would no longer attend them if they were ill or hurt. He walked away without them and, when they rushed after him, catching him just as he reached his destination, he thought that they had responded to the threat.[28]

Blechynden's sense of responsibility applied outside as well as within his household. At work, when a snake bit Callindy, head of the team of women responsible for beating out *surky*, Blechynden made some effort to calm her and finally succeeded by administering to her, for want of brandy, a container of well-stirred water as a placebo.[29] In 1805, the sircar Ramnarain told Blechynden that his fellow sircar Cassinaut had 'a purging' and his servant the cholera morbus; Blechynden prescribed for the servant an equal measure of water and tincture of 'Columbo' root (a remedy for dysentery, actually from Mozambique) with six drops of laudanum. Going even further from his own employees, in 1796, he ministered to Tiretta's boy Alberto when he appeared to be 'in the last stages of a consumption'. He ordered for him each morning an egg yolk beaten with three tablespoons of rose water, sweetened with 'Sirop de Capillaire' and a little nutmeg, and a 'diet of sapo with sugar candy' and some candy mixed with spermaceti, a fatty whale extract. He said Alberto ought to sleep in a dry, airy room facing south instead of his 'Dog hole under the stairs' and that if he recovered, he should be sent on the river for a change of air. Later, as the late Mrs Tiretta's room was still empty, he asked Reta to suggest that Alberto be put in there. After another day, the patient, who had to be urged to take his medicines, thought that he was improving.[30]

Most telling in regard to household intimacies was the responsibility Blechynden would take for his servants and associates not only in regard to their work but also, without distinction, in their private affairs. He may have gone further than others, but many Europeans supported their Indian associates and servants before the law and against other Europeans. They would help to varying degrees and Blechynden, too, had his limits. There will be more examples in the next chapter. Close involvement with servants, both by employers and by the authorities, extended over almost all aspects of life.

A wide-ranging example occurred when Blechynden's head groom, Gofarrah, became estranged from his wife, Champah. It combines our themes of concern, proximity, private and public interference, and moral-ity, especially over marriage. Blechynden's neighbour Mary Wade said that Champah had told her that Blechynden had banned her from visiting her house, calling her a 'curbee' (prostitute). He was, he replied, incapable of such a thing. Privately (undermining his denial) he objected to being interrogated not only about his servants but his servant's 'strumpet' and complained that there was 'not a *fart* so to say let in my house but she [Mary] knows of it'. He declined an invitation to tea. The story was that he had intervened in a quarrel between Champah and Gofarrah, who was complaining at the time she was spending at the Wades', ostensibly to bathe in their tank, but he suspected so as to consort with her servants. Blechynden had called in Champah but she had nothing to say in her defence and so he banned her from the Wades' and told Gofarrah that she should not stay in Blechynden's house. She had gone but had slipped back in with a key, opened the bearers' house, and stolen all Gofarrah's copper plates and other belongings. Now she accused Blechynden, in a petition sent to him by the sitting justice, of making Gofarrah turn her away while keeping their children.

After this, Blechynden encountered Gofarrah himself at the end of Bow Bazar, crying and being shoved along by a police peon. He took the peon's number but urged Gofarrah to go with him quietly. At home, the durwan and other servants told him that the peon had called Gofarrah names and treated him very roughly, even though he had not resisted him. Blechynden sent his writer Gopey and a sircar, Seebnarain Bose, to find out what was going on. They came back and reported that the proceedings had ended before they arrived and that the lawyer C.F. Martyn was the sitting justice. He had directed the couple to make it up, but on Gofarrah's refusing to speak to his wife, had told her to go and take the children with her. The peon prevented Gofarrah from complaining about his treatment of him.

A little later, a verbal message from Martyn directed Blechynden to give up Champah's clothes. He considered asking for a written note but decided instead to reply in writing to say that he had complied, adding that Gofarrah complained of his wife's keeping both the children and perhaps the mother could have the daughter and the father the son. He also reported that the peon had used Gofarrah very badly and suggested that such behaviour should be prevented. Martyn replied, begging Blechynden to spare him from being pestered with such complaints and telling him that he should sort out the matter himself. Blechynden thought that rather difficult after a magistrate's order had been issued.

A couple of days later, not having managed to see Martyn, he raised the matter with another magistrate, Charles Rothman (of Burgh, Barber & Rothman), who promised to do justice to Gofarrah when it was his turn on the bench, in three weeks. Blechynden said that he would prefer that he spoke to Martyn for him, rather than wait so long. But five months later, he was still asking another justice of the peace, Matthew Louis, about Gofarrah's complaint and giving Gofarrah a chit for him. He finally lost patience after a further ten weeks, when Champah took out another summons against her husband. Blechynden told Gofarrah 'to go to Jericho'; he was, he said, 'the plague of my life'. A few months after this latest summons, a mali told Blechynden that Gofarrah had run away, decoyed by Champah, or so Blechynden imagined, and he ordered another grasscutter to be hired instead.[31]

## CRIME AND PUNISHMENTS

Servants were beaten in India; they were also beaten in Europe. Sometimes the punishment took on a quasi-judicial character and, at other times, it was just a matter of lashing out in irritation. Blechynden had views about appropriate punishment—his own always being just, of course. He did not take kindly to other Europeans beating servants excessively. Once Charles

Reed, an up-country timber merchant, was lodging with Blechynden (reluctantly on Blechynden's part). Reed flogged his *hircarrah* (messenger) so severely that he ran away. This irritated Blechynden. What was worse, the hircarrah fled through the house garden, leaving a gate open, allowing deer and goats to get in. The malis did not discover this until morning, when they had a great job of catching and removing the animals, which, meanwhile, had entirely cleared the garden of roses, cabbages, lettuces, and so on. Blechynden resolved—for the moment—never to have 'another person in my house'.

Blechynden's own bad temper was the other side of this coin. One May day, finding his bearer not at home, he ordered a peon to carry his umbrella for him as he was going out. The man refused: it was 'not his Business'—an alternative view of his role and status. Blechynden 'gave him 8 or 9 lash[es]' with his cane, after which 'he thought fit to carry it'.[32] Another time, when Blechynden discovered 'not a soul' at his building work at ten o'clock, he beat the steward and the foreman 'by way of refreshing their memories' and 'slippered' the woman, a sweeper or *metrany*, who pounded bricks to make mortar; perhaps it was the Callindy he treated for a snakebite. Once, he found no palankeen bearers on returning from a journey on the river. He made his way home on foot, discovered the bearers 'carouzing' there, and gave their chief one good stroke with a horsewhip. (On another occasion, Blechynden's house steward himself beat one of the bearers for being drunk.) Again, Blechynden gave the cook three or four stripes with a cane when he had been asleep all day and not prepared tiffin. The meat at dinner that day was so foul that Blechynden refused to eat it. His son Arthur tried some and felt so ill that he wondered if the cook had tried to poison them. The cook refused to sample the meat, knuckle of veal, saying that he would lose caste if he did; Arthur and Blechynden made do—not for the first time—with bread and cheese.[33]

One night, Blechynden was awoken by a mali, Baddinaut, who told him that the buck deer had escaped. This 'piece of impertinence' made Blechynden very angry. He later found that the mali had been expressly forbidden to go into his room and disturb him. Baddinaut said a woman whose cow had been seized in Blechynden's garden had offered him four annas to let it go, perhaps the real reason for waking his master. Blechynden told him to go away and look for the deer. He could not get back to sleep, however, as Baddinaut had opened his bed curtains and let in mosquitoes. Blechynden called him back to drive them away and, when instead he whisked ineffectually *under* the bed, slapped him in the face. Baddinaut ran off and Blechynden sought out another mali, Keenoo, but he was missing from his house. Blechynden cleared the bed of mosquitoes himself as best he could and had a very bad night. Next day, the malis were caught and he 'served out striped jackets to them'. Later, he was informed that Baddinaut had been caught selling Blechynden's grain at Saum Bazar and had run off, fearing the consequences. In going, he had let in the deer, which destroyed the rose bushes yet again.

One quasi-judicial incident reinforces the link between violence and close living within the household. Taking out his razor to shave one evening at his garden house, Blechynden found it covered in dirt, with some black hairs sticking to it. He called the (clean-shaven) malis, who were in charge of the house. They denied all knowledge; they were shaved at Saum Bazar, they said. Blechynden tied them up and gave them each a lash alternately with a cane. Gopaul suffered six and three were delivered to a substitute for Gopaul's colleague Rogonaut. The dooria was called and he too said he knew nothing; he was in charge of the dogs, not the house, and so he escaped punishment.

Lilloo was set to inquire further and to bring a barber for Blechynden. Lilloo's suspicions fell on Deenoo, the manservant, because (the malis claimed) he was seen fastening his turban at the hall mirror while they were in the gardens. Blechynden determined that if his guilt were proven, he would give him a 'woful flogging for his insolence'. Next day, Deenoo pleaded his innocence: they could cut off his nose with the razor if he were guilty. Next, the dooria was said to have gone to Lilloo at his house. Lilloo came in and reported that the dooria had stopped him at the gate and said that if Blechynden forgave him this fault, it would never happen again. If this were true, Blechynden concluded, he would give him a 'smart jerking' for letting his fellow servants be punished in front of him. Forty-eight hours later, Blechynden was back at the gardens: he would hold a 'court martial' the next day. When that day came, however, the malis told him that the dooria had gone out at noon and not been seen since; he had sold his bed on the day he confessed to Lilloo and now had taken everything away with him. The malis were held responsible for letting him go and Blechynden stopped all wages until he was caught. Several months after this, his razor had been used again. Blechynden told the malis and dooria that they had been in charge and one of them must have been responsible. He had them tied up and threatened to have them flogged unless the guilty one confessed. They remained silent and so he had the peon give each of them eight strokes with a cane. They would get no more wages, he told them, until the culprit was found.[34]

Most reprisals, even when impulsive, did relate to actual misbehaviour. Several years later, when Tiretta and his servants were living at Blechynden's garden house, a circumcision ceremony was held there for a boy, Allum—in Blechynden's absence—with sixty or seventy guests at the feast, and another twenty at another the next day after the Bakr Id (the Muslim festival celebrating Abraham's sacrifice) and at a nautch in the evening. The manservant Deenoo came under suspicion for the robbery of many tablecloths, towels, and other belongings. Tiretta's servants were anxious to blame him. He was also under suspicion for having slept in the house while Blechynden was away. His mouth almost too dry to speak under interrogation, Deenoo claimed that he was there lighting candles for Tiretta. Blechynden sent for the *chaukidars* and ordered Deenoo to give up everything that had been entrusted to his care.

Blechynden was opposed to 'proceeding to extremities' (a court case and possible death sentence) and therefore at first he confined Deenoo. But Deenoo—obviously given to these gestures—threatened to cut his own throat and also could offer no security that he would appear before the magistrates, and so Blechynden reluctantly sent him to the *thanadar* (in charge of the police post). Blechynden had a sleepless night, 'much vexed' at Deenoo's 'ingratitude'. Deenoo still had the keys for the breakfast things and to get them back next morning, Blechynden sent for him to the thana and tried to get him to name his accomplices; he refused to confess to anything, except to say that Currim, the hookabadar, had put him up to pretending to cut his throat in the hope of persuading Blechynden to release him. Hearing that, Blechynden dismissed Currim.

The magistrate, Blaquiere, advised Blechynden to get rid of all his staff, as he could not identify the guilty ones; Blechynden thought it unreasonable to punish the innocent. Many more attempts were made to get Deenoo to confess; he refused and almost toppled Blechynden by catching hold of his feet, begging forgiveness whether he had or had not stolen anything. Blechynden sent him back once again to the thana, next morning had him released, and then dismissed him. Later, when he requested a reference, he wrote merely that Deenoo had served him as ketmutgar for nearly seven years.[35]

The impression is of a losing battle to maintain control. The garden servants continued to offend. Years after he fled, Baddinaut re-entered service. Blechynden went to the gardens unexpectedly on a Thursday and found absolutely no one there. He could not even gain admission: no malis were to be seen; the dooria was fast asleep. A brother of Gopaul, one of the malis, appeared and received four stripes. Baddinaut could not be found and was once again dismissed. In 1813, after a long period when Blechynden had been unable to go to the gardens at all, he found the house in a shocking state, panes of glass broken, some doors and windows stolen, all the floors covered with cattle and jackass dung, the walls defiled with the 'most shameful bawdy', and no malis to be seen. Baddinaut, however, had still been employed just before this; he came to tell Blechynden that water was rising in his tank again after he had ordered the breaching of a dam built across a public drainage ditch.[36]

Earlier, in 1805, when deer got into his garden and ate the roses yet again and no one would admit having left the gate open, Blechynden fired both the malis. The same day, he dismissed a peon, Ashraf, who had come from town without the newspapers and then claimed wrongly that none had arrived: it is, reflected Blechynden, 'sufficient for a servt. to come into my service [for him] to be no longer good for anything from too much indulgence—but I shall turn over a new leaf'. In 1800, Doman, hired to exercise horses, had been similarly absent and Blechynden had reflected that 'this arises from my having forgiven all his faults hitherto—find my system is too lenient—I must not consider these ungrateful black servants as humble friends but use a moderate degree of severity'. Acting on this new resolution, he then dismissed Doman immediately he arrived, at eight o'clock, and a couple of days later hired a new boy (Buxoo) who styled himself the 'coachman'.[37] It cannot be said that this quick reaction was typical. Blechynden was still threatening to dismiss servants and admitting to himself that he probably would not do so in 1819, when no peons arrived and the sices refused to accompany him on a shoot. One by one, the peons turned up later.

## SERVANTS VERSUS SERVANTS

Blechynden had little patience with quarrels between servants and objected particularly if they sought to involve members of his household other than himself. When the sice Morad complained to Blechynden's then bibi Isabella over a quarrel with some grasscutters, Blechynden dismissed him and the grasscutters. Both Morad and his brother were impossible, he decided, always quarrelling and sometimes drunk; they had even had 'the impudence' to appeal to him to decide between them on some argument. But Blechynden refused Isabella's demand that he dismiss two other servants, Govindram and Gopaul, saying that he could not turn someone away who was not at fault.[38] Blechynden's justice could be rough, but was carried out with a semblance of due process.

His interventions might also be inconclusive. There were mysteries not to be penetrated. On one occasion, a mali came from the gardens and told Blechynden that Doncaster's people had seized Blechynden's old sice and the dooria and had whipped them—the old man so badly that he had vomited up blood. The story grew with the telling and next day it was said that Doncaster's mali, Panchew, had come with two or three hundred coolies and snatched Blechynden's men from his own compound. Blechynden summoned Panchew, who claimed that the dooria had gone on to Doncaster's land to strip after he had been accused of having tobacco secreted in his clothes. He and the sice had been taken on the main road, not from Blechynden's compound. Blechynden gave up trying to get at the truth and docked his own staff's wages for deceiving him. His whipped servants, if they were whipped, stayed unavenged.[39]

But servants' quarrels often revealed more than they obscured. Where they might lead was illustrated by a series of incidents in 1801, after a man appeared in Blechynden's garden house compound with a Bengali petition. He was a *daffadar* (supervisor)[40] who had not been paid his arrears, but the petition concerned his wife, who (he said) was being kept at Blechynden's gardens by Mangoo, the dooria, and the malis Baddinaut and Gopaul. The woman, being sent for, admitted that she was the daffadar's wife. Blechynden told Mangoo that it was infamous to keep her and he replied that he had no desire to do so. The sice Morad became the spokesman and said that the man starved his wife and would not give her clothes. But she was plump and better dressed than her husband, who would earn only three rupees a month. Blechynden got the boy Buxoo to tie up the dooria, as he had no peons with him, and give him six strokes with a cane on the back and, when he turned his back to the pillar, seven on the thighs. He then told the husband to take his wife; he might still complain to the magistrates if he wished for the injury and loss of caste. They went off, with the man pushing his wife a little to move her along.

The dooria then appeared to faint and Blechynden, alarmed, ordered the sice Buxoo to throw water on him. He waved it away and lay on the grass, his eyes closed. Blechynden ran in the heat to fetch C.K. Bruce, trained as a doctor, who came and inspected Mangoo; he said that the problem must be an infection as there was scarcely a mark on his back and legs. His pulse was seventy-two a minute. He was given brandy and a phial of salts, but Bruce declared that he was shamming. Blechynden was still alarmed, but after a while the dooria recovered, took some brandy, and asked for food. Blechynden asked why he had pretended to be ill and he said that he had not. The flogging had not hurt him, he claimed, but he had been overcome at the woman's leaving. He had felt sick in the stomach and his head was swimming. This eased Blechynden's mind, though he was put off striking servants for a while, starting with the durwan that very day though he 'deserved' punishment because, 'intoxicated with gangah or bang', he had failed to deliver a letter until one and a half hours after it arrived. Mangoo lay down on his cot, and later walked to the market for oil and exercised the dogs. Blechynden had a disturbed night, thinking and dreaming about the incident.

Less than a month later, the woman was back with the dooria. Blechynden ordered his peons to watch them and sent for the husband, thinking he would refer them all to the magistrate, Macklew, if the dooria feigned illness again. When the husband came, the woman was not to be found. Blechynden threatened Baddinaut with the magistrates and she appeared. The husband, a bricklayer, said that his wife absconded while he was at work. Mangoo claimed that she had come back with him unasked when they met at the bazar. The husband took away his wife for a second time. Again, Blechynden said that he would support him if he complained to the magistrates, but the man preferred to 'go off quietly with his worthless wife'.

General discord followed among the servants at the gardens. One tetchy Sunday, Blechynden overheard a quarrel in which Baddinaut accused Gopaul of stealing Blechynden's fowls, bamboos, firewood, and wine. Gopaul retorted that Baddinaut was bringing women into the house and lying with them on Blechynden's couches. Blechynden feared that he was going to have to make an example of someone or he would be 'plundered of everything'. The next quarrel was between Baddinaut and the deaf hookabadar Panchew over a sheet belonging to the latter. It turned out that the sice Morad had taken it, to shelter (he claimed) from the sun while he went to Saum Bazar. Robbing him was fair game, thought Blechynden, but robbing each other was too bad. He called a chaukidar and put Gopaul into his charge, and told Panchew to do the same with Morad. Gopaul pleaded and promised until he was let off, but after the arrival of guests, Meer Abul Kasim and his nephew, Blechynden was reminded of the loss of his books to white ants and decided after all to commit Gopaul into custody. A third quarrel broke out, the other servants blaming Baddinaut for having got Gopaul into trouble. Baddinaut pointed out a peon, Soonarullah, in particular, and so Blechynden dismissed him. Next day, the sircar Rammohun Chatterjee tried to intercede for Gopaul, but on Baddinaut's evidence, he was dispatched to the thana. However, a couple of months later, he was still employed and managed to get himself gored by a deer.

Blechynden sent him to Dr Shoolbred in a palankeen; he returned with an ointment, saying his injuries were slight. Blechynden told him to take a hog spear to protect himself in future and then killed the deer himself. Venison was served to a large party some ten days afterwards.[41]

In mid-1805, Gopaul foolishly left his cloth on the couch in Blechynden's dressing room, revealing that he had been sleeping there; he got a slap in the face for it. Blechynden then went looking for Baddinaut too, sure that they had both 'been making a thoroughfare' of the room, but he ran off. Orders were given that Baddinaut should not be readmitted, and a substitute mali, Ourjun, was called from Calcutta. Not long after this, however, Ourjun was found to be sleeping with a woman on a couch in Blechynden's dressing room. Gopaul denied this had happened but the sircar Cassinaut and the dhobi both confirmed it. Blechynden arrived to discover the woman's husband and another relation there, claiming that she was in the house. He searched but could not find her until he told the dooria and a grasscutter that they were dismissed for letting a woman in and concealing her, whereupon the dooria pointed to her hiding place in a little hole under some of the steps. Cassinaut reported that Ourjun had been for sending her away, but Gopaul had said that it was too risky to do so in daylight. Blechynden delivered the woman to her husband in front of the large crowd that had gathered.

Cassinaut's further inquiries revealed that the dhobi was also involved with the woman, but could not get to her when the malis took her into Blechynden's house. Jealous, he had come in on pretence of taking away the sheets to be washed, had found her sleeping in the dressing room, called the chaukidars, and made a fuss. Blechynden decided that they would all have to go, especially as dismissing the dooria after a similar incident seemed to have had no effect. The chaukidars had taken the malis to the *cutcherry* (court house), where they were due to appear before the magistrate, Edward Thoroton. Ourjun's brother reported that they had settled with the husband and appealed to Blechynden to prevent any official punishment lest Ourjun lose caste. Blechynden replied that the husband must have lost caste himself and so he would wait and see what he wanted done. For a start, Blechynden would compensate him from the servants' wages. The husband came and definitely did not want any punishment of the offenders by the authorities. On that basis, Blechynden gave him a letter to Thoroton, who, having also asked the husband, released the prisoners. The husband was willing to accept fourteen rupees in compensation. Blechynden owed five to Gopaul, two to Ourjun, and three to the dhobi, and so he paid the husband what he wanted, a certain

Nillunder standing security for the balance of four rupees. When a new dooria was found, Blechynden dismissed the old one and the grasscutter. They may have considered themselves lucky. Years later, Calcutta was agog when a married sice, a 'fine Patan' of about twenty-three, was murdered and his genitals cut off by one Townsend, a native Portuguese, for having committed adultery with his wife. Townsend was taken to gaol. His wife went out to dinner.[42]

## HONOUR AND INGRATITUDE

Evidently, the entanglement of master, servants, and law had mixed consequences. In the backdrop to these examples are not only the difficulties of managing large households, but also differences of perspective and expectation. In return for his accepting an employer's liability, Blechynden came to equate timekeeping, loyalty, and duty in his workers, with mixed results. One day, in his building work, he insisted on having ten painters rather than two, and next day found that twenty-five had turned up. On another occasion, he found all six bricklayers 'skulking with the Servants and 2 of them in the Cookroom'; he took their names and had them struck from the list of workers for the whole day. It was 'very provoking', he complained of yet another absence; not only were 'former advances not worked out', but further money had only just been paid, three rupees per workman. The excuse was that 'someone had died and they had been to the feast', 'What Rascally Souls these natives have,' he wrote, 'What wretches—as if they were not bound in Conscience to give me the whole of their labour for a day's pay instead of working idly.'[43] This may be taken as a motto for Blechynden and his household servants, a concatenation of disputes, derelictions of duty, and punishment.

Servants tried Blechynden's patience repeatedly. His regular tailor, Dyam, was irregular in his attendance. Once, during his period of mourning for Tiretta's young wife, Blechynden had to borrow black stockings from Tiretta as his own were badly split and the tailor had not been near him for three days. It was five days before he reappeared.[44] When a troublesome buggy horse broke one shaft and fell on the other, Blechynden could not persuade 'the stupid cowardly sice' to hold its head to keep it from beating itself and the buggy to pieces. He had to kneel on the horse himself—the exertion putting him into a profuse perspiration—while the other grooms came and unbuckled the harness. Once, another sice, Dullal, supposed to be accompanying Blechynden on a ride, was so drunk that he could not stand. Blechynden ordered that he should not be admitted to the house.

He did not reappear the following day, and so he was dismissed and a replacement found. When one servant reappeared after a long absence, saying that he had lost a child, Blechynden made no answer but went over to Tiretta's, borrowed seventeen rupees, and paid him off.[45]

The sices were a frequent source of trouble. Even the head groom, Gofarrah, having been the most reliable of servants, began to complain of ill health. In February 1797, a sign of favour to Gofarrah, or perhaps of his incipient weakness, was his being permitted to ride Blechynden's horse Padre, at his own request, behind the buggy on the way to the gardens. At the time, it was an issue whether Blechynden could afford to keep an extra horse; and sices normally ran beside their masters. Now, in April, Gofarrah said that his head was swimming, his skin was 'lazy' (*soustie*), and he could no longer carry out his duties. Blechynden replied that he would get no wages if he stopped working; but if he was ill, Blechynden would find medicine for him and allow someone else to do his work until he was better. Gofarrah would say nothing more about his condition, but suggested that he did not want to leave Blechynden's service and instead would take over being sice to the horse Johnny. Blechynden said the pay for that post was a rupee less (four rupees) than he was getting, but Gofarrah agreed. It must be idleness, thought Blechynden, or he had got himself 'into some scrape in Calcutta'. He was not very happy with the replacement sice: he could not keep up with the horse in a short ride through the streets of Calcutta. Three weeks later, Blechynden found Gofarrah stupefied with ganja (cannabis): his eyes were fixed and he was hardly able to speak. 'I fear the Boy is going to the Dogs,' Blechynden wrote. He survived in Blechynden's employ, however.[46]

We have seen enough of the problems with the staff at the gardens, but more immediate domestic arrangements were also very often fraught. Blechynden's manservant Kyroo was so drunk one morning that he could hardly stand and half-filled the teapot with tea leaves, which Blechynden fortunately noticed before the water was put in. Kyroo had a man called Daulat do his duty for him and so Blechynden hired him on the spot and sent Kyroo 'about his business'. However, Kyroo was still in his employ five days later, when he was so drunk that Gofarrah had to deputize for him that day and also the day after, when once again he was drunk at breakfast time. He seems to have been replaced some time later.

In January 1800, Blechynden had a sirdar bearer called Collypersaud. By September, a new servant, Panchew, was looking after him. When ill, he provided 'a very foolish locum tenens' who did not bring breakfast until near 9 AM. In December, Panchew did not appear because he had been arrested by the guards the previous night for being in possession of some of Blechynden's spoons; one could not blame them, thought Blechynden, but he sent to Blaquiere to have Panchew released.[47]

When it came to difficult servants, the ketmutgar Emaundee was in a class of his own. A successor to Kyroo, he had responsibility for organizing meals and serving at table, apart from dressing Blechynden's hair and looking after him personally as a valet. Emaundee would go missing for days at a time. In 1795, he was dismissed; but the replacement, Cummoo, soon left Blechynden, 'not chusing to remain for 5 Rs a month & he cannot tye hair!', and the long-serving sircar Lilloo brought back Emaundee. In July 1796, Emaundee was granted a holiday one Thursday on condition that he return the next day so that another manservant, Hingun, could have leave. He did not return but Hingun also disappeared anyway; another servant, Bhilow, was already missing. Blechynden was suffering from an upset stomach and had no one to attend him. Hingun returned on Monday, saying that he had been ill, and came again on Tuesday, the sixth day that Emaundee and Bhilow had been missing. But Hingun had no keys and Blechynden was obliged to dine on a slice of dry bread and a tumbler of water. After another two days, Emaundee sent to say that his head hurt and to give Hingun the keys. Blechynden resolved to make his *back* ache when he appeared, and if he did not come the next day, to send a chaukidar for him. That day he turned up at last, claiming to have been sick, but 'his countenance belies him', Blechynden thought. He sent for a couple of sices and had him flogged. For the umpteenth time, he decided that he must discharge him. Emaundee went missing again the next month and again kept his job. In November, he was even given a day's holiday and stayed away for two. 'I always threaten never to allow him another [holiday],' wrote Blechynden, 'and yet the expression of I am thy servant, disarms me.'

Blechynden obviously made allowances, perhaps (given other examples) especially for his personal staff. Various traditional holidays were respected. Peons and bearers were granted holidays for Id in August 1818. In March 1797, Emaundee was allowed three days' leave for Id and provided another temporary replacement, who did not appear at all. Because of the Muslim festival, Blechynden could not find a barber to tend his hair. Later, when a manservant (Buddoo) reported that his mother had died, he was given a day's leave and eight rupees. Emaundee, however, was 'at his usual tricks' once more early in 1797, going out at 9 PM and not returning until next day at three o'clock. He claimed to have buried someone from his house that day, but 'he always says so'. Blechynden sent a servant to check and, finding the excuse was untrue, gave Emaundee '3 or 4 blows' with his whip. He also directed the durwan to keep him in the house all night and in future to stop him from going home before ten—Blechynden had usually let him go at seven or eight.[48]

The new regime may have proved too arduous for Emaundee. More than once in April 1797, Blechynden had to dress unaided as Hingun also did not appear and Emaundee had not been seen for days. Hingun's excuses on one occasion, when he returned after four days away, were perhaps too elaborate. He said he had had a fever and his house had burnt down; Blechynden did not believe him. Another five days' absence two months later cost him his job, until Lilloo pleaded for him 'as being very poor' and Blechynden took him back. Finally, in April 1797, Blechynden hired as ketmutgar another Emaundee, formerly servant to Proctor, at six rupees per month. This did not solve the problem. In June, after two days without a manservant, Blechynden was forced next door for breakfast. In August, he was employing Ameer as ketmutgar as well as Emaundee. One day, Ameer turned up at three in the afternoon and Emaundee not at all. He came at sunrise next day and Blechynden ordered the durwan to confine him all day and night. By 1801, when the manservant was Deenoo, he slept out of the house, against orders, and so was sometimes not at work when he was needed to dress Blechynden's hair: at least once a barber had to be called. In 1805, the manservant was called Rumjohnny and Blechynden gave him one or two cuts with what he described as a soft, worn-out horsewhip when he did not appear to tie his hair. His failure to attend Blechynden at dinner at a friend's once again produced the refrain: he *must* dismiss him.

Decisive action was sometimes taken. One day, a servant ran off 'with the bazar'—three rupees' worth of food bought for a meal. The manservant at that time, Deenoo, brought chickens and other food out to the gardens for a late dinner and a few days later presented the missing servant to Blechynden. The man claimed to be mad, but Deenoo said that when he captured him at his house, four of his brothers had 'sallied out' and attempted to rescue him. In his opinion, the family lived by 'depradations of this kind'. The servant admitted that they had eaten the meal and promised to pay for it. Blechynden put him in the custody of a peon, who later brought him back saying that he had talked to him rationally, trying to persuade him to let him go. Blechynden decided to leave the man to Deenoo, who was responsible for the three rupees, and gave him a chit for the magistrates. Next day, Martyn sent back a note saying that the man had repaid the money but that he had sent him 'to a house of correction for 15 days'.

In March 1801, when Blechynden paid all his household servants, he deducted forty-five rupees from them for a silver case of mathematical instruments that had gone missing. The case was mysteriously presented to him by his servants, saying—or rather (he said) pretending—that they had found it in his old palankeen; he paid back what he had retrenched. Buxoo, the boy hired to ride the horse Captain, complained about this deduction of pay and so Blechynden dismissed the 'little brat', thinking to exercise the horse himself. He did so, but was too heavy for it. Shortly afterwards, therefore, he rehired Buxoo 'on his pressing entreaty and promise to behave better': decisive action gave way to compromise, as so often. Soon after, he thought that Buxoo was absent on pretence of sickness and so sent him to the cutcherry. He then ordered his release because he was involved in another, more serious case on the day Buxoo was due to come before the justices. About six weeks after this, Buxoo 'teazed [his] heart out to take him back' and he did so once again because Captain needed exercise.[49] The details become blurred, but the repeated pattern of offence, complaint, punishment, and forgiveness is plain. Behind it, stereotypes were being shaped.

## ROBBING THE MASTER

Blechynden was repeatedly and consciously trying to create a climate of trust, even 'humble' friendship, with his servants. But problems over perfomance and honesty would drag on for months, and even so, malfeasance was frequently forgiven. The first Emaundee complained that he was indebted to a moneylender for sixteen rupees. Blechynden ordered Lilloo to pay. Lilloo demurred because Emaundee had already had forty-one rupees for bazar expenses in a month when Blechynden had been seldom at home. Blechynden was 'much vexed' at this 'villainy'. On another occasion, finding a dinner furnished for eight annas and comprising fowl, shrimp, curry, hindquarters of mutton, potatoes, and boiled gherkins, he exclaimed: 'How my Servants must have cheated me!'

Confronting Emaundee, he referred to his diary, with its catalogue of meals, and claimed that it was worse 'to rob me whom they saw struggling with the severity of distress, and by that means injuring my Creditors'. He admitted that his service was not the most desirable—as at this time he could not pay wages punctually—but (contrary to the record in the same diary) he defied them to say when he had ever had them beaten or denied them a holiday. Emaundee blamed his father. Blechynden made no comment on the evident loyalty of Lilloo on this as on other occasions, but harangued both men on 'the heinousness of robbing a Master who was placed by Providence in the situation of a father to counteract to the Servant the pains of Servitude'.[50] We may assume that they thought his notions of duty and contract odd or even immoral, for they were unlike many prevalent South Asian ideas about employment and obligations, resting as they did on advance payments, caste requirements, reciprocal duty, or bondage; and (at this time) as much on fluid as on fixed status and roles.

Certainly the lesson was lost on Emaundee. In 1796, Blechynden discovered his tobacco supplier was receiving a rupee a month for tobacco and half an anna for '100 gools', whereas Emaundee was charging him four rupees in his accounts. Blechynden complained that 'these people have no sense of honour or honesty': Emaundee had the heart to cheat and rob him when he knew he had no income and was in 'the extremity of distress'. After discussion, Emaundee agreed to furnish the hookah for two rupees a month.[51] On another occasion, he was accused by the durwan of stealing one of the bibi's copper dishes and a silver spoon; he denied both offences, claiming that the dish was one of his own that he had taken with some food to the servant Bucktar. It was impossible to get to the bottom of this: the loss of the spoon had gone unreported for eight months. There was another hubbub about stolen property in 1817, when one of the ketmutgars had lost two handkerchiefs and they were recovered from the bundle of the mate (assistant) to the cook, along with pieces of silver and brass buttons belonging to Blechynden. The man denied everything and Blechynden was not entirely sure of his guilt as the servants had been at the gardens some weeks since the items went missing and he could not see where they could have been hidden during that time. He ordered the mate to be sent to the thana overnight and had a sircar investigate. Next day, however, he ordered the man released as there was no proof against him, and 'no knowing what desperation might have driven him to'.[52]

More serious theft was discovered in May 1797: only five of about sixty pairs were left from two boxes of 'fine brass Europe hinges'. The durwan, being summoned, said he knew nothing. He was given over to the chaukidars to be brought before the justices. Lilloo was set to making an inventory of the stores. The durwan persisted in his denials before the justice, Andrew Macklew, and was held for further questioning. Next day, security was taken from him by another magistrate, Thomas Boileau, but he still denied that he knew anything of thieves or the goods. His offence was to have either taken the hinges or allowed them to be taken (because he guarded the entry to Blechynden's premises). Boileau was inclined to send him to the Herringbherry for a fortnight, but advised Blechynden that he would do better to cover his losses by deductions from the fifty days' pay the durwan was owed, as that would have to be paid to him in full if he were sent to gaol. Blechynden agreed to this. Boileau then said that Lilloo, the sircar, was the more guilty of the two and ought to be punished for being careless of Blechynden's property. Boileau wanted Lilloo to be sent in; he was not.[53]

## SIRCARS AT BAY

A couple of years later, the long-trusted Lilloo was ill, 'or pretending to be', and the other sircars were unable to read his writing. Blechynden busied himself with the accounts, but was 'much distressed' by them, such 'sad cheating' had he found. Later he asked Gopey what he thought Lilloo had done with his money. He lived in a straw hut and did not seem to be building a house. Gopey said that he gambled and in one year had lost Rs 3,000. He had covered the debt by debiting Blechynden's account with cash for tradesmen whom he had not paid and by overcharging on quantity for the materials supplied. Blechynden resolved to leave Lilloo to deal with those he had cheated over these payments and supplies. Later he discovered that, after receiving eight rupees from him to pay two peons, Lilloo had carried them on his own account with the cash keeper, Ramjoy Muckerjee, to offset a debt of forty rupees that he (Lilloo) owed to Ramjoy. Blechynden called in Ramjoy and paid Lilloo's debt in full. He also found his brick merchant was still owed Rs 400 though Lilloo had charged the payment to his accounts. He made Lilloo grant him a bond for the sum and a receipt relating to all the demands outstanding.

Such subterfuges were evidently very common. Around this time, for example, a chaukidar brought Blechynden his mali Seeboo with two planks and seven empty bottles that the chaukidar claimed Seeboo had stolen from Blechynden. Seeboo denied it at first, but admitted it when the sircar came. He was dismissed. Lilloo's dereliction was greater and more troubling; but he remained for some time in Blechynden's service, presumably paying off his debts. When he was dismissed, Blechynden received in quick succession a recommendation for a replacement from the lawyer Forbes and (as noted earlier) a possibly pointed visit from a former sircar, Andiram, who, however, merely commented that Lilloo was a fool, not dishonest. Blechynden decided to practise the economy of doing without a sircar. Quite soon, the indispensable Lilloo was back.[54]

Next, during major work on Calcutta's roads and several other significant projects in 1801, Blechynden made very elaborate inquiries into theft, cheating, and corruption, taking advantage of ill feeling and tale-telling among the sircars and contractors. Among those doubted were Rammohun Chatterjee, the gambler Lilloo, and the supposed plunderer Jaggernaut. One of the informants was Ramtonoo Ghose, a former pupil at Blechynden's charity school, who told him incidentally that the Brahman teacher was cheating him also, having only about ten boys instead of the hundred he had had in the past—information that proved correct.

Blechynden investigated his sircars' corruption himself rather than committing the culprits to the magistrates. His hope was he might thus recover more money and avoid disruption as far as possible. The accounts made to the government for major road building and other works were called into question. The sircars' papers were sealed up on 25 May. Lilloo and Jaggernaut provided and renewed security. Lilloo advised dismissing a 'rascally' temporary servant, Teen Courie, as a thief after a watch went missing and then reappeared damaged. Blechynden told Lilloo that he was 'surrounded by thieves of every denomination'.[55] Blechynden exclaimed also at the ingratitude of another person caught up in this, who had been bribed—one Goyram whom he had 'brought up from a boy' in fulfilment of a promise to his father. The issue dragged on. Blechynden was visited by Jaggernaut and Lilloo as supplicants, and they tried unsuccessfully to proceed against him through Blaquiere and the Supreme Court. Lilloo then presented his great distress with poignant lamentations and promised to be faithful if re-employed. Eventually Blechynden agreed to accept his bond for what he considered he owed him, and re-employed him to pay it off. He was still employed in 1805.

Meanwhile, even the new sircar, the trusted Cassinaut Ganguly, was accused of cheating on the purchase of timber. Sircars were expected to charge a commission, 'dustoory', on purchases they made for their employer, but at set rates. For construction and other work, they received three rupees or two per cent, plus a 'gift' of one per cent. Earlier, Cassinaut seemed caught out when the bibi of that time reported her shoes cost two annas, including 'dustoory', but the sircar charged two rupees. This 'unhinged' Blechynden against Cassinaut but he said nothing, only ordering Gopey to put nothing in the books unless Cassinaut produced a voucher for every item to be debited.

Later, Rammohun Chatterjee also came under suspicion, but long continued working for Blechynden. His alleged dishonesty in Blechynden's service was eventually the subject of a trial at the Court of Requests, instigated by Davy Naug, in March 1805. Blechynden's whole house was in 'uproar' at the summons to give evidence (and hence swear an oath, anathema to any 'good Hindu'). On another occasion, Blechynden was very sorry to have forced Gopey to be sworn in as a witness and felt he must make amends. Rammohun eventually absconded, going to Isherah. From there, he wrote to Blechynden protesting his innocence. He was still trying for reinstatement in 1807, on hearing Cassinaut was under a cloud. Later he tried to implicate the even longer-serving Davy Naug in corruption, telling Blechynden that he had made a great deal of money while his master (Blechynden) made nothing, and he had even built a shrine at his country house at a cost of Rs 20,000. Blechynden did not believe it.[56]

## FROM CONTRACT TO SENTIMENT

The never-ending disputes over honesty, time, and attendance were always close to concerns about conscientious completion of the task or about spheres of responsibility—and may be revealing about different perspectives and expectations. Thus, there was approved compassionate leave, as it would be called today, and other agreed absences or holidays; but policing them was always contentious. The draughtsman Hurry was given leave, 'of course', to bury his brother-in-law, which greatly delayed urgent work; he returned eighteen days later and then, along with Gopey, immediately took two days' holiday for the hook-swinging ceremonies, during which there was always one day of 'Bengali holiday'. The then bibi, Krim Simone, took a palankeen to attend.[57] Festivals, therefore, were accepted reluctantly as a legitimate reason for absence. In addition, however, there were extended holidays and unexpected disappearances, which caused disputes. For example, Gopey asked for twelve days' holiday for the Durga puja in 1796; Blechynden said that would cost him wages. In the end, he was away between 5 and 24 October. In 1798, when the Durga celebrations were on 19 October, he ended his holiday on 5 November. In 1801, he went home ill on 9 September, returned, was advanced Rs 100 for Durga puja (with Blechynden telling him that he ought to be spending money on his children instead), and then stayed away without formal leave between 20 and 26 October. In 1803, he took fourteen days' holiday, and in 1804, when the Durga puja occurred on 14 October, he returned to work on 20 October. During one month in 1805, he was absent for his father's funeral, then said he was ill, next wanted a holiday for his son's birthday, and then wanted two days to take his children to his family home—'*toujours quelque chose!'* complained Blechynden. In October, he returned to work on 8 October, asked for leave again on 23 October because his nephew was very ill—a request that could not 'in humanity' be refused—and then declined to come the following day as the nephew had died. He did not appear on the next, though he had promised to be in early.

In 1798, too, Gopey failed to appear for work and again wanted to go home to Nadia. Blechynden set the chaukidars after him. Davy Naug claimed that he was shamming illness. Blechynden said that he would not be allowed to go home until after he had returned to work: he sent Jaggernaut, who reported, however, that Gopey had already gone. Examining the cash books, which Gopey was responsible for writing up, Blechynden found entries had stopped over a fortnight before. Tiretta's writer was also missing, which added to the confusion. Lilloo and Jaggernaut told Blechynden that he would have to write to the judge in Nadia to get him to send Gopey back, so as to ensure they were cleared of any irregularities in the accounts; Blechynden did so, though the district judge was Arthur Hesilrige, with whom he had no wish to correspond.

Gopey returned after about ten days, professing ignorance of any process against him by Hesilrige and begging to be let back into Blechynden's service. This time Davy Naug was his advocate. Blechynden pretended to be inexorable, but agreed. Gopey returned to work the next day, saying he had had a serious illness; Blechynden told him that Hesilrige was a very good doctor. Gopey had been telling the truth on that point at least, however, because Hesilrige wrote a polite letter back to Blechynden, enclosing reports in Persian and Bengali, saying Gopey was not to be found in his district. Eventually, Gopey was heavily in Blechynden's debt, and so in 1809, when he sought three months' pay, including nearly two months in advance, and ten day's immediate leave, Blechynden refused to pay him beyond the present day.[58]

The rigmarole of absence and incompletion of duties hinted at more fundamental misunderstandings. Blechynden, especially irked by wasted time, thought progress was achieved only through knowledge, effort, and innovation. Were attitudes to work different in hot and in temperate countries? Frederick Cooper, African historian, claimed: 'a clash of different notions of time and work occurred in the context of colonialism ... The confrontation was read by white commentators as ... laziness ....'[59] In Calcutta and with Blechynden, the story was more complicated. The year itself was regulated, not or not only by a harvest rhythm, but by other prescriptions. One time-pressure was exerted by the indefinite departure of ships for England, for merchants and bankers, and because this was when letters had to be despatched.[60] More generally, there were locally published almanacs and calendars (including Hindu and Muslim feast days).[61] Blechynden's personal clock was mainly a natural one, despite the scientific calculations he made to find the correct time. Typically he would rise at 4.00 AM, write 'till Daylight', and punctuate his day with such markers as 'Gunfire', 'Breakfast', 'Dinnertime', 'Sun Sett', and 'Candle light'.[62] Despite this partly seasonal daily rhythm, he insisted upon the attendance of domestic servants and workers at particular hours. His employers constantly wanted him to speed up his building work, and in turn he insisted on timekeeping, even for workers being paid at piece rates. His irritation with late or missing workers was frequently expressed in cultural terms. He criticized indolence and unreliability in fellow Europeans as well, but it was as if that critique was sharpened by the perceived shortcomings of Indians. Climate was something to be resisted (as by mad dogs and stereotypical Englishmen).[63]

Obviously the servants of Europeans operated within parameters set by Europeans. Blechynden's experience shows how the management of labour was an important arena of conflict and misunderstanding. His idiosyncracies dominated his household for good or ill. Concubines too had to comply. More or less indirectly, they were subject to the mores of the age, laws of marriage, and European men's rights over children and property, and also affected by laws relating to employment, as shown in Sex and Sensibility. Servants were particularly subject to contract law and its offshoot, master-and-servant rules. This they had in common with other employees in categories the law was generalizing and reconstituting, alongside the continuing plethora of indigenous titles and responsibilities. Early Calcutta households thus provide a kind of prehistory of the redefinitions of the public and private spheres and of rights and morals converging around employment, as they were around property and space, in colonial India and in Europe.[64]

Contract was important to Blechynden as an idea; but above all, he was concerned with purposeful management and schedules. This had a positive as well as a punitive side. At the margins, the state and law were surprisingly closely involved and were already beginning to recognize duties of care for the employers, even while they focused on disciplining employees. More important, norms of conduct implied a reciprocal responsibility on the part of the employer. This too constituted conditions for servants, including slaves and bibis. Blechynden's attitudes were encapsulated when he was accidentally given letters that had been dropped in the street.[65] They read:

Dᵣ Sir

You Will Greatly Oblidg Me by Letting Me Know Wither You tack in Black Slaves Gerals into The Horspattel as Miss Porter ave a Slave Gearl Gave Her that as Venerl Diseas Verrey Bad...

Sir, I am Yours trouly,
J. Porter

Sir

Natives of all Sex are received into the Hospital, but it is a very improper place for the femail ones to be sent, and there is a charge of Eight Rupees per month to be paid for each patient which will soon come to the price of a Slave as times goes.

Yours truly
Thos. Meredith

Blechynden commented:

Ergo! It is more economical to let her perish of a Cruel Malady communicated to her by some inhuman Monster than lay out 8 Rˢ per mensem for her cure! Benevolent Mr. Meredith! Aimiable Mr Meredith!! He is the more guilty in this Case not only from the assurance that he gives that he would not save a wretched fellow Creature from the Grave for 8 Rˢ but for actually preventing or at least attempting to prevent another from doing so, when the money would not come out of his pocket.

Blechynden soon had the opportunity to put this theory into practice. His slave girl, Mary, complained of being ill and 'after many hums & haws' admitted 'it was the Clap'. Blechynden 'examined her and found it even so'. She declared that no man had been near her and it had 'come of itself'; but then admitted she had had the same condition 'once with Addy'. Blechynden provided her with medicine. A few days later, when she said that she was very well and would take no more, he warned her (and the bibi) that 'if she chose to take the symptoms of amendment for Cure & shut the Wolf up in the Sheepfold, they must expect no assistance from me when it returned with increased violence'.[66]

   Four conclusions may be drawn. First, servants were not ciphers subjugated to the master's will—they expressed too many opinions, took too many active steps, and secured too many compromises. Secondly, the European experience of servants was one of interdependence, as between the white and black towns of Calcutta, or for that matter between mixed-race children and their wet nurses, or later British colonial infants and their ayahs. Thirdly, Blechynden, with perhaps more soul-searching than most, recognized that it mattered little that his relations with Indians were contractual but a great deal that they depended on trust. Finally, breaches of trust—the irritations of poor timekeeping, unreliability, and dishonesty that comprised the servants' contractual failures—became clamorous advocates in European minds for stereotypes about Indian character and the contrasting virtues of European conduct and institutions. Taken together, these conclusions also represent the inevitable interplay between cultures whereby cultures evolve. This was not the facile 'either/or' of perpetrator and victim. So too colonialism used to be treated only as something done *to* India, but now is also seen as something done *with* it.

# 4

# Law and Disorder

Were we to be driven out of India this day, nothing would remain to tell that it had been possessed, during the inglorious period of our dominion, by anything better than the orang-outang or the tiger.

—Edmund Burke[1]

## CALCUTTA RULES

Like the rulers of the colonial empire, the employers of Calcutta's slaves, paid servants, and concubines operated in an atmosphere of both sentiment and conflict. The undercurrent of suspicion and mutual rivalry was awkwardly managed by negotiation and law. It is worth dwelling on the law because it underpinned so much conduct in early Calcutta. It implied a public oversight of private activities. Courts were gradually regulating labour even in domestic settings, as well as civil disputes and crime.

We cannot ignore the scurrilous tales of abuse, affecting both daily behaviour and the longer-term impact of colonial rule. The magistrate Levi Ball, for example, caught his bibi having sexual relations with one of his peons. He took their two children from the bibi and turned her out of the house. Then he arrested the peon and sent him to the House of Correction for three years—which Blechynden thought was (if true) about double any sentence Ball was entitled to pass. This story passed around Calcutta at a remarkable rate, not least by exchange of news among bibis, which was how Blechynden heard of it.[2] In such an atmosphere and with such 'law', Europeans and men, especially men of influence, had very clear advantages.

A revealing case concerned the notorious W.T. Jones, an attorney whose vindictive behaviour plagued Blechynden for several years (described in *Sex and Sensibility*).[3] He was alleged to have killed his durwan by flogging him. Tried for murder, he escaped punishment because a doctor, Hill, gave evidence that the durwan (who had not died immediately) had had 'something very like arsenic' in his stomach. Some time later, Jones was said to have killed his *mater* (a sweeper, the lowliest of the servants) by striking him on the temples and then pinching his throat to keep him silent. Blechynden was immediately interested in the mater's death because his then bibi had decamped to live with Jones. The *chaukidars* had ordered the body taken to the *cutcherry* on the father's complaint. Blechynden inquired at the Police Office. Crowds started gathering in the street. Sepoys arrived with fixed bayonets to deal with Jones if the inquest should take that turn. He had been very alarmed when the man was brought in dead, but perhaps had little reason for concern.

When the inquest began, Jones's durwan gave evidence that he heard Jones striking the mater, who came downstairs and showed him a splinter in his hand from a broom. The mater went home that evening and was dead next day. Jones's clerk, Tom Lloyd, sent a chit to call Jones and, while they waited, entertained the inquest with an account of how Jones struck a servant with his fist, split his nose, and when the bleeding stopped, wanted to tear the wound open again to make it worse. Blechynden wondered that Matthew Louis, the coroner, had not silenced Lloyd. The court writer spoke to Baddinaut, the former and future mali of Blechynden, then working for Jones. Baddinaut shook his head. The writer whispered to Lloyd, who stared at Baddinaut and then called Jones's cook, who had been upstairs with Lloyd earlier, being trained in 'what answers to make'. He came, in dirty Bengali clothes with an old black coat over them, and to everyone's surprise said that he was a Gentoo (Hindu) when called upon to swear. His evidence echoed the durwan's: he had heard the beating but not seen it. The coroner decided that Jones had no case to answer.

R.C. Statham, Examiner in the Revenue and Judicial Department, later told Blechynden that he thought the mater *had* died of sickness. Blechynden pointed out that he had given evidence on oath to that effect to the coroner and so he hoped that he really did think so. Statham said that Jones was fond of the boy as he had 'knocked and thumped him about more than all the rest and yet he never left him!' This 'proof of Jones's attachment set [Blechynden's house guest] Powell into a laugh'. Blechynden objected that the inquest was negligent. Several witnesses to the assault were present but only two were called and their evidence was wholly inconclusive as to Jones's guilt. A man would not die of a splinter in the hand, unless from lockjaw or gangrene, and so there should have been a post-mortem examination to ascertain the cause of death. The surgeon Roger Keys was in the court. Blechynden concluded that as coroner, Lloyd was 'more versed in the Gentoo than the English laws', citing one part (ch.3, s.9) of the 'Pootee or Ordination of the Pundits' that he said permitted perjury to preserve life except where a Brahman was murdered, a cow killed, or a Brahman had drunk wine.[4] As Jones had killed only a durwan and possibly now a mater, he was entitled to perjury!

Jaggernaut brought more information. He reported hearing Lloyd tutoring the witnesses. Baddinaut had said that he would tell the truth, at which Jones's *consomah* remarked to Lloyd that he must be cautious what questions were put to him. Lloyd replied that the coroner would ask the questions and all the servants had to do was to say that they knew nothing. Baddinaut repeated that if he were sworn in, he would tell the truth, which was why he was not called. Jaggernaut said that Jones's servants all appeared in black coats to cover the marks on their backs from repeated floggings. The consomah himself had been knocked down and had not been near Jones for three days, but could not leave as he was owed four and a half months' wages. Jaggernaut said that the mater's family, also not called at the inquest, claimed Jones had half throttled the man so that he could not eat and died shortly afterwards. They intended to petition the Supreme Court for justice. Gopey added that 'all the natives present were much dissatisfied at the manner in which the inquest was conducted— particularly those belonging to the police office who are acquainted with the English routine of examining witnesses &[ca]'. Blechynden warned him not to get involved—it would 'embitter the rest of his days if he were the means of depriving Louis of his post & Jones of his life'. Gopey said that he had no intention of meddling; he was just repeating what was being said.

Blechynden, faced with the strong indication that Jones was a murderer for the second time and indeed now accepting it as fact, nonetheless cautioned Jaggernaut too to keep out of the matter and resorted to pieties he would have dismissed as absurd on other occasions. His new doctrine of criminal law was: punishing Jones would not bring back the dead man; Jones would have to answer to a higher tribunal. As well as Indian observers, even some Europeans disagreed. Charles Rothman, later discussing the acquittal of the poulterer of the Indiaman *Bengal* after he had killed the ship's third mate, told Blechynden that Lord Wellesley had commented: 'it required a great deal of Interest to get hanged in this country'. A scavenger, Mackay, had also recently been acquitted, and Rothman said he was quite of his Lordship's opinion, citing as further proof 'what's his name?—the Attorny who killed his Durwan and latterly his Mater? The Gallows has been groaning for that man for years—and yet he has hitherto escaped.'

Everyone, Blechynden and the Governor-General included, believed Jones guilty but recognized that any attempt to make him answer for his crime in the Company's Calcutta could rebound on the advocate of justice and not the murderer.[5]

Despite such examples, unprivileged people were not always affected negatively. Evolving theories placed government under the law and prescribed equality before the law. As European power settled down in India, building a new state, it had to decide who was entitled to the benefits of law. Could a Shylock enjoy the same rights as a Christian? Who was a citizen? The question concerned variously infidels, 'barbarians', slaves, or commoners and had been asked in Europe at least from the sixteenth to the nineteenth centuries. Clearly, debate became more active in England as the notion of a national law and polity developed. But the question was being asked too in early modern India, when states sought legitimacy, or people debated the lawful response to unjust rulers, or Hindus objected to Mughal tax discrimination and asked if rulers' or subjects' rights were limited by their religious duties.[6] Under colonial rule, Calcutta was served by institutions that made a show of not seeing social or racial difference but applying other distinctions instead. The jurisdiction of the Supreme Court had to be laboriously proved in each case, at much benefit to the lawyers, but the primary criterion was residential, not racial.[7] As a consequence, rights were being defined generally and by specific, objective criteria, such as over landed property.

There was enhanced social and political control for the British; but Indians could and did use the law against Europeans and between themselves. They were notoriously quick and prolific in using the courts set up or developed by Europeans, taking no notice of partisan claims that English jurisprudence was, as James Mill said of penal law, 'utterly repugnant' to India's existing laws and customs.[8] Blechynden, though claiming to detest oppression of any kind, was of that prominent school— found from taproom to council chamber—that believed arbitrary but benevolent government suited Indians best. They needed 'Vigour beyond the Law'; they failed to 'relish equal and humane' justice. Therefore it was a mistake to entrust the policing of society to lawyers who would 'entrench themselves ['trembling'] behind an act of Parliament'. However, as Blechynden also recognized, that was increasingly where the East India Company and the Board of Control were placed; and in fact Blechynden was always ready to instruct people on legal principles.

One day, he encountered Andiram, the contractor foreman (*mistri*) of his painters, who had been taken in charge by a peon who identified himself to Blechynden as belonging to Bernard Smith, a magistrate. He could not produce any paperwork nor a chaprasi (a badge-holding, official messenger) to give credence to this claim, and when Blechynden sent for a chaukidar, the peon admitted he was Hurry Sing, a servant of Datteram Chuckerbutty, who wanted him to seize Andiram for debt. The chaukidar arrived, Blechynden sent a chit to Andrew Macklew, justice of the peace, and the peon was so alarmed that he asked Andiram to intercede for him. Blechynden took the mistri aside and told him to let matters go ahead: 'our Laws are very careful of the liberty of the subject', he explained, and 'he might depend upon the obtaining of special damages'. Andiram objected that Datteram was a great man. Blechynden retorted that 'great men are the proper subjects for the cognizance of the law as they cannot plead ignorance' and ought to set an example to others. On this occasion, he 'talked to the wind'. Andiram went off with the peon and Blechynden sent the chaukidar away.[9]

Others were less shy of British procedures. A former employee of Blechynden's sued his one-time steward for unpaid wages and Blechynden supplied an affadavit that he had been in his employ:

A Sircar whose face I recollected called and told me that he was my Garden Sircar under Harrypersaud Chowdrie—but who has never paid him any Wages—and on his Summoning him to the petty Court declares he does not even know him—what villainy—gave the man a Certificate of his being my Sircar under Harrypersaud for the Months of January, February and March 1792.

There were other instances: his bearer applying to the court after being burgled, or a mistri, Rammohun, suing one Addison over debt. Blechynden's one-time house guest Grant hired a *dhye* as a wet nurse, but turned her away because she had no milk. She complained to the justices that he beat her and wanted to ravish her. He was summoned to court. Louis, presiding, ordered him to pay the woman—whether damages or arrears of wages Blechynden did not know.[10]

Poor employees and even women and children had a limited redress against oppression. They needed it. Apart from the many problems of contractors, labourers, and servants, there was a good deal of casual violence in Calcutta—among Indians, but certainly also involving Europeans. One day, Blechynden narrowly avoided being injured by a drunken sailor in a buggy; a few paces further on, he came across an Indian who had been run over by the buggy and much hurt. Blechynden attributed another incident that he witnessed to the unusually choleric disposition of one Fitzroy, who had taken a house on the Cossitullah. He was apparently annoyed by a small boy who looked at him. The boy was not more than six or seven years of age and was wearing a gown (*jama*) and red turban. Fitzroy fired one barrel of a gun at him, missed, and threw a large brick, which also missed, 'fortunately'. He then ran after the boy and struck him on the back of the head with the butt of the gun. The boy fell on his face almost at the feet of Blechynden's horse. Blechynden fixed Fitzroy with a steadfast stare in hope of shaming him. He took no notice.[11]

Another early instance of road rage reinforces the impressions of a spread of order as well as the readiness of Indians to appeal to law. While he was riding with his friend John Wales, the partly deaf Blechynden was hit from behind by a buggy wheel. One of the passengers struck out as he passed. Wales chased after and, unseen by Blechynden, returned three or four blows. A crowd gathered and seized Wales's horse from outside a friend's house. The travellers in the buggy, who were Parsis, complained to the magistrate's clerk, John Miller, that they had been insulted and assaulted; they had seized the horse so as to identify the offender. Blechynden too had reported the incident. The magistrate summoned Wales and Blechynden to attend on him. Blechynden had to confiscate an 'extraordinary' intemperate reply from Wales and substitute a version of his own. The Parsis, meanwhile, were bent on prosecuting the case before still higher authorities.[12] The incident blew over and Wales recovered both his temper and his horse; but the case shows the importance placed upon dignity, the readiness of the Parsis not only to raise a crowd but to complain to the Company authorities, and the requirement that Europeans answer their accusation: in short, how the city tried to regulate space and conduct by law as by measurement. Violence was somewhat restrained, just as property was defined, urban space demarcated, employment formalized, and labour disciplined. For Europeans, this was often the expected transplanted; for Indians, it was sometimes the unfamiliar made everyday.

The law's widening remit extended to servants, but not unchallenged. Once, Blechynden's cook Chand got drunk with the dinner money and was discovered lying naked with a *metrany* (prostitute) in the street in Tiretta's Bazar. Blechynden returned home with a guest to find no dinner prepared. Unable to persuade a sice to deputize, he had to repair to an inn. Chand had been given three rupees to furnish dinner. When he returned, he begged to be punished at home rather than have the public disgrace of the magistrate's court. The other servants supported him in this; but Blechynden was adamant and despatched him with the *chaukidar*. The magistrate's clerk, John Miller, then explained that the Chief Justice had told him that the justices must 'leave the Masters to correct their Servants'.

Sir John Shore too had instructed the magistrates not to 'punish for private faults' or intervene unduly to assist employers in disciplining servants. Accordingly the magistrate asked Blechynden for proof. He said: 'I did not expect to be called upon to produce a Blackman to corroborate what I had written and signed with my name.' The culprit was released for want of witnesses.[13]

A slave girl, Sophy, provides a different story. Blechynden bought her for Rs 200. She then had a child by the manservant Emaundee. A second slave girl, the venereal Mary, was also acquired, as a gift. Both women ran away from time to time and the durwan had been forbidden to let them leave the house. On one occasion when they disappeared, Blechynden sent peons after them. A gatekeeper also vanished somewhat earlier. Five days later, the women were detained. Mary claimed that she and Sophy were carried off by force by the gatekeeper and Blechynden took no action against her. He had Sophy's hair cut off as a punishment. Later Blechynden heard from Gopey that the former gatekeeper had also been caught. He had not only satisfied 'his own lust' with Sophy, but 'to make a property of her—having taken all her silver Joys' (jewellery)—'prostituted her to a Grasscutter' working for another European ('Mr Shakespear'). The gatekeeper refused to reveal the silver ornaments' whereabouts and was taken by the chaukidar before the justices. Gopey then reported that a woman who had Sophy's ornaments was planning to leave Calcutta for Balasore. Blechynden wrote to the magistrate to have her stopped too and she was captured. The magistrate 'desired the Girl to be sent to name the property taken from her—but this', wrote Blechynden, finding some scruples over privacy, 'I would not consent to & rather preferred the man's keeping them'. The gatekeeper and the woman were both released for want of evidence.

Finally, in the early hours one morning, Blechynden was wakened by his bibi, saying that Sophy had run off again. She was caught once more by the chaukidar and taken before the magistrate. The sitting justice, Bernard Smith (with whom Blechynden had had disagreements in the late 1780s), asked her why she had run off the first time and she replied that she had been decoyed by the groom of a European (Shakespear again). She had run off the second time because Blechynden and his concubine beat her, she claimed. Blechynden asked that she show the marks of this beating, which she could not. She had taken a knife, she said, to cut her throat if caught. Smith told Blechynden that 'she was a bad bargain & the sooner [he] got rid of her the better'. Blechynden agreed. He was afraid to take her back, he said. She was so desperate that she might poison the children. But he wanted her punished. Smith said that he could do nothing as she was a slave. As an absconding servant, she would have been liable to a month's imprisonment. Further interrogation ensued, at Blechynden's request, to clear him of mistreatment. Sophy admitted that she had had plenty of food and clothing, as good as her mistress (the bibi), and denied that her trinkets were gifts. She claimed that she had bought them from her savings. Smith pounced on this. It implied that she had had wages, which made her a monthly servant, liable 'to be sent to a House of Correction' for breaking her contract. He was happy to oblige.[14]

This domestic cameo is revealing—about the meaning of slavery (here bonded domestic service, with some pay); about the household as a guarded and regulated space; about the living conditions, relationships, and wilfulness of servants; about their employer's motives and fears; about coercion, flows of information, and the roles of various Indian allies; about the policing of Calcutta, despite other evidence of lawlessness; and finally about the limits of Company law and European understanding. Whatever the instructions from on high, legal interventions did extend to household crimes, especially absconding, and provided sanctions against improper conduct, even for slaves (supposedly excluded from master–servant law).

Sentiment seems to be missing. Yet three months later, Blechynden saw Sophy near his old house, 'sitting on a Stool in the Street Rags and Wretchedness of a common Prostitute and that of the lowest kind'. 'I could not help pitying her,' he wrote, but 'on seeing me she turned herself around—after I had passed I looked back and saw her laughing but I turned my head away directly.'[15] It was an enigmatic encounter.

## ROUGH JUSTICE

Law was frequently invoked, then, with mixed results. The question that arises is how far it mattered that, in practice, it fell far short of its ideals? It did so also of course in the Britain of this day, due to the arbitrary and largely unaccountable power of magistrates and judges; the ambiguities and conflicts of common, statute, and other law; the confusion of jurisdictions between courts; the lack of robust laws of evidence or codes of procedure; and the generally weak or uncertain rights for defendants even to be heard or represented in criminal cases. British India inherited these quirks and failings, mixed them with generous doses of imperfectly understood local law, and applied them with large dollops of corruption. It did this in a rapidly developing commercial and social world of very great diversity.

Recourse to law was therefore in Calcutta, even more than in London, a triumph of hope over experience and not without personal risk to the plaintiff. In January 1798, for example, a durwan, Mahomed, whom Blechynden had dismissed the previous July, sued him in the Petty Court for arrears of wages (less than twelve rupees). Blechynden assumed that the *sircar* would have paid and sent him to give evidence; his accounts showed that Mahomed had been overpaid. The durwan was sent to prison. Blechynden had directed that no action should be taken against him and so presumed that the sentence must have been for non-payment of court costs.

Some stories about the lawyer and justice of the peace C.F. Martyn show how very rough-and-ready the system was. According to John Miller, the justices' clerk, Martyn lived rent-free with few servants, as he ate out for every meal, and earned Rs 800 a month as justice, Rs 600 as Advocate for the Paupers, plus 'douceurs', and income as a barrister. He was reputed to call in prostitutes and always refuse to pay them. On one occasion, he used his cane on an Indian who was appearing before him and who as a result entered and then dropped a case against him. He was then prosecuted by Martyn before the Supreme Court for having brought an action and not gone through with it. Martyn lost this case 'against a black-man' and appeared at the police house in a fury, with 'his face as red as a turkey'.[16]

The generally chaotic nature of law in practice was illustrated also by an action against Martyn before the Supreme Court. It was for assault, brought by a man by the name of Crimp, who secured Indians and forced them to become seamen under the law that also applied in England. He had been before the justices for pressing lascars for one ship, then enticing them away and pressing them again for a second ship. The alleged assault by Martyn consisted of an order that Crimp be 'slippered' five times (too lenient, thought Blechynden) for a violent assault on a lascar and also a woman with whom he was in bed, after which Crimp had had the lascar imprisoned in a police cell. Crimp claimed that he had a decree for debt against the lascar in the Petty Court, which, as Blechynden observed, was irrelevant to the assault on the man and even more so to that on the woman. Much as he hated oppression or attempts to sell justice (he reiterated), on this occasion he thought a magistrate was entitled to protection when he gave someone moderate punishment 'for the good government of the town'. Even worse was that the case against Martyn had been cynically brought for Crimp by the lawyer W.T. Jones merely to secure his own costs. In consequence, Jones himself no longer struck or punished his servants but repeatedly referred them to the justices. There were at least a hundred chits from him awaiting processing in the Police Office. If he now argued (for Crimp) that magistrates had no authority to punish offenders, then those referrals could only be regarded as an attempt to entrap the justices.[17]

The Swiss merchant Henri Aguiton, to take another example, once told Blechynden a revealing tale of servants and the law, and perhaps also of the conflict between different understandings of employment. Matthew Louis, the justice, had sent a chaprasi to seize one of Aguiton's bearers. Hearing a commotion in the street as this was happening, Aguiton asked his sircar what was going on and when the bearers and the chaukidar came into his compound, he spoke to Louis's man. He was told that the bearer had undertaken to serve a Dr Munro and now would not attend his duty. Aguiton said that there must be some mistake, as the man was his servant, and sent the chaukidar to give this message to Louis. He then inquired further of his own people and found that in fact, at that moment, he was not employing the man. He had been with Aguiton for about four years, but some time before had put his brother in his place while he went home; he was now waiting to take over again from his brother. A letter came back from Louis. In fact, two letters came, but the first was refused by the servants as it was a folded paper without an address, which the servants had been forbidden to accept to avoid the equivalent of junk mail—for example, lottery and subscription papers. Louis stated that the man had quit Munro's service and desired that he be delivered up. Aguiton sent him with his own note, explaining how he had employed the man and that (as he had now been told) he had never entered Munro's service. The man's *jemautdar*, the leader who controlled the bearers and their hiring, wanted him to work for Munro, who, however, refused to pay in advance (as was the custom for this caste) or to keep the eight bearers thought necessary for someone living, as he did, at Chowringhee. The bearer had never seen Munro, nor been near him or his house, he claimed.

When the bearer reached the Police Office with this message, Louis ordered the man confined. Hearing this, his brother and fellow bearers crowded round Aguiton and begged him to intervene; but he would not. Next day, however, he himself received a summons from Louis. He went to the Police Office. Louis addressed him loudly and in 'very magisterial manner', and accused him of interfering with a chaprasi carrying out his duty. This sort of thing might do very well in France or Mauritius, but it would not do in Calcutta. Aguiton asked what the conduct of the French had to do with the case. Aguiton was a Frenchman, said Louis. He was not, said Aguiton. He had been in France, Louis supposed. He had, but that no more made him French than long residence in London made him English, replied Aguiton. Louis said that he had 'the happiness to live under English law & English magistrates'. Aguiton retorted that he had always done so, but in seven years in Calcutta had never had the humiliation of being summoned by a magistrate nor had any complaints laid against him by others.

He had, Aguiton said, merely told the chaprasi—who had neither summons nor warrant with him—that he thought there had been an error. This did not satisfy Louis. He had the jemautdar's and the chaprasi's depositions taken. The Armenian court writer pointed out how much they contradicted each other. So Louis had the record scratched out and proceeded to ask each witness leading questions until their testimonies nearly coincided. Aguiton questioned this procedure and was told that he was impertinent. Louis then committed the bearer to detention for a month. Aguiton asked if the man should not be heard in his own defence. Louis said that he could have nothing to say that was not in the letter he (Aguiton) had sent. Aguiton said that that was a response to Louis's message and did not refer to anything since given in evidence to the court. Louis ignored this. He went on to ask the chaprasi to point out which of Aguiton's people had refused to receive his unaddressed letter. A peon was identified and Louis ordered that he be taken down and beaten with five shoes. Aguiton protested that the peon had merely been following his master's lawful orders and was not in any way at fault himself. But again Louis took no notice. The servant was duly beaten in sight of Aguiton and in consequence quit his employment at once and left Calcutta, fearing that his family would think he had been guilty of a crime.

Aguiton drew up a statement of the case, intending to submit it to Sir Henry Russell, the Judge, with whom he was acquainted, to see if he could obtain any redress. Blechynden agreed to correct the English in his petition, but not to be involved further. In the event, Aguiton's letter came back with a note from the Sheriff (Walter Ewer) saying that it should be addressed to the Chief Justice, Sir John Anstruther. By this time, the bearer had been released and Aguiton was at a loss as to how to proceed. He was unwilling to write to Anstruther, whom he did not know. Blechynden said that he might as well drop the matter and himself tore the letter in two.[18]

A similar victim of partial justice and quixotic behaviour was Doncaster's 'little knock-kneed' sircar Rammohun Chatterjee, later employed by Blechynden. The story also illustrates something of the relations between Indians and Europeans. Rammohun had been given Rs 500 to carry from Calcutta to Serampore. The boat in which he was travelling (he said) was run down by another boat under sail and capsized. The money was lost but no lives. No complaint was made about the lost money at first, but one was entered as soon as Matthew Louis began his week as magistrate. Rammohun produced proof of the capsizing of the boat, but Louis ordered him locked up in the thana, with a peon who had accompanied him. Rammohun offered the names of several respectable natives who would put up bail, but Louis would have none of it. Rammohun spent a day confined without food and was brought before the justice again next day, after which he finally persuaded the *thanadar* to let him go out to eat, in the charge of two chaukidars. On the third day, again brought before Louis with Doncaster present, he was allowed out on bail. The peon, Harroo, remained in custody. The boat had been recovered, damaged, but not the money, which was said to have been in a bag on the seat between the two men. Rammohun appealed to Blechynden for help; Blechynden told him that he needed a lawyer.

George Reed (a young Anglo-Indian working with Doncaster) told a different version: there was no overturned boat, the witnesses were perjured, and Rammohun had the money. There would be a criminal prosecution. Rammohun would hang, he predicted. Blechynden recoiled: he would not 'take away a fellow creature's life for 10 times 500 Rs'. Rammohun turned up, protesting his innocence, to give Blechynden various lurid details of Doncaster's affairs, including a private prosecution for a huge sum that he was said to have purloined from the Company in a fraudulent salt operation. Rammohun's case had now been put off until Louis would be back on the bench: evidently he was hardly neutral in the matter. Blechynden offered to lend Rammohun money to cover any that was missing, but he refused it, insisting that he knew nothing of the lost sum and believed that it went to the bottom of the river. He said this so solemnly that Blechynden could not help believing him. A little later, Doncaster sent his 'pimp' Netaije to threaten Rammohun again with prosecution and to say that he would prevent him from getting any further employment. Blechynden advised Rammohun not to see Netaije again without witnesses. Rammohun came so often to Blechynden that he began to worry he might be supposed 'his abettor', however much he felt for his situation. About this time, however, Netaije returned and told Rammohun that Doncaster was not going to interfere any more; that Rammohun should not mind what Doncaster said when he was angry; and that he might forgive Rammohun.

The crisis then eased for a time. Rammohun and Harroo (the peon), one after the other, came to tell Blechynden that they had been released, Rammohun gleeful and Harroo in great anger. They had been summoned again by Louis. He took the whole case to Sir Henry Russell, who required him to release the accused. Reed was present at the cutcherry when their release was formalized and was very annoyed, wanting them committed to stand trial at the quarter sessions. Louis spoke to Reed privately for a long time. Both Rammohun and Harroo were now talking of petitioning Russell. Blechynden told Gopey to mark that he was not advising them to do so. He had a prediction for Rammohun: within a week, he and Doncaster would once again be 'as thick as two Inkle-weavers' (weavers of linen). Rammohun swore that he would never enter Doncaster's house again.

Blechynden was wrong, as it happened. He was shortly beset with Rammohun asking him not only to lend him money for his Durga puja expenses (he did not, advancing fifty rupees to Gopey instead when he made the same request) but also, in the absence of any other patron, to assist him over a writ taken out against him by George Reed—which writ Blechynden regarded as 'precious malice'. First Rammohun's brother, who had helped put up bail, and then Rammohun himself appealed to Blechynden to help with the draft of a petition to Russell. He read it noncommittally, but the Accountant-General's assistant John Dowling, who was present, was 'less fastidious' and made various suggestions for improvements. Blechynden's friend Bishop[19] informed Rammohun that, having been bred in the law, he had no hesitation in saying that Rammohun would be hanged. They all had a hearty laugh at the rage this produced in Rammohun. Later Robert Downie also helped with the draft: Blechynden thought it was as good as if Downie had written it for himself, which to his mind was going a bit far. He warned Rammohun never to let Doncaster see a copy with the corrections. Still unwilling to give advice himself, he wrote a chit in the name of Rammohun's uncle to ask if Downie's attorney would defend the action for Rammohun. Accordingly, Rammohun made an arrangement with an attorney, Forbes, who needed seven gold *mohurs* for the counsel's fees. The lawyer's sircar might have been able to advance the money, but Rammohun appealed instead to Blechynden.

Machinations ensued, illustrating the support that would be provided for an Indian acquaintance of middling status, and its limits. Blechynden was concerned about becoming liable for costs, the reason he had also kept his distance from the petition, and said that he would not provide the money even if he had it; but would stand as security if Downie would advance it. Downie proved willing to provide money, but against a draft from Blechynden. Hearing this, Blechynden suggested that Rammohun apply to Henry Tolfrey, his own attorney, who would advance whatever was necessary. Blechynden did not have an account with Forbes, with whom Rammohun had already signed up, and so when neither Forbes nor his sircar could provide the advance, Blechynden went to Tolfrey with Rammohun, who signed him as his attorney, getting back his warrant from Forbes. Blechynden agreed to underwrite costs up to the seven gold mohurs, after which Rammohun would have to be responsible himself. Blechynden took out a quarter ticket in the lottery to try to cover his costs, telling Rammohun that if it won a prize, he would conclude he was innocent. Rammohun said that in that case, it was bound to win. (It did not.)

Rammohun later claimed that Reed sought out the boat that swamped his, hired it, and took it over to Doncaster's. There, Reed got the master into the cabin and offered him ten rupees to give evidence in his favour. The *mangee* refused, saying he had already given his evidence: it was on record in the Police Office. Rammohun had two witnesses to this attempted subversion of justice and had told Tolfrey. The omens were looking better. Reed challenged the bail, but it was upheld. Downie described Reed to Louis as a 'scorpion' who was trying to ruin a poor sircar. Louis however claimed that Reed had proof—never produced in court, it must be said—that Rammohun and Harroo had brought the money ashore and divided it between them. He blamed Blechynden for giving Downie wrong information, something he later said half-jokingly to Blechynden himself. Instead of mentioning that he had the story from Rammohun, Downie replied that Blechynden was only doing what any humane person would do, which gave the very impression that Blechynden was trying to avoid, that he was helping Rammohun.

He had not much liked Rammohun ever since first meeting him in 1784, but thought that he must either be 'a compleat villain, or a very oppressed man', and so let him into his house out of charity, on the assumption that he was the latter. Meanwhile Reed, now living in Doncaster's house, paid a call on Blechynden as a neighbour. He said that he would be represented in the action by Burroughs and Rammohun by Ledlie as advocates. Blechynden resolved to contrive to hear Doncaster's evidence and in due course did so. He intervened too when there seemed a problem at Tolfrey's over the payment of counsel, using his guaranteed seven gold mohurs. He reflected that Ledlie had only two days to study the brief. Eventually back home, he was greeted by Rammohun catching hold of his feet and saying with great joy that Reed's case had been non-suited. Blechynden remarked that did not entirely prove Rammohun's innocence, but sent him off to his family to celebrate. Louis still believed Rammohun guilty and said that he deliberately kept back 'two of the most material witnesses against him', from which Blechynden concluded that Louis was either hindering justice, contrary to his oath as a magistrate, or was cruelly casting aspersions on Rammohun's character. Later, Blechynden entrusted Rammohun, along with Lilloo and Jaggernaut, with managing the construction of Calcutta's Circular Road.[20]

Once again, the law was revealed as frighteningly confused and partial. It had much propensity for creating discomfort and loss, even when the outcome was eventually favourable. Financial backing for legal action was difficult to obtain and fragile. Despite that, quite humble workers appealed to law. In several ways, that fact is remarkable, given the very strong hierarchies of power as well as the obvious corruption and capriciousness of the systems of justice. Sometimes the magistrates' venality and slack grasp of the law aided defendants; sometimes not. One man caught in the act of robbing a house was taken before Louis, who recognized him as a habitual offender and ordered that he be given some 'rattans' (be caned). The complainant was outraged, told Louis that he knew nothing of English law, and sent the man to the Supreme Court. The offender was tried in four days and hanged a week later. Blechynden once again complained at the 'very fatal' character of the judge's sentences and could not see that the loss of a few rupees was ever worth a man's life. On the whole, however, workers seem to have fared better when the judges and their much-maligned English law were involved. On one occasion, a trivial case of assault was taken to the Supreme Court because of the known corruption of the magistrate, Martyn; the defendant was connected with one of his 'bottle-holders'. Yet the Court too could be inflexible and unjust.

Blechynden copied out an *Extra Gazette* of December 1805, marking the retirement of Sir John Anstruther as Chief Justice. Though he conceded that Sir John might be a lover of justice, Blechynden remarked that most people complained of his 'violence' and 'arbitrary decisions'. The *Gazette* quoted Anstruther on the relatively law-abiding nature of Calcutta, which he attributed 'to the example of morality and good conduct shewn by the higher orders of the British inhabitants'. William Fairlie, the merchant, speaking as foreman of the Grand Jury, praised Anstruther's term of office, during which 'improved and more active administration of justice [had been] introduced, an efficient police established, and the British character advanced in the esteem of its Indian subjects'. Fairlie claimed that Sir John secured 'to the inhabitants of one of the wealthiest and most populous cities in the world the practical blessing of the English law' and diffused 'the sense of its protection through every part of those extensive Provinces which are subject to the Supreme Government of

Bengal'. Blechynden wondered why this exchange of compliments had started with Anstruther and, cynically, what law had been infringed when his predecessors Impey and that good man (Sir Robert) Chambers, had received no such speeches. Rumour had it that Anstruther himself engineered and indeed drafted the Grand Jury's flattering address. Several members refused to sign it because it was 'full of unfounded assertion'—which Blechynden agreed it was.[21]

## MEDIATION AND MISRULE

It seems it was as much what was *claimed* for English justice, rather than its practice, that encouraged Indians to risk making use of it—coupled no doubt (as Blechynden found to his cost) with the lack of other remedies in extremis. Let us explore further this question of Indians and the law. It mattered, as said, because of the wide net cast by the law over Calcutta's residents, both rich and poor, and also the laxity and corruption of the courts. Important, as already noted, was the support European employers gave to their Indian servants and acquaintances. In many ways, they were the brokers and interpreters of a new and imperfect system as it was being introduced. Their conduct reinforced the role of law in both private and domestic causes, and spread new ideas and practices from European to Indians, in some ways just a different context for the same phenomenon.

Occasionally employers were challenged at law. Blechynden himself was subjected to legal scrutiny. One day, a 'classy [khalasi] named Himut' put into his hand a petition presented to Mr Justice Royds against Blechynden and his former sircar Seebnarain Bose. It was for arrears of wages (Rs 107) due for work at Hamilton & Aberdein's buildings. Blechynden had Gopey explain to Himut that he should find Seebnarain and bid him bring his accounts so that they could see if anything was due. Seebnarain eventually appeared; Himut's account was inspected. It showed that he was owed forty-nine rupees and Blechynden ordered him paid fifty. Himut wanted more because he claimed six rupees a month for the *tindal* (chief of the *classi*es), arguing that his pay had been raised in line with what Tiretta gave. Blechynden appealed to Durgaram, Tiretta's sircar, who strongly denied this. Himut had taken himself off by this time, but Blechynden was inclined to believe Durgaram, remembering Tiretta asking him what *he* paid, so their costs would be the same.[22]

More often, Blechynden would help those caught up in legal action. When one of his mistris, Sultan, was arrested in possession of two guns, at first Blechynden would not 'interfere in justice'—Sultan had nothing to fear if innocent, he said, and a note from Blechynden would not help (or at least, he hoped not). But then, being in debt to Sultan, he could not refuse to put up bail for him. On another occasion, in Bandel, outside Calcutta, four drunken Muslims assaulted one of Blechynden's servants, his then manservant Rumjohnny, robbed him of money, and broke Blechynden's hookah snake. Three of the attackers escaped but Rumjohnny held on to one of them and delivered him into the custody of two of the classies stationed with Blechynden's *budgerow* (barge). Together, they complained to the local magistrate, Sir Charles Blunt, who had Rumjohnny's assailant confined. He was released on security by the *daroga*, however, and the chaprasi demanded security also from Rumjohnny. The three men who escaped then took out a summons against Rumjohnny for assault! Next day, their case was heard by Blunt, who refused to hear Rumjohnny in his own defence, let alone investigate the charges he had laid against the men. Blechynden wrote to Blunt on Rumjohnny's behalf and also complained to the Company, in the person of George Dowdeswell, Secretary to Government in the Judicial Department.[23]

A similar instance occurred when the sircar Tilluck was working for Blechynden on some bridge building. He complained of a man called MacArthur, who had come to his house after dark and flogged him; he then gave him some brandy to put on his wounded back. MacArthur was summoned by Blaquiere and the case referred to a Grand Jury. MacArthur first said that he had never set eyes on Tilluck and then that Tilluck had interrupted some of MacArthur's workers who were removing planks.[24]

On another occasion, Blechynden sent four witnesses to support his peon, Mahomed Ali, when a drunken sailor tried to invoke the Police Office against him. The witnesses certified that the sailor had in fact assaulted the peon when he told him not to urinate against Blechynden's gate. Martyn dismissed the sailor's complaint as frivolous.

Once, another drunken European seaman staggered against Blechynden's peon Currim in the Bow Bazar. The man then started hitting Currim with a cane, somewhat held back by a 'kind of' mulatto who was supporting him. Blechynden demanded the cane and was met with abusive language. He stopped at the guardhouse nearby and asked for a sepoy to restrain the seaman until he sobered up. Returning to Currim, Blechynden found him being attacked by a tall European in white jacket and trousers. The man knocked Currim to the ground and made to go back into the punch house he apparently had come from; but the sergeant accompanying Blechynden had seen the assault and had the sepoys arrest the man. They put him and the drunken seaman in the guardhouse. Next day, at the justices' offices, the sergeant told Blechynden that he had the two Europeans confined below. Levi Ball (one of the justices) wanted to speak to him. In the committee room, where all manner of police, judicial, and municipal business was conducted, Ball asked Blechynden about the assault and, hearing the story, decided that he should imprison both the assailants. Blechynden said that one night in the cells was probably enough to teach them to 'be more circumspect'. Going away, he reflected that by rights, he should have consulted Currim as the person assaulted.

Blechynden eventually lost patience with Currim. Early in 1800, he appeared in Blechynden's compound, crying, with an iron chain round his leg. He said his uncle had put it on, claiming he was mad. Blechynden thought this a good way to make him so and had one of his contractors file it off. He let Currim stay with his durwan. After a couple of days, Currim came upstairs to Blechynden and said that he wanted leave to go to his father, whom he had not seen for a long time. Blechynden gave him five rupees as a tip and 'bid him trouble me no more'. Two weeks later, Currim was at his gate again, talking incoherently and 'quite deranged'. He followed Blechynden round all day: there was no silencing him, even when he was threatened with arrest. About six weeks afterwards, Currim was in the house again. Gopey reported that he had been seen the day before, quite naked, outside Weston's Bazar. Blechynden sent him downstairs to the durwan, whom he told not to force Currim to leave but if he went out, not to admit him again.[25]

By contrast, Blechynden consistently backed Cassinaut Ganguly. Cassinaut said that he had borrowed Rs 250 for a person from his home area in Nadia and mortgaged all his property there, worth Rs 4,000 or 5,000, which his creditor proposed to seize. Blechynden agreed to lend him the Rs 250 for a year and gave him leave to go to Nadia to settle the matter. Blechynden was uneasy, given the very much larger amounts regularly passing through Cassinaut's hands, for example to pay workers, and so questioned him closely about his accounts. Cassinaut assured him of his honesty and also promised to pay back Blechynden's money early, because he himself was owed some Rs 4,000 for copperplate printing that (letting 'the cat out of the bag') he said he carried on at home. He was either worth money or considerably indebted, thought Blechynden.

A potentially more serious threat to Cassinaut arose in 1806. He was accused of dacoity and of absconding. Blechynden was very alarmed to hear this from the magistrate of 24 Parganas, Edward Thoroton, who told him not to warn Cassinaut. Blechynden replied that he would never shield anyone from justice but also he would not presume a man guilty without proof. It was 'hard to answer for Blackey' but he really had 'as good an opinion' of Cassinaut 'as of any native' he knew. He described how long he had known him and how he came into his service. He had been a sircar to the printers Stewart & Cooper when Blechynden carried out work for them in 1786. When their business failed in 1790, Blechynden was appointed a trustee and saw Cassinaut almost every day at Cooper's house. He bought a share and afterwards the principal part in the business himself—this was the *Chronicle* press and newspaper. Cassinaut worked for him at first; but stayed with the press in 1793 when Blechynden sold out, having ruined himself. Blechynden went on living in the *Chronicle*'s premises for some time, however, and so was still in contact with Cassinaut.

When the business finally closed, Cassinaut went to the engraver and mapmaker Aaron Upjohn. After Upjohn's death, Blechynden came into contact with him once again while he was administering the estate as principal creditor. Cassinaut pleaded poverty because of what Upjohn owed him and Blechynden told him that he could not favour one creditor over another. He had suspected him of hindering the recovery of his own debts during Upjohn's lifetime, but changed his mind. Cassinaut mentioned that he had pawned his own wife's jewellery to buy dinner for Upjohn when he was greatly distressed. This show of loyalty so impressed Blechynden that he appointed Cassinaut to superintend the repairs of the Court House, on which he was then engaged. Cassinaut had remained in his service, from one job to another, ever since.

Thoroton listened to this account and said it altered the case very much. It was quite untrue that Cassinaut had absconded—he was going about Blechynden's business as usual—and the accusation of dacoity turned out to be a piece of mischief invented after Blechynden had ordered a beating for a convict worker who had wilfully damaged an embankment and flooded the work of 600 men. Soban Ali, the jemautdar in charge of the convicts, threatened to make Cassinaut 'repent', believing that he had informed Blechynden, who had complained to the acting Governor-General, Sir George Barlow. Later, not knowing what was afoot, Cassinaut himself came to Blechynden for advice, hearing from a friend that a 'trick' was going forward against him. Thoroton dropped his investigation. The case shows why an employer's support mattered in such a legal system. Properly, Blechynden complained, Thoroton should have pursued the real wrongdoers, giving Cassinaut a chance to clear his name and confront those who maligned him. Thoroton did warn Soban Ali that he would be dismissed if Blechynden made any more complaints against him.[26]

## ORDER AND MORALITY

Many things were revealed in the stories of this chapter and the last. We saw how servants behaved around their master and in his absence. We saw their relations among themselves, including rivalries over women and the celebration of festivals, and the close proximity in which entire households lived, including the Europeans. One conclusion is that European and Indians thereby formed opinions about each other, feeding into the familiar stereotypes. By interpretations embedded in the narrative of his experiences, Blechynden construed the English as caring and just and the Indians as often unreliable but improveable and potentially grateful.

Turning to the role of law, we saw other ways in which stereotypes were formed and norms transmitted. Indians presented 'petitions', for example to Blechynden, using a European form of appeal, and sent their fellows to the magistrates; but also negotiated with masters and officials. They made choices among themselves about ways to regulate conduct. Blechynden similarly appealed to the authorities while also dispensing summary punishments himself. Finally, these examples remind us yet again, amidst the impositions of a standardized order upon Calcutta's diverse people, that arbitrary misrule, powerful interests, and personal whim also shaped the conditions of life. Others have noticed how the *trappings* and indeed the principles of Western jurisprudence were taken up by Indians convinced of its practical injustice and partiality in colonial hands.[27] The moral is that the law was increasingly hard to avoid, Europeans actively promoted its ideas to Indians with whom they were associated, and some Indians sought to make use of it.

We should not ignore one major caveat often illustrated in these pages, namely that the expansion of the state's law—in whatever form—still competed with a confusion of private actions. In this sphere, as in most others, the public and the professional were not obviously distinct from the private and the amateur. Blechynden not only appealed to magistrates in his domestic affairs, he also dispensed 'justice' himself every day. Another telling instance will suffice. In 1801, he came across an old woman in the street. Her head was bleeding after she had been struck by a boy as he tried to snatch some fruit from her. The boy was working on Blechynden's road-building project. He had him seized. He gave him a long lecture about robbery and its likely consequences and about the sin of raising his hand against a woman old enough to be his grandmother. He ordered him to be given three strokes with a cane, made him do salaam upon the woman's feet, and then dismissed him from his employment. He thought that 'the boy will be better for it—there was something ingenuous in his countenance'.[28] This improving circle ran from ethics to punishment to education to reform, and back again. Blechynden offered a universal moral of European devising but (in this case) cross-cultural credibility and he co-opted Indian custom—touching feet as a sign of respect—as one of his strategies to get that message across.

At this time, in all these aspects, jurisdictions were still unclear: what belonged to Indian and what to universal (meaning ideal European) norms; and how to disentangle the overlapping remits of the official and the domestic. As he dispensed summary justice in the street and mixed the laws of employment, crime, and public order, it did not for a moment occur to Blechynden to doubt the propriety of his actions, even though (or possibly because) he was very often anxious about contracts or habeas corpus in his private life and frequently produced an imitation of judicial procedures in managing his business, family, friends, and staff. So too, quite unconsciously, he constructed a seamless web of English and Indian, public and private, punishment and reformation. The result was not only an arbitrary but also a nuanced exercise of power. With the thieving boy, he dealt informally with an offence for which the Supreme Court might have imposed imprisonment or even death.

The ideas, goals, and ethics promoted by Blechynden *were* overwhelmingly European in origin, and in their operation, critical of Indians (and also Europeans). Englishness was partly constituted in law, and a supposed Indianness by the need for it. Ambiguities in the exchange of ideas and practices in Calcutta should not blind us to the direction of travel. It seems exaggerated to claim that early colonial law and government were largely just a continuation of previous practice. There *were* survivals and accommodations in what developed in India, just as the experience of India and the exigencies of colonial administration helped change European ideas and systems. But, as Nandini Bhattacharyya-Panda has shown for Hindu law, the new systems being introduced and taken up by Indians were fundamentally imported inventions in their character if not their content, related to theories of the unitary sovereignty and standardized authority of the state.[29] That is one reason why many of the exchanges and influences demonstrated in this book revolve around colonial rules of law and of behaviour.

# PART II
## *Senses of Self: Blechynden's Children*

# 5

# Raising a Family

I must do my duty by these innocents.

—Richard Blechynden[1]

Among other subjects, the first part of this book approached the question of English identity through narratives of the shortcomings of Indians, in the guise of servants, ironically juxtaposed with the corruption of Europeans. A parallel might be seen with the ways in which bourgeois morality in Europe was defined against the supposed inadequacies of subordinate classes. In both cases, social- and self-improvement were key goals. Part Two of this book places more emphasis on the means of constructing identity in the English context, again in ironic juxtaposition with practice. These chapters concentrate on the children in the Blechynden household, using not only Richard's diary but also the shorter diary of his son Arthur.

The diaries permit none of the structural analysis that has been made the basis of family history by Peter Laslett and others; but they touch on several points of the rich canvas painted by Laurence Stone and those genres concerned with individual lives, with emotion, with relationships, and with identity, the kinds of subjects approached by the contributors to Roy Porter's collection *Rewriting the Self*. In the children, we see too how differently from their mothers, the bibis, they were placed within the current set of ideas and customs. Bibis could be reformed perhaps; but children must be formed. A practical application of sentiment was intended to shape them, through nurture, education, and socialization, according to particular values and rules of conduct. These principles were in the process of evolving and were closely and overtly associated with the development of British character and the creation of a British empire.[2]

## PATERNAL LOVE

Richard Blechynden had six illegitimate children who survived infancy. The mother of the eldest children (Arthur and Sally) was an Indian Muslim who died after giving birth to Charlotte, and was greatly missed. The mother of the younger son, James, was an Indian or Eurasian, Mary Anne. The mother of two further daughters, Harriet and Emma, was an India-born but European or plausibly Eurasian bibi, Isabella. Arthur Blechynden was born on 7 February 1790; his sister Sally or Sarah on 21 November 1792. Their sister Charlotte followed on 10 January 1796 and their half-brother James on 20 November the same year. Of Isabella's daughters, (Jane) Harriet was born on 23 December 1806 and (Lydia) Emma on 2 May 1809. Blechynden was attached to these children, in partly sentimental ways common in these times. He fretted over their illnesses and thought seriously about and invested in their future. Their father's care, their education, and their social involvement all marked these children as belonging to a European milieu.

This does not mean Blechynden's concern was always overt, at least in terms of what he thought worth recording in the diary. For example, the birth of Sarah produced no further comment and other arrivals were scarcely more elaborately noticed; anniversaries too were often very casually marked, as for that matter were Christmas and other festivals. Moreover, when his baby son Sidney died in March 1793 and Blechynden had no way of returning to Calcutta from Serampore, he merely sent a chit so as to secure an undertaker who had advertised cheap funerals. However, the baby was buried among notable Europeans, near Short's monument in the Park Street cemetery. On the night when he heard of the death, Blechynden wrote: 'I could not compose myself to rest, thinking of the child' and worrying about the funeral arrangements. True, the death was a 'very happy release' for one who had always been ailing, but for that he blamed the very bad wet nurse, taken on because the mother would not suckle the child. This was a diary entry typical of many others that reflect rather than express or analyse his agitation. In blaming the wet nurse and indirectly the mother, he was echoing the perennial opinion of experts in Britain, if not the upper-class fashion; but he was also revealing his emotional state, the thoughts going through his mind as he tried to sleep.

Lawrence Stone claims high mortality rates forced parents to limit their emotional involvement with infants—and cites one case from the 1770s of a mother, devoted to her older children, who hardened her heart against a sickly baby thought unlikely to survive. Infant death rates began to fall in Britain after the 1750s, but anecdotal evidence suggests that that was far from true in Calcutta even for well-to-do European families, even though its European doctors adopted improved obstetric techniques and smallpox inoculation was widespread (factors associated with the improvements in Britain). Certainly Blechynden's record of his response to Sidney's death not only showed emotion, but also that he did not dwell on the tragedy—very much his stance as he followed the frequent funeral processions for his adult acquaintances.[3]

More generally, Blechynden could be quite distant from some aspects of his children's lives. Because he was particularly strict in applying limitations of propriety to his bibis, they and their babies largely occupied their own world. Infants were breastfed and coaxed through teething and early illnesses by their mothers or, more commonly, a wet nurse. Harriet, for example, had a *dhye* who finally left when she was eleven months old. The bibis exchanged visits and even engaged in businesses, as well as looking after children with varying degrees of reliability; and Blechynden seldom interfered. When Arthur and Sarah were young, financial and other complications meant that they were brought up in a small house adjoining their father's rooms in town—brought up very largely by their mother and her servants. Subsequent bibis, including Europeans, managed similarly for Charlotte, James, Harriet, and Emma. Blechynden's children's first language, and the main language of his household, was Hindustani and not English, with the possible exception of Harriet and Emma.[4]

On the other hand, this gives a far from complete picture. Blechynden was certainly warm in his relations with women. His relations with his children also could be tender. Above all, they evoked his strong sense that he must show care and the children gratitude. In short, his example indicates that the greater closeness of families, noted from the eighteenth century onwards, also applied in some measure to a mixed-race household in Calcutta. Blechynden asserted himself, obviously, over his children's names, which were not just English but often meaningful in family terms.[5] At other times, the father was recalled from his work or wakened in the night to deal with his feverish and teething children. When unable to treat them himself, he called European doctors to tend their illnesses, though sometimes a bibi would do so on her own initiative. There are touching details: at 2 PM on 3 November 1802, Blechynden marked two of his children's heights on a wall in his house (Charlotte 3 ft.10 $^3/_4$ in., James 3 ft 7¾ in., without shoes) and, having moved, he returned in 1805 to copy the marks.[6]

He had all the children baptized and inoculated against smallpox, as was the custom. These two rites of passage were managed in quick succession for both Charlotte and James. First, their heads were shaven; beds were prepared; and the children were inoculated by Dr Hare. Both developed a fever a couple of days afterwards, but they were doing well as the pocks began to appear. Secondly, Padre Lee had been sounded out about the christening and was willing, provided it was kept secret from Padre Brown, who would be angry if he knew. Blechynden too wanted the ceremony to be quite private, even to the extent of doing without godparents, as (he claimed, incorrectly it seems) Padre Clarke had permitted for the two older children. Lee replied that they were necessary, but he could be one godfather and any male over fourteen the other; baptized Christian servants were acceptable. Additional men could not stand in for the godmothers, he said, in response to a further query, and Blechynden decided that he would have to contrive to get a couple of girls from Mrs Copeland's school as he could think of no other possibility. The pretence, it should be noted, was all about form, as with his relatives in England: everyone knew the children were his and illegitimate, but great efforts were made to ensure that no one was forced to acknowledge the fact. Mrs Kennedy and Mrs McDonald, two friends, would not have this, however, and plotted to breakfast with Blechynden on the day and serve as godmothers themselves. Blechynden was touched. The whole party laughed heartily at his trying to describe the children as his niece and nephew. Charlotte and James were duly baptized, standing quietly while Lee read through the entire service without raising his eyes from the page—the quietness was particularly remarkable in James, who was suffering from an itch for which Hare had prescribed an ointment. In 'return for his kindness', Blechynden gave Lee a plan and elevation of Lee's brother's funerary monument, drawn by Blechynden's draughtsman Hurry.[7] The two youngest girls were baptized similarly, on 28 March 1807 and 5 September 1809.

Gradually, therefore, out of their quasi-Indian environment, the children came to be socialized into their father's circle. Unlike their mothers, they did not have to be invisible. They visited neighbours and were clucked over by visitors—Arthur was a 'very pretty child much petted' by such guests. The children and the current bibi would come to the garden house and spend weekends en famille or with house parties of male friends and sometimes their female companions as well. While still very young, Arthur accompanied his father when he went to shoot birds for the table or when he and friends went bathing in his or a neighbour's tank. Their mother's death brought the two older children into closer contact with their father. They went more frequently to the gardens than when their mother was alive. At Blechynden's town house, it seems a child's bed was normally in his room: it was moved out when he was preparing to have a hydrocele operation. As Arthur became older and was attending Mr Purchase's school (at twelve rupees per two months), he was taken to the gardens over the weekend for 'a change of air and scene'. One evening, he was sent for to join a dinner with William and David Mills (the watchmaker), various others, and the child of Jackson, a tailor.

Against this backdrop, we may assess the extent of fatherly duty. There were many problems with childcare, for example, and these provide further expressions of concern and, paradoxically, involvement. The first issue was the unreliability of servants. Sometimes it was just a matter of logistics: the ayah was very ill one day at the gardens and went back to town, leaving a replacement. Often it was more serious: one servant, Ramzanny, was reported for abandoning the children for several days in 1800 and consequently dismissed. A similar instance occurred when the children had no food cooked for them for two days running in September 1796 because their servant, Mary, went out at 10 o'clock the first day and had not returned on the second. When she refused to come back, Blechynden had her arrested by a *chaukidar* and sent her with a chit to the magistrate, Macklew. He asked if Blechynden would take her back, in which case 'he would give her a few Brooms and return her'. If not, it would be best to 'let her beat Surky' (the mixture of crushed brick and lime used in house and road building). Blechynden said that he would not take her back but the punishment should not exceed the crime. Macklew committed her to the Herringbherry for a month, which Blechynden thought far too long. He asked Macklew to commute twenty days of the sentence, as he thought even ten 'more than sufficient'. Macklew promised to do so. At this time, the bibi Mary Anne would have been about seven months pregnant, but even if she had not also been absent, she was evidently not well suited to ensuring the children would be cared for.[8]

There was a clear need for supervision. The burying grounds proved how dangerous Calcutta was for children. One day in 1801, Blechynden arrived home to the gardens to find his daughter Charlotte screaming that she had drowned her brother James. He ran to the tank and found the *dhye* pulling James out of the water. Charlotte had pushed him off the steps. Blechynden upbraided the dhye, who said that she was had been bathing the bibi. He 'whipped Charlotte smartly' and gave James 'a cuff or two for going there'. After this, Blechynden also seems once again to have had the time or the need to play a somewhat larger part in the children's care.

One night, he was frantic to discover James missing from his bed, not relieving himself in the 'necessary', and nowhere to be seen in the house, though Blechynden searched every room. He wondered if he had fallen out of a window, trying to make water, and so also searched the grounds, the stables, and the durwan's house. James was found fast asleep under Blechynden's own bed, the consequence, it seemed, of a glass of undiluted wine given him by Samuel Jones.[9]

A second complication, perhaps explained by the difficulties with servants, was associated with the extended visits by the children to other households where there was a woman who could be in charge. These arrangements caused Blechynden much disquiet. Some time after their mother's death, for example, Arthur and Sally were staying with W. Collins, or rather being looked after by Mrs Mulder, his bibi, so called because she was not married to Collins.[10] Blechynden suggested that he might send the children to them if Mrs Mulder wished, and Collins replied that she would be glad, a little vexed that he had not sent them before. They went off two days later. A couple of weeks after this, Mrs Mulder asked for Sally to be sent to her; she went with Arthur for company, as (Blechynden said) she would only cry without him.

Perhaps, for the moment, he was glad to have them out of the house. The day before, the children had scribbled on the last blank page of the duplicate of a letter sent to Europe and had been beaten. Gopey too was reprimanded, because it would not have happened had he appeared for his copying work, as he had promised. Having sent the children to Collins, Blechynden followed them to dinner and when he was about to depart, found them asleep and was obliged to leave them. Their sojourns with Mrs Mulder then became more extended. Arthur was returned eventually with his hair cut: 'nothing can be more frightful—sheep shearing is twice as comely'. But Collins refused to return Sally. Blechynden did not like this at all: it created a kind of obligation and opened 'a fine door for pretending great attention' was being shown to him.

Drawn-out manoeuvres ensued, revealing of father–daughter relations, domestic arrangements, and the influence of a determined bibi. Having inquired after Sally, a little after Arthur's return, Blechynden was forced to accept an invitation to eat with Collins, against his will, in order to see the child, which he 'very much' wished to do. He decided that she looked thin and definitely uneasy, and hinted that he would have to have her home. There was no response and so, after a couple of days, he asked for her to be brought back to him the next day. Collins said Mrs Mulder 'cannot do without her'; Blechynden must come to them to see her. As he was sure

Sally was miserable, he decided 'some other expedient' would be needed to extract her. He hit upon saying that she needed to go to Mrs Tiretta's sister for a few days, but Collins still insisted that Sally stay with him as she was company for Mrs Mulder. By this time, she had been with them fifteen days; the situation was 'very disagreeable' for Blechynden. When once he got Sally home, he resolved, she would never go near Mrs Mulder again. The next day, he dined at the Collins's and thought Sally in better spirits, though yellower in appearance. But—it was 'very provoking'—there seemed to be no extracting her until Collins moved back into town.

She was still there nearly a week later, and this time Blechynden chose to turn down all invitations to dine with Collins until she was returned. This seemed to work. After almost three weeks, Collins asked if he had offended him. Blechynden made various excuses for not having visited and it was agreed that he would take Sally back next time he dined there. However, she was still with Collins at the start of September, after two months, again looking a little thin and yellow—either she was bilious or she was being allowed to run about in the sun. Her father offered to take her home but, looking repeatedly at Mrs Mulder as if seeking consent, Sally said that she would come the next day. She did go home and Mrs Mulder sent after her various pieces of her linen that had been with the washerwoman.

At this time, July 1796, Blechynden heard of his formal appointment as Tiretta's deputy. He was now attending the justices, receiving their commissions, and perhaps was busier than before. After barely a month, he agreed to send Sally again to Mrs Mulder, but took her home with him at the end of his own visit the same day. Mrs Mulder asked for Sally to spend Christmas with her. Blechynden had intended to take the children to the gardens, but sent both to Collins on 24 December. On Christmas morning, Collins, Mrs Mulder, and the children all came to the gardens in a buggy for breakfast and then went back to Calcutta.[11]

Blechynden was equally concerned for his two younger children and again faced practical and social difficulties, partly of his own making. His patriarchal authority over children, so apparent at law and in major decisions,[12] once again did not always extend to the everyday, even (or perhaps especially) when a child's mother was no longer present. If Mrs Mulder had been importunate in her demands, that strong-willed woman Mary, 'Mrs' Wade, seemed to render Blechynden almost powerless.[13] With Charlotte, he complained, Mary tended to do as she pleased. She 'tiezed my soul out', he wrote, to have Charlotte stay with her; he used all the excuses he could think of but 'it would not do'. Two days after this, when he visited Charlotte at Mary's, he found that she had shaved her head: 'she does as she pleases', he complained. Charlotte had the usual childhood problems: in May 1997, she was feverish and 'purging' (presumably vomiting or suffering from diarrhoea). Dr Hare's partner, Williamson, called and prescribed rhubarb and magnesia. Mary then claimed that Charlotte was troubled with worms and Blechynden called in Hare. Mary afterwards summoned Dr Dick as Hare had not returned, which made Blechynden angry for the indelicacy to Hare and the danger from having two doctors prescribing at the same time.

By the turn of the year, Blechynden regarded Mrs Wade as looking after Charlotte. He ruled a cash book for her as it would look unkind to refuse in the circumstances. Next month, on the same argument, he agreed to take his milk from Mary even though it was disagreeable to turn away his old milkmaid. Later Mary reported Charlotte was getting 'stout' again; but she was 'thinner than ever' the following March. Blechynden objected to Charlotte's being in the sun. He still made allowances for Mary—sending her peaches, for example—because she was looking after the child; but wrote 'I wish to God I had it away'. Two days later, he saw Charlotte 'sitting cross-legged upon the damp tiles and as thin as ever' and again wished he had her in his own house.

At the end of May 1798, he found Mrs Wade feeding her rhubarb because the child felt a little warm and he 'begged of her in Godsname to give it no physic but leave it entirely to itself and if ill to send for Dr Hare'. Mary said she preferred Dr Dick. Blechynden told her abruptly that Charlotte was his child and Dr Hare was his physician. Yet again, he went away wishing he had her home. By June, he had finally retrieved her and, after a trip to the gardens in the buggy, remarked that she was 'already so much benefited as to walk a little' if held by the hand (at two and a half). The dhye led her 'once or twice up and down the hall' and even Wade 'could not help expressing his surprise at her improvement'. Mrs Wade was said to be very angry, having thought Blechynden would never take Charlotte back, and to be even angrier that she seemed to be thriving. Meanwhile, in February 1798, an ayah replaced the dhye who had been looking after James, who seems not to have enjoyed Mrs Wade's attention.[14]

## SENDING THE CHILDREN HOME

Sending the children to England was a third reflection of parental care and also a mark of the children's expected status. Knowledge of English and English background obviously would aid employment in a British colony. Therefore, even before Blechynden was granted official employment as

Tiretta's deputy, he had determined to send his two eldest children to England for their education. He received letters from his English relations 'containing very agreeable news' and this too helped make up his mind.[15] When a Mrs Darly wrote to him asking if he would send the children to her school, he replied that they were 'on the wing to Europe'. Arthur and his sister Sarah (or Sally) would stay with relations in London and elsewhere.

They were young, but no younger than many who were sent on this adventure. Arthur, the elder, was growing up. He had been taken riding and shooting; he had swum three-quarters of the length of the tank at the garden house, with his father and Bruce. One day, almost as if he recognized the change in identity involved in the journey to England, though ostensibly from fear of changes wrought by the 'enlarging of his features', Blechynden made 'a small artificial mole' in Arthur's shoulder—running a needle into his skin and rubbing in china ink and spirit when the blood appeared—a 'private mark to find him out' when he returned to India. Thinking of the passage home, he also sounded out his friend, a ship's officer, William Farrer. Blechynden said, ostensibly making conversation, that he supposed people would think Rs 600 a lot to transport a child to England as it meant nearly Rs 150 a month 'for dieting an infant'; he believed that the *Cronberg* and other ships had charged only Rs 500. Farrer said that Lloyd would not charge less than Rs 800, and Blechynden remarked that Lloyd's ship was very full of passengers and had little room. When it came to sending his own children, Blechynden would have to see the ship before he settled anything.[16]

Blechynden agreed on the passages to England with Thomas Bishop, captain of the *Maria*. Blechynden asked what he would take to transport the children to England. Up to you, was the reply. No, said Blechynden, he must fix a price. Bishop suggested Rs 1,200 for two. Blechynden got him down to Rs 800. Bishop then gave instructions as to 'what is requisite for them'. Blechynden began the preparations promptly, as time was of the essence—he found, for example, that the shopkeeper Aguiton had only fourteen pairs of children's stockings left and was unsure of their price. (Much later, Blechynden bought thirteen pairs, all that then remained.) Aguiton—speaking perhaps as an importer concerned about the safety of shipping in wartime—was strongly against Blechynden's trusting his children to the *Maria* unless she went in convoy. Blechynden inspected the ship with Bishop a few weeks later and decided that it was small but its accommodation very good.

The departure date was uncertain (as ships awaited full cargoes), but in mid-June, Bishop said it would not be later than 5 July. Blechynden then wrote to the responsible Sub-Secretary of the Company to have an order for his children to embark, and received it next day: 'Capt. Thomas Bishop, commander of the Honble Company's Extra Ship Maria' was 'permitted to receive on board for passage to England Master Arthur Hesilrige Blechynden and Miss Sarah Blechynden', by order of the Governor-General in Council.[17]

Money had to be found not only in future for the children's keep in England, but for the immediate costs. Matters were made worse when Blechynden was told that he could get nothing for his salary bills for May 1797—the Company often did not pay in cash, even for money laid out, let alone for salaries, and instead issued notes in arrears that had to be exchanged, commonly at a discount. There was also a last-minute hitch over payments on account, needed by Blechynden for the building of a new Stamp Office and supposed to be drawn in the name of Tiretta, who was away.

To collect the necessary money, first Lilloo and Gopey were instructed to work out accounts and to check on Blechynden's own debtors and ask for payment with appropriate degrees of civility and emphasis. Tell him, said Blechynden in one case, 'I positively cannot wait any longer, and have 2 children to send to Europe without a rupee to pay their passage or provide their necessaries'. Some debtors complied; some borrowed from others to give cash; others equivocated. Blechynden pleaded with the most prevaricating (and dishonest) Aaron Upjohn, for even the '*smallest* sum he could spare or raise' *now*, as a lakh of rupees was no use to him after the *Maria* had sailed. He thought it 'cursed hard that I must beg & solicit what is due to me'. He feared he would have to take to law to get money from one Scawen, who had long owed a large sum to him and Tiretta jointly, and even more separately to Blechynden, for work on a house. Scawen was not making them any payments, despite 'fooling money away in outcry purchases' he did not need, at twice the price he would have had to pay in the bazar. Blechynden struggled without success to make Tiretta pursue this claim with urgency.

Secondly, Blechynden took on extra work, for example, drawings and a possible new auction rooms and stables for Dring, Cleland & Co. A sum begged from the stables' owner Deletang was a delicate matter, as it was expressed as a loan, but Blechynden regarded it as payment for a translation of a text on farriery that he was undertaking. He was also building a monument for the recently deceased wife of Charles Rothman, a fellow principal of the languishing *Chronicle* newspaper. Blechynden asked if he could be paid, because he was in great want of cash. Rothman shrugged and said that everyone was the same, but he would see about it the next day. He apologized a fortnight later for not paying, but hoped to be able to do so in a few more days. Blechynden cannot have had high hopes: Dickson, the undertaker, told him that *he* had still not been paid three months after Mrs Rothman's funeral.[18]

Thirdly, friends and acquaintances suggested advancing sums to help. Aguiton offered Rs 200 without being asked. Tiretta was surprisingly unforthcoming, and when Blechynden dropped rather obvious hints, Tiretta replied that he himself urgently needed about Rs 1,500, which he was trying everywhere to raise.

Finally, Blechynden began borrowing amounts more formally on his own account.[19] At last, on 5 July 1797, he paid all that was due to Bishop and received his receipt.

Blechynden feared that the children would be badly provided for because of his lack of money. His neighbour, Mrs Wade, had been consulted about the children's clothes and busied herself buying cloth and organizing tailors to sew it. William Mills (from whom Blechynden also borrowed money) gave him a small trunk of clothes that he had had made up for a child (perhaps an apprentice) whose father had now taken him away. Blechynden 'pleaded for the child—as being guiltless of the father's follies', but Mills said that he would burn the clothes if Blechynden did not take them, and so he did. One night, with the departure confirmed for ten days ahead, he gathered as many as ten tailors and kept them at work by candlelight at his house, and himself was busy among them '*like a woman*'. (They had all fallen asleep when he rose at midnight.) He also began marking all the children's articles in Indian ink. In the end, he had gathered quite a collection of garments, linen, and bedding. For Arthur, there were fifty-three shirts, twenty-one stockings, sixteen long drawers, and nightwear; at least twenty-nine jackets and trousers of various kinds, old and new; fifteen pairs of shoes and two hats; and various sheets, towels, pillow cases, a blanket, a quilt, and a mattress—in all 228 pieces, not counting soap, gaiters, and so on. For Sally, there were fifty shifts of two kinds, seventeen frocks in five varieties, eighteen pairs of stockings, fifteen pairs of shoes, and a cap, plus bedding as for Arthur, making up 149 items. Blechynden added a 'keg of mangoes'.[20]

All this frantic activity at least took his mind off the main matter, that Arthur and Sally were about to leave. In July, Bishop announced his final, delayed departure date and also that he was not after all taking a doctor, McLean, with him, which made Blechynden apprehensive. Bishop said that 'whoever goes with him must stand the same chance he does—I pity the children', commented Blechynden. At the end of June, he took them in a palankeen to dinner at Bishop's, presumably in order to introduce them. On 16 July 1797, a Sunday, Blechynden rose at 4 AM after a restless night: 'the separation with the children lay heavy' at his heart. He dressed and had Arthur called and dressed. Mary Wade came over, bringing Sally. Mary too was much affected by the imminent parting, so much so that Blechynden eventually thanked her for all her attention to the children but begged her to go home as she was upsetting them and him too. She went but stayed by the gate to see them leave. Arthur wanted to ride his pony rather than go in the palankeen, but when they were still in the Bow Bazar it started to rain and he joined his father and sister under cover. They went to the house of the recently bereaved Samuel Jones, because his son Sammy and daughter Harriet were also travelling to England on the *Maria*. The ayahs told Sammy this for the first time just as the Blechyndens arrived; he burst out crying and could not be comforted.

The whole party, which included Bishop's wife, then left for the quayside, little Sammy Jones still crying, but his sister 'very merry' and Blechynden's 'poor lambs grave and silent'. Blechynden handed them into the *budgerow* (barge) that would take them downriver to the *Maria*. 'Summoning up all the *man* in me,' he recalled, 'I suppressed so much of the *father* as merely to have my eyes moistened when I kissed them & bid them farewell.' He had a premonition that it would 'be an *everlasting farewell*!! Pray, God Almighty forbid it.' He prayed also that the children would become 'worthy members of society', which was of course the main point of the exercise. Bishop squeezed his hand and promised to 'do his duty by them'. Blechynden went up on the Esplanade to take a farewell look as the boat pulled away. Jones came and dragged him off. They are gone, he said, 'we can do no good'; 'what is the use of our staying here', he asked. Blechynden left, feeling 'very uneasy', 'very melancholy'.

Before dinner, 'precisely 9 hours' after the separation, Blechynden employed himself with desultory inspections of building works in progress and then at his papers, sorting Upjohn's letters and planning retribution over his debts and deceptions. He continued fretting about the children. Jones told him that Bishop had said he was going to stop at Archipore, meaning after a boat journey of perhaps fifteen miles, and then proceed to the ship on the morning tide. Why was that, Blechynden worried. Where would the children sleep? He had originally intended to put them aboard the *Maria* himself off Calcutta to 'avoid accidents and mishaps', but Bishop had persuaded him that they ought to join the ship on the river in the 'bight' just below the Fort (presumably just before Tolly's nullah, the

Kidderpore docks and Garden Reach). Unbeknownst to Blechynden, he had then sent the *Maria* downstream, so that the passengers had to follow after it, at the height of the rains, perhaps as far as Fultah, some thirty miles by river, or about ten miles above Diamond Harbour, its customs house, and the open estuary. Blechynden was not pleased. That night, having hardly slept the night before, he hoped to get some rest, but (he wrote) 'could hardly close my eyes thinking of my poor children—& how they will get to the ship'. At one o'clock, it came on to rain and blow very hard; Blechynden wrote that 'my heart ached for the children. God knows if they were in a house at Archipore or were left to pick out a soft plank in the budgerow'. Possibly, he thought, Bishop might already be underway, for it was ebb tide. The children would catch cold and there was no doctor on board!

When day came, he could not 'catch' his scattered thoughts, missed the children very much, and was still uneasy about their getting to the ship. In the evening, he could not work at his translations 'not for want of *time* God knows [but] for want of spirits'. Worse was to come. Jones told him that Bishop had been back in town *on Tuesday*, looking after his men, and the budgerow had not reached Archipore until that morning. All their party had to eat on Sunday after leaving and on Monday was the cold meat Jones had given them. What a situation 'for the poor children', thought Blechynden. Mrs Bishop was said to be unwell—unsurprisingly. Better news followed. Jones received a letter saying that they were all safe on board and the children were playing together. He then heard from one Nagle, surgeon of another ship, the *Heroine*, that he had been on the *Maria* and seen the children, who were all well, though Sam cried very much when Nagle left and wanted to come away with him. The *Maria* was reported to be at Kedgeree and then in Channel Creek, where the pilot would normally leave it.

A few days later, Blechynden was told that his children's names were listed in one of the papers in a passenger list for the *Maria*. He checked and found that they were in the *Telegraph*. He thought it 'very improper to insert illegitimate children's names in this manner' and resolved to 'give Mr McKinley [the editor] my sentiments very freely on the indecency the first time I meet him in Company'—he did not trust himself to write. Such a thing was 'an insult upon public morals' and people would think him responsible. Worse, Arthur's name was given in full (Arthur Hesilrige Blechynden), though he and Arthur Heselrige (now a Senior Merchant of the Company) were no longer on speaking terms. He went on: 'I call a man keeping a mistress in a very private manner a *failing*, but when he does so openly and publicly, a *vice*—what then must I feel when I see the names of my illegitimate children stuck up in a public print. Lax as morals are in this country, it must surely be offensive to the public eye. I am pained at the thought.' Despite this ethical wriggling—his ability to overlook the discrepancy between his scruples, actions, and emotions and to ignore the possible effect of such attitudes on the children he cared about—in August, he was relieved and proud to get a letter from Bishop. Arthur had been seasick, but Sally not at all. He had 'never in his life' seen quieter children, wrote Bishop—unlike those of his friend Jones, with whom they were having 'a deal of trouble'. They would cry all hours of the night for something or other, and Harriet in particular had 'a trick of laying eggs, which makes it very disagreeable'.

There may have been a pattern here. In January, one of Jones's children had been reported 'dying', covered in blankets and shawls; Blechynden looked in and was unconvinced; and the child was quite well two days later. A couple of years before, in an easily recognizable scene, one of Jones's children got hold of a buggy whip at Blechynden's garden house and was thwacking the table with it, at great risk to the glasses, tableware, and hanging lamps. Jones wrestled the whip away, whereupon the child grabbed the playing cards from the table. Jones got those away as well, and 'frightful screams' ensued. Mrs Jones took the child's part and there was a 'furious altercation' between husband and wife. Blechynden felt embarrassed for them and the 'harmony of the Company was entirely interrupted'. On board ship, apparently, the Jones children's ayah was a 'very good natured & careful woman', but she had so much difficulty with Harriet that she had asked to be put ashore. Well, they had to have patience, said Bishop. He would not fail to give Blechynden's children the 'utmost attention' and to write to him punctually. Blechynden was gratified by his account of Arthur and Sally, which he interpreted as reflecting on his 'manner of bringing them up'. He took the letter and read it out to Tiretta.[21]

The *Maria* was damaged in the Bay of Bengal. Bad weather drove it to Pulo Penang, where it stayed for some weeks. When it reached Madras, leaking, it again had to put in for repairs. But a Captain Richardson reported seeing the children and that they were well. The next report came from Cape Town, where the *Maria* stayed three days in January 1798 before proceeding to St Helena. Arthur was said to be 'taller & stouter'; Blechynden doubted 'stouter' if he were taller, as he was already very tall for his age. He was drawing ships every day upon the deck. Sally was 'perpetually singing—A song she has made "Englishmen—very good man" &c'. This letter—and perhaps, subliminally, the last point especially—relieved Blechynden's mind a good deal; but the effect was only brief. A few days later, the return of the Jones's ayah, probably from Madras, with 'heavy complaints' to Jones, made Blechynden once again sorry that he had sent the children with Bishop.

In August 1798, he heard by overland despatch that the *Maria* had reached England on 17 March, and a little later, that Jones's children had been taken in by Jones's late wife's mother, now herself remarried. Blechynden himself had 'never been so anxious' for a letter. Eventually, at the end of October, one arrived to say that his children had 'arrived safe, in good health & well received, thank God!'[22] A further letter arrived just before Christmas 1788, reporting that they were still well, 'thank God' again, followed swiftly by an ayah who had been to England with another man's children and who said she had seen Blechynden's children and left them both happy and in good health. A letter of 13 March 1800, received in September, reported that Arthur was advancing 'surprizingly in his learning—but' (added Blechynden, meaning, I suppose, the downside to this good news) the expense of maintaining the children at home was very great. He told himself not to grumble. He had brought the cost on himself and must have occasioned the same burden for his own parents.[23]

## MORE OF THE SAME

Arthur had been not yet five when his father started planning to send him to England; when he left India, he was seven. Sally was only four years old, still four months short of her fifth birthday. Their history was repeated in 1802, after their cousin Marmaduke Blechynden offered to take Charlotte and James to England with him. During the year, a pattern of greater involvement with their father had begun for both the younger children, as before with their elder siblings. Blechynden took them to the gardens more often, sometimes at their own request, for a change of air. Their transfer to England had been on his mind. A year before, when his aunt Mrs Theobald asked him to send some 'fine Indian cotton thread' to knit stockings for his children in England, he wished she also wanted 'legs for stockings'—he did know what to do with his children in India. Six months after that he asked Captain Sharp, of the *Bengal*, if he would take them. He replied that he would take the boy for nothing but not the girl, as she would need an ayah, who would be too much of a temptation on board. Captain Cummins might agree to take a girl, he thought; but it transpired that Cummins was taking no passengers. Blechynden would not send James on his own, and so the plan was postponed. (Later he saw some girls were going home after all on the *Bengal*, which he thought 'not kind' of Sharp.) The children's departure was hastened by Marmaduke's offer, therefore, and much less of a strain financially, but otherwise followed the same pattern as for Arthur and Sally. James was a couple of months over six and his half-sister Charlotte was just seven.

Captain Richardson, Marmaduke's commander on the *United Kingdom*, was reluctant to take the children, having—it seemed—no passengers himself. If he were accept them under Marmaduke's aegis, it implied his newly recruited third officer would be paid Rs 1,000 or Rs 15,000, officers having a quota of passenger and cargo space at their disposal. (One suspects Marmaduke's offer owed more to that calculation than to a sense of family obligation.) Richardson apparently commented that he did not know why he should put so much money into Marmaduke's pocket, knowing nothing of him. Through the first officer, whom he invited to dinner, Blechynden explained that the money would not go to Marmaduke but to pay his cousin's debts in Calcutta and possibly England, and it was no loss to Richardson as Blechynden would send the children next season with another captain if they did not go now with Marmaduke. Richardson then agreed, but said £14 must be paid 'to the [ship] owners' for each child. Obtaining the money against his rupee account at the merchants and shipwrights Gillett & Edwards, Blechynden gave Marmaduke £100 (Rs 1,500) to cover this owners' fee, the children's food, and other bills, and also for delivering them to Captain Powell's wife at Kingston in the event that their relatives did not accept them. Marmaduke agreed; Blechynden set about preparing clothes for James and Charlotte and securing the Company's permission for their departure.[24]

When it was time for the trip to England, Blechynden had both children's hair cut short for the journey and took a 'very affectionate leave' of them. Charlotte rode with him in a palankeen and James on his pony. At the boat that was to take them to the ship, they had to wait for some time and Blechynden thought to get his sircar Cassinaut to tell James that as Marmaduke did not understand Moors (Hindustani), he must be an interpreter for him when necessary. Cassinaut began to explain this and James stopped him, saying: 'I believe you think I am a fool? Did I not hear what my father said to you? I shall certainly interpret for all the gentlemen.' Cassinaut reported this to Blechynden, who had not heard it but had seen Cassinaut smile when interrupted. Blechynden called to James that 'since he is so proficient in English he must repeat in that language what I said to Cassinaut'. He did so very correctly, to Blechynden's surprise. Charlotte, though older, had not made as much progress in English. James then complained to Cassinaut for reporting what he had said, adding that 'I am *sure* from that, that you think me a fool merely I suppose because I am a little boy—but by & bye and I shall be as tall as you and then I shall come back & and very soon too and be a Captain, command many men and acquire burrah naum' (presumably *bara naam,* great renown).

Blechynden kissed the two children again on the boat and bade them farewell, reflecting sadly that he might not live to see them again. A more immediate worry was that Marmaduke was far from the ideal guardian. He had already forgotten to give James a hat or even to sit him on the shadier side of the buggy when taking him to the gardens. As we know, he repeatedly did not pay his servants, a 'swindling trick', especially when his cousin had given him the money. At the departure, Blechynden told the boatman to go straight to the ship and not let Marmaduke visit other boats on the way; but then he heard that Marmaduke stopped alongside one to get some tea and stayed there from 7 a.m. until 3 p.m. It was going to be 'a miracle' if the children reached England safely 'under such patronage'.[25]

Blechynden received a letter: they were on board; the children had cried a great deal and wanted to return to Calcutta. That seemed to make it worse and Blechynden felt very low. Then there was another message: all was well and a young woman on board had agreed to take care of the children in return for food from Marmaduke's mess. Later, Blechynden was sorry to hear that by May 1803, his 'poor lambs' had only reached Cape Town, rounding Africa in winter when they should have been halfway to London. Then he was delighted to find that they had arrived and Mrs Theobald had been willing to take them in as an amusement for her. They had not had to stay with Mrs Powell at Kingston; Marmaduke stayed there for a fortnight instead. Mrs Powell wrote and returned Blechynden's order for £50 drawn on Mr Theobald. A further report confirmed that Mrs Theobald was remarkably fond of the children and took James with her wherever she went, though, displeasingly, Blechynden's sister Mrs Whitchurch declined to see them.[26]

Six years later, long after Arthur had returned, Blechynden—impatiently awaiting news of Sarah, Charlotte, and James—was wondering about sending Harriet home. Just after New Year 1811, when Blechynden's relations with her mother Isabella were suspended, the merchant Robert Downie offered to take Harriet with his family. Blechynden objected that he would not have time to prepare her clothes and other belongings; Downie added that that was no matter, as he had plenty, having three children of his own. Perhaps he *would* send her, Blechynden thought, and almost at once raised the subject again, asking if it would not inconvenience

Downie. He replied that, on the contrary, he had a spare berth as a child was not travelling as expected. The price was Rs 1,500 but he would charge Blechynden only Rs 1,000 and cheerfully pay the remainder—it was a fixed matter, he said, when Blechynden objected. It was still a high cost, but Blechynden thought it worthwhile, for Harriet would have that 'great thing', the Downies' protection. He mentioned the 'probability' that Mrs Theobald would not be able to take in Harriet and the 'possibility' of her death; and Downie said that he himself would take the greatest care of her, and of her sister too when she was sent home. At this Blechynden agreed, but advised Downie to take Mrs Downie, Harriet, and his own children to visit Mrs Theobald, see if she perceived any likeness in Harriet 'or if nature speaks in her heart', and to act accordingly. Downie promised 'great prudence'. He had taken entire charge of Harriet by August 1812.

Soon after, Blechynden had a long chat with Harriet's mother, Isabella, about sending their daughter Emma to England: she expressed alarm but less aversion than he had expected. He advanced this justification:

Wisdom is most certainly the principal thing [*Proverbs* 4, 7] and as it is not to be acquired in this miserable country I am under the necessity of sending my children to England to obtain it—painful separation! Doubly so at my time of life, and with my bodily ailment, as it considerably diminishes the hope of my seeing them again! But I must do my duty by these innocents.[27]

The transfer to Europe thus indicated Blechynden's parental concern, sometimes as understated feeling and sometimes directly. It was also expressed as conventional hopes for the future, spiced with conventional pleas to the deity. A constant concern for the welfare of all his children and a keen appreciation of their qualities, good and bad, ran through his diary to the end. Clearly most other parents agreed, though not quite all. When Blechynden's friend Richard Ecroyd was considering sending his half-sister to England when she was thirteen, her mother, Mrs Maxwell, demurred: the girl would be too old to go to school and was already too old to travel safely amongst sailors. She wanted her with herself, the more so as she already had four or five children in Europe who never wrote and did not propose to return. Ecroyd prevailed, however.[28]

There was nothing at all remarkable about sending children away, nor (contrary to some accounts) was it peculiar to British people in India or solely a reaction to social and geographical distance. From at least 1500, according to a source cited by Alan Macfarlane, a majority of English children had been sent from home at an early age, between seven and ten, to boarding schools or to work as servants or apprentices, often for other families of similar rank. Macfarlane was studying a seventeenth-century cleric, Ralph Josselin. It is interesting that nonetheless, he found regular contact and even emotional ties within the family.[29] Stone concludes, unsurprisingly, that the practice diminished the ties of affection between children and parents; he is also pessimistic about the prevalence of romantic love. On the other hand, he describes the greater 'ease and warmth' emerging in the eighteenth century.[30]

If sending his children to England was a mark of Blechynden's attachment and not a denial of it, then it seems that—problems of childcare apart—the main issue was the malign influence of Calcutta and even of Blechynden's household. It was partly a 'foreignness' of culture and language, which definitely included the Christian but India-born Isabella. Blechynden repeatedly recalled his duty to provide for his children. English education was a paternal choice, as in other matters where he asserted his rights, if necessary against the children's mothers. It was a *project*. When a ship's captain was leaving for England and his last words were that he would bring out Arthur, Blechynden replied that he certainly should, 'if you find him fit for it'. He regarded an English education and experience of England as essential to establish his sons in a profession and to ensure suitable marriages for his daughters.

English contacts would be made. In 1805, Blechynden met a young man who said that he had been at school with Arthur, just as Blechynden himself encountered school fellows from time to time. Later, when news came of the death of the Reverend James French, Arthur's teacher, Arthur was in tears and his father offered some 'consoling talk'. Though he and French had never met, Blechynden too was upset, knowing the 'happy bias he had given to Arthur's mind' and thinking that he would miss his influence on James. Arthur thanked God for 'such a valuable friend and schoolmaster' who completed his education. The children also needed social skills, the skills of gentlemen and women. As if to test their level of accomplishment, Blechynden wrote Arthur and Sally a letter in French in 1803. A Captain Bidon brought letters and drawing books from Harriet and Emma in October 1821, not long before Blechynden's death. He was grateful to see their improvement. England was countering the moral influence of Calcutta. Typically, on Emma's birthday in 1813, he wrote: 'may God make her a virtuous woman'.[31]

Blechynden's plans for the children were unremarkable, but that is interesting in itself, given the irregularity he himself perceived in his domestic circumstances. First, most of his children were Eurasian; yet Blechynden—who was quite aware of skin colour in others—seems hardly to notice the fact. It was an exceptionally rare acknowledgment when in one arbitration, the disappointed party claimed that Blechynden had decided against him because he was not European. Blechynden retorted by asking what his own son was, which quite confounded the litigant. But secondly, more usually, when musing on sending Arthur to England, he had reflected: 'surely my relations must have more liberality of sentiment than to refuse to notice him because he is illegitimate—that is not his fault it is mine.' When Sally had her face savaged by a dog, he was saddened at the likely permanent blemish, which would be hard, he thought, 'particularly in an illegitimate child'. Indeed, daughters *were* said to be more of a problem. At least in higher social circles, it seemed that, as Lord Mulgrave put it in the Lords in 1800, 'bastardy is of little comparative consequence to the male children'.[32] Blechynden was determined that it should not be of consequence to any of his children.

# 6

# Jobs for the Boys

*Labor vincit omnia.*

—Richard Blechynden, 1 July 1809[1]

Blechynden, with this unattributed tag from Virgil, was expressing a hope that if 'labour conquered all things' it would overcome the 'devil' hindering the construction of a bund (embankment) at Sealdah. Various supernatural explanations were being given for his difficulties.[2] He might equally have applied the motto to his extra efforts in his duties as Superintendent of Roads and his ulterior motive, which had more or less borne fruit by this time: securing a place for Arthur. In these efforts, we see a major example of his paternal ambition and his concern with his children's immediate and future well-being, but also their character.

## SECURING THE SUCCESSION

In 1802, Blechynden had been told plainly that if Tiretta succeeded in his attempt to secure himself a large pension, it would reduce the salary Blechynden would be paid as Superintendent of Roads, even though the expectation was that he would carry out significant reforms in that office. He was also informed that a deputy would be provided for him, whether he required one or not: he ought to be able to siphon off a proportion of the sum (Rs 150) allowed for the deputy's pay by finding some indigent European willing to work for very little. It was expected that he would do this as compensation for the abolition of the post of Civil Architect, which Tiretta had also held, and so the deputy's post would be a sinecure, or at least of low status, merely relieving him of the 'heavy dirty part of the duty'. His response was that the first priority ought to be a generous settlement for Tiretta and that he did not want a deputy, as he was educating a son at home 'purposely' in his own profession so that he might become his deputy and then his successor. If he 'at all answers the expectations that are formed of him and profits by my instructions here', he went on, it would be in the magistrates' interests to keep him rather than any other. Blechynden was asked his son's age—thirteen or fourteen. It was pointed out that that allowed plenty of time for another deputy, whom his son could succeed. Blechynden objected: such a deputy would merely hinder him if ignorant, and if not, could not properly be turned out in favour of his son. Serjeant Mackenzie was forced on him nonetheless.[3]

One morning in October 1806, a palankeen arrived at Blechynden's house. As so often, he tells the tale without hindsight, as if he were writing the narrative in a novel. Seeing the palankeen, he thought that a friend had come and he called for breakfast, but then saw a stranger walking into the house. The bibi Isabella ran away and Blechynden rose to greet his visitor. He did not hear what he said, but as he seemed well-dressed (meaning of the right class to invite to a meal), pointed him to a chair. The visitor, misunderstanding the gesture, took his hand. Blechynden shook it 'frigidly' and racked his brain to think if he knew the guest, reflecting that he would hardly have offered to shake his hand if they were not acquainted. Perhaps he had met him at his old friend Brightman's? He waited to know the man's business and was bemused when he sat silent. He then said something and Blechynden, raising his ear trumpet, had to ask him to repeat it. Captain Cook desired him to pass on his compliments, said the stranger. 'You came out in the *Hope*, did you sir?' asked Blechynden. 'Yes, Sir,' the man replied. Another silence followed. Now Blechynden wondered what had brought a country-born lad—that is (here), one of mixed race—to his house so soon after his arrival in Calcutta.

Then it struck him: This could not be his son, Arthur, could it, sent to England aged seven for his education? Mrs Theobald had written that she was sending him back on the *Teignmouth*. Might he have come earlier, on the *Hope*, instead? No, that could not be, as he would have brought letters from home or at least mentioned Mrs Theobald; and surely Cook would have sent a chit—'Dear Sir, I have the pleasure to send you your son', or some such. Blechynden eyed him as he ate. Did his nose resemble his, or his profile? But he had black hair, and Arthur's was brown. But something was going on: there was an unusual hubbub of servants on the stairs. The stranger got into conversation with Ladd, someone also at breakfast, and Blechynden dashed away to ask Isabella who it could be. She asked if it could not be Arthur. Blechynden sent in a chit to Ladd: ask him his name. Ladd glanced at it, put it in his pocket, and, in the course of conversation, put the question as instructed. The stranger told him and added that he was Blechynden's son. 'Why Blech,' said Ladd, 'this is your Son.' Blechynden exclaimed, '[G]ood gracious Arthur is this *you* and is this our meeting after so long a separation—why did you not tell me your name [and] deliver Mrs Theobald's letter to me?' Arthur replied that he had left his letters on board.

Arthur was now sixteen. Blechynden took him out after breakfast, introduced him to clients and friends, ensured that he had a meal, and during the afternoon, called him to a bridge he was constructing. The conversation soon turned to news from England and then to Arthur's future in India. It was his intention, said Blechynden, to bind Arthur as apprentice to himself, if he liked the profession. He very much desired that, said Arthur. He was set to copy out his own articles of indenture. Next day, as if to symbolize the new start, they went to the gardens, of which Arthur had faint memories, and Blechynden had him 'well scrubbed in the tank', which he much needed. There were then annoying costs and delays in clearing Arthur's belongings through the customs house. Included in his luggage was a theodolite to replace one Blechynden had broken and six yards of blue broadcloth to make Arthur coats.[4]

Getting him a place was much more complicated. New establishment had to be signed off by the Governor-General. There were inevitable delays with the death of Cornwallis, the temporary appointment of Barlow, and the eventual arrival of Minto. However, the appointment of a Committee for the Improvement of the Town of Calcutta provided an opportunity.[5] It was proposed to allow Blechynden two assistants. Immediately, he requested the Judicial Secretary, George Dowdeswell, that one of them should be Arthur. The other would have to be Mackenzie, for menial tasks; but Blechynden urgently needed the second to be a professional, one who could survey and make plans. As he admitted, he had been readily expanding his duties in order to make a place for Arthur. A salary of Rs 300 a month was envisaged. Blechynden also lobbied W.C. Blaquiere, who, when the Committee considered the matter, duly moved that Arthur be appointed, which was agreed. When the proposed salary was mentioned (the same Blechynden had received as Tiretta's deputy), Dowdeswell decided Rs 100 would be enough. Blaquiere reported to Blechynden that he had said he would be afraid to make such an offer—it would be regarded as an insult—and suggested that Rs 200 was the very least that could be offered. Nonetheless, Dowdeswell insisted on Rs 100.

Blechynden was thunderstruck at this 'shameful trick'. The scavengers who could not read and write earned Rs 150 each, he said.[6] He needed a

deputy in whom he could have confidence and his son was 'fully adequate
to the duty, of unimpeachable integrity and in addition to his natural
willingness to work would have the dread of a father's displeasure—and its
probable consequences at his death—hanging over his head to stimulate
[him] to exertion and to rectitude'. Blaquiere agreed with all that and said
that he would not give up. Blechynden told him that the magistrates had
uncovered 'their frauds' and he despised them. He had hitherto (he said)
'worked like a slave & cheerfully—trusting to see my son my successor—
but they have now broke the back of my zeal & I shall drudge a regular
round like a horse in a mill, confining myself to my Calcutta duties and for
every thing beyond that referring them to the Engineers'. After Blaquiere
went away, Blechynden stayed in the compound, violently flushed in the
face and feeling unwell.

He wrote a long letter for Blaquiere to show the Committee, enclosing
drawings executed by Arthur and a list of the bare minimum of equipment
he needed: theodolite, spirit level, drawing instruments, protractor,
plotting-off scales, two measuring chains, brass parallel ruler, colours, and
camel-hair pencils, which had cost Arthur almost £58 in England, plus
drawing boards, paper, T-squares, surveying flags, and so on. Blechynden
pointed out that he had two or three times the work of Tiretta, who had
been paid Rs 950 and allowed a deputy on Rs 300. He was paid only
Rs 700, and had to that conclude the offer of a deputy on a salary of
Rs 100 was a 'soft refusal' of the appointment. How could a gentleman live
on Rs 100? How many years of savings from such an income would it
take to pay for the necessary equipment and its wear-and-tear? Was *he* to
provide the instruments, which Tiretta had not done for him? Blechynden
had trained his son, he said, trusting former promises, in the hope that
he would become the Deputy Superintendent and Surveyor, as was
desperately needed. Arthur could readily find employment elsewhere at
twice what was being offered. Blechynden was writing, therefore, because
of a need for his services and not to seek a maintenance for his son at the
public expense.

The letter, with its reference to the actual costs of the duty and to the
public interest, was an attempt to counter the assumption that Blechynden
wanted the Committee's backing for casual nepotism. Martyn told him
that the salary, though small, was regarded as a favour to him to help him
maintain his son, an increase to his own salary rather than a regular salary
for a real deputy. Blechynden said that they were making a thief of Arthur:
he could not live on the salary and so—though he 'hoped he was above
such infamy'—they were tempting him to be corrupt. That of course

would also have been typical: the salary attached to an office was often the most trifling of its perquisites. Twenty years before, Blechynden said to Martyn, he remarked to an *amin* (court official), Nemo Mitter, now dead, '[*Y*]*ou take bribes I am sure*' (as he spoke the words again, he fixed his eye on Martyn for some seconds, 'which made him look *queer*'). The amin replied, 'Sir—let the Company fill my belly and I will be honest—I have a wife and four children—my salary is 25Rs per mensem and I pay 30 for my bearers.' Martyn, though one of those who two days earlier had agreed to Arthur's appointment, now asked if he had been educated in his father's line. Arthur and Martyn had not been introduced, and Blechynden wondered if Martyn was hurt by the omission. Blechynden explained Arthur's training and its motivation. Martyn offered to speak to Dowdeswell. Blechynden said that he had already written to him.[7]

Arthur completed the first year of his apprenticeship on 27 October 1807 and started going on his own to supervise the building of a house for a Company servant, Samuel Middleton. (This was a large project, over which Middleton effectively defrauded Blechynden; Arthur remarked that he seemed honest and they had ignored warnings about his character.)[8] Before the Improvement Committee on the same day, Blaquiere brought out Blechynden's letter, which he had not yet passed to Dowdeswell. Blechynden asked him also to show Arthur's drawings, but Blaquiere did not have them with him and appeared to have lost them, large though they were. This was disappointing (they remained missing) as the issue of professional competence was significant to the salary: Mackenzie earned eighty rupees and one of the Company's junior engineers would probably not make Rs 100. Later, Blechynden met Dowdeswell, Blaquiere, and Martyn in the course of business. Nothing was said about the terms of Arthur's employment. Blechynden started asking directly if anything had been decided.

At the Committee meeting the following week, it was said that they could not raise Blechynden's salary by more than Rs 100, an allowance for his extra trouble; he was free to use the extra as he pleased. Blechynden responded that there must be some mistake, as Arthur had been proposed as his assistant. Dowdeswell said that Rs 100 was sufficient for Arthur as a start—the amount might be raised in future—and, inconsistently, that this was not the time to apply to the government for an assistant. Was it a permanent appointment, inquired Blechynden, thinking that at least that would prevent anyone else being brought in. It was not an appointment at all, said Dowdeswell, but (he repeated) an allowance for Blechynden. This setback had the effect, Blechynden felt, of tricking him out of all the extra work and expense he had undertaken in order to justify having Arthur as his deputy.

Arthur continued to work independently, for example surveying some ground for Sir John Royds of the Supreme Court; he was also studying Bengali. The diary is fragmentary in these months but it is safe to assume that Blechynden did not let the matter rest. A couple of months later, he sent another letter to Blaquiere, making a formal request for a deputy. At some stage, this was supported by the magistrates and forwarded to the Governor-General-in-Council. Blechynden was now heavily engaged, not only on private buildings, monuments, and other works, but in the repair or construction of public roads, drains, and bridges. When Blaquiere grumbled to him about the state of the Chitpore Road, Blechynden complained in turn about the prevailing system of so-called 'contract repair' on many established streets—it took him three days a week, he said, to check that all the work was being done that should be done, and he wished the magistrates would require by letter that he or the Deputy Superintendent make a weekly report on these roads. This was a device to have Arthur's work and status recognized; it would also justify the allocation to him of a couple of peons. The Chitpore Road was undoubtedly in a bad condition—Blechynden's bibi Isabella was in pain and almost suffered a miscarriage after travelling over it—and work was started, the task consigned to Lilloo.[9]

Next, an unseemly dispute over the appointment of scavengers, with strong evidence that Martyn was taking bribes for providing posts, was followed by a resolution of the justices, ordered by Dowdeswell, putting the administration (for a time) on to a more regular basis. Blechynden was given responsibility to ensure the cleaning of the streets and drains, to control the scavengers and contractors with their carts and bullocks, to report defects, and to propose efficiencies and improvements. Arthur was appointed as Deputy under the Committee for Improvement, to be paid from the lottery established to raise funds. Blechynden's ambitions for his son had coincided, eventually, with a growing recognition that the extra work he had been undertaking was not only a device to ensure Arthur's appointment, but a necessity given the corruption, confusion, and inefficiency of Calcutta's petty administration and the appalling condition of its public roads, bridges, and drains. That is not to say that the seriousness of the situation had guaranteed a proportionate reaction. Blaquiere acquired a deputy himself in 1809, at an initial salary of Rs 500, said to be due to increase. The happy holder of that post was one David

Andrew. After the appointment, he was permitted to remain at his indigo factory, to be called upon 'when wanted'.

The Committee next offered to pay Blechynden an additional eighty rupees to Rs 100 that he could use for a deputy of his choosing to help with measuring and reporting on roads and securing the payment of residents' contributions or tax. Blechynden immediately considered trying to keep this post (if it were permanent) for his son James, but reflecting that it would involve responsibility for money, decided for now that he would need to appoint Arthur. Blaquiere said he should employ him, then. Blechynden remarked that he had no written instructions for all this work; Blaquiere said that he was 'glad' of that, as Blechynden would not have to undertake all the writing and calculations he was so fond of. However, when Blechynden mentioned the idea, Dowdeswell responded that Arthur had enough to do already. The post would mean mustering *bheestis* (water-carriers)[10] every morning, among other things. So Blechynden decided to set Serjeant Mackenzie to the work in return for the eighty rupees he already received, for which he did nothing, in Blechynden's view. Eight months later, when he found 200 bheestis sitting at his gate and his servants told him that it was a demand to be paid—presumably the custom of *dharna*, whereby the weak try to shame the strong into responding to their grievances—Blechynden told them that he would not pay them (he had not even seen their *jemautdars*' bill) and sent them to Martyn for their 'disgraceful insolence'. But using Mackenzie presumably meant that Blechynden retained the extra allowance himself; and later he managed a further increase in his pay from the Committee for Improvement as well as the recognized deputy's position for Arthur.[11]

## PROFESSIONAL COMPETENCE

Professionalism, qualifications, and experience could help with these efforts and were sometimes a small bulwark against corruption. In 1811, on the subject of a replacement bridge at Kidderpore, a difficult assignment, a certain Mr Jones, who claimed to have been asked by some Committee members for his proposals, said that he had a diploma in his pocket, which was more than Blechynden had, and could build a handsome bridge on a different site, away from what was the worst quicksand he had ever seen. Captain Wood of the Engineers said his diploma must be in 'ignorance, insolence and self-sufficiency'. Blechynden's plans had been approved by the Vice-President-in-Council, the Engineer Officer on the Committee for Improvement (himself), the Chief Engineer, and the Commander-in-Chief. Dowdeswell, very red and loud, said that the government was 'extremely offended' at Jones's insolence and demanded to know who had commissioned him. Wood and Blaquiere that denied they had. Martyn said nothing but was very pale, his lips white, a blue circle under each eye, and big beads of sweat on his forehead. Blechynden hardly knew when he had felt so pleased. Jones's letter, he noted, was 'well-imagined nonsense'.

Arthur's place similarly had to be confirmed by his own excellent work, especially for the Committee for Improvement. His first sole charge was work on a canal: he felt his character and future prospects were at stake, especially chances of future government appointment. He expected he and his father would lose Rs 15,000 on the work. The canal was finished two months after the original deadline, but they were able to justify the delay because, in the meantime, the government had decided to widen the canal. Over the next months and years, Arthur gradually established himself and increased his earning capacity.[12]

The situation of both father and son became quite comfortable. An official salary was far from being the only or even the main source of income even for employees who were not corrupt. Just as they had to provide all their own equipment and many of their costs on professional duty, so too they had many opportunities for additional earnings—for the Blechyndens, surveying for the Supreme Court, taking commission on public or private works, and so on. This income was, by nature, occasional; but significant enough for Blechynden to become choosy. For example, when one Ghulam Hossein asked him to build a mosque at Amrutullah and, more immediately, a warehouse for him, Blechynden explained that nowadays he would work only on contract or for a fixed amount, his unfortunate experience with Middleton having cured him of working on commission. Ghulam was indignant and asked if Blechynden compared him to Middleton; Blechynden answered that no one had seemed more just at the outset but he had been 'woefully deceived' in Middleton and was now 'very cautious'. Ghulam offered to pay Rs 15,000 on top of actual costs, only slightly less than Blechynden proposed. Blechynden then asked for a written agreement. Arthur spent some time planning and costing the work; but in the end, his father refused it, having been told Ghulam was a 'tricking man' and fearing legal complications. He remarked, as was evident from a reluctance he would not have shown in more hard-pressed years, that neither he nor Arthur was anxious for employment, not even for the promise of a profit of Rs 15,000.[13]

On the other hand, despite—or, arguably, because of—the availability of ancillary income, official posts were never completely secure. An additional allowance of Rs 300 had finally been provided to Blechynden; he had transferred it directly to Arthur by 1812. But in 1814, changes in the Police Office took away the Deputy Superintendent's salary altogether, cutting Rs 300 from Blechynden's pay and returning it to Rs 700. It seemed a step backwards from a reasoned and progressive approach to the town's administration and reflected a prolonged period of in-fighting. Blechynden could see why the previous justices, namely Macklew, Blaquiere, and Thoroton, had been appointed—they were Persian and Bengali scholars—and even Martyn might have been intended as a kind of moderating influence because of his legal training. Now justices were being appointed, Blechynden complained, to bulk out the 'overgrown salaries' of a 'greedy phalanx' of men who accompanied the new Governor-General (Lord Moira, or Hastings) and who knew nothing of the 'language, habits or customs of the natives'. This charge seemed to include the 'good looking but very young' Sir William Rumbold, who later proved an ally.

The changes included the establishment of two new committees, for conservancy and roads, alongside the Committee for Improvement (or Lottery Committee), supposedly to benefit Blechynden by returning to him the overall authority he had once had over the roads and extending it to Calcutta's suburbs. The latter reform was thwarted by the animosity and self-interest of Blaquiere and also successively by the highhandedness of newcomers in the Police Office, such as John Eliot, judge and magistrate of 24 Parganas. Blechynden's zeal outran his judgement (he would begin on work before receiving the advances for it); yet it proved impossible to restore his unfettered oversight or to recover Arthur's post. Blechynden was bitter about this. When he heard of the death of his aunt Mrs Theobald, he blamed in part Arthur's loss of office and his own reduction in salary, matters in which she was keenly interested.

However, he decided that an open confrontation about their situation and the general working of the office would probably multiply his enemies rather than improve his position. Also, he 'had too much spirit' to try to restore Arthur's post by grovelling, 'as some mean wretches do'. Instead, perhaps underlining his problem, he complained of his lack of influence to Rumbold, whose rank in the service gave him access to 'the first members of the Government'. Blechynden recognized that, as he said, 'partly from domestic habits, and partly from knowing that go where I will I carry a nuisance about me in my deafness, [I] rarely visit, and never dine out, and therefore have no opportunity of wiping off the dirt' that might be thrown. Blechynden repeated this on another occasion, saying that he was disadvantaged because he had no time for 'ceremonious visits'; his deafness was 'a nuisance to every person' he conversed with; he hated dining out; and could hardly do so with his large family, 'like a detachment of an army'.[14]

Despite these setbacks, this was also a time of hesitant progress towards a more regular, official surveying establishment in which other opportunities might arise. In 1813, Arthur was sent on a survey on behalf of John Hayes, then Magistrate at Sylhet, in what was promised to be a 'comfortable vessel', drawing on the Master Attendant for his charges and costs. Daniel Templeton, Registrar in the Military Department, said the government used Arthur very ill to send him off like this and there was some doubt about getting payment from the Marine Board. Arthur went with James on a good cutter, but Blechynden regretted their departure, fearing that they would fall ill of a jungle fever or some other incident would happen to them. He promised himself that he would be miserable till their return. In the event, they arrived back a little early, after Blechynden's palankeen had returned from the dockside without them. Arthur was already in his room shaving and James had gone for a ride to shake off the chill of the morning. They had had a difficult time: the survey was hard (all ravines, trees stumps, and shoots of new vegetation) and the boat journey long and rough. Blechynden mentioned their travails to Captain Scott of the Marine Board. Hayes said that he was pleased with Arthur's report and promised they would be handsomely rewarded.

A couple of years later, another possible opening for either Arthur or James occurred with the death of Captain Reynolds, Civil Architect of the Western Provinces. The indigo planter Brittridge suggested that one of them apply for the post.[15]

Arthur continued to work with his father, was even called upon for services by the justices (though in what capacity, Blechynden wondered), and remained Surveyor to the Committee for Improvement. He tried to remedy the situation himself when his wife wrote to the Countess of Loudoun and Moira and received a reply: the Governor-General would make inquiries of Rumbold; they might expect justice. However, the matter was not resolved while Blechynden was alive and it continued to rankle. When Alex Smith, Head Clerk at the Police Office, stopped working for the Lottery Committee, he was due to lose Rs 200 in pay, but the magistrates had him draft a letter saying that they recommended he nonetheless retain the money 'on account of his long-standing in the Office, and his good conduct'. This caused Blechynden to ask bitterly what 'bad conduct' it was of Arthur's that caused him to lose his entire Police Office salary and what he himself had done that three-tenths of his pay should be retrenched after thirty years of 'faithful & laborious service'.[16]

## EMPLOYMENT AND MORAL TURPITUDE

The fair-skinned and precociously ambitious James, though fairly often ill, seems to have been a forthright and venturesome child. Once Blechynden found him lying on the bare terrace with a violent fever. He refused to let his father take him to bed. It was 'improper' to leave him in that state, however, and so Blechynden wrote a note for the doctor. Hare's son came and ordered a powder for the boy. Blechynden put James to bed and gave him the medicine with honey. Soon afterwards, the boy got up again and came out, refusing to lie on the bed: a 'chip off the old block'. On another occasion, when Blechynden was awake at 4 AM, having slept only since one o'clock, he found James at his elbow and reflected that he needed as little sleep as his father.[17]

It was a sign of things to come, perhaps, that James's return to India was delayed. In 1812, when Blechynden already expected his return, he heard that James had been expelled from school, supposedly for fighting another boy's battle and then refusing to be flogged as a punishment. Instead of being sent to India, he had been enrolled by Mrs Theobald in another school at eighty guineas per year.[18] By 1813, when James was at last expected but had still not appeared, Blechynden had 'very faint hopes' of getting him appointed as his assistant—if he were to apply for support now, others would be forced upon him, backed by one or other of the justices. On James's account, he felt that he could not cut with men he regarded as his enemies among those in charge of Calcutta's public works, but he was frustrated to have awaited James so long: six months, he considered, by July 1813. If he had come at once, Blechynden thought, it would have been sufficient for him to be three-quarters as 'exemplary' as Arthur; now he would have to be his equal. He was expected on the *Providence*, but did not appear when it arrived at Kedgeree in early July. At last, he wrote from Madras to say that he was staying with a clergyman by the name of Davis. Finally, he reached Calcutta with a Captain Price of the *Arabella* at the end of the month.

He had become 'a manly youth & a little taller than Arthur'. He had a surprisingly exact memory of places and occurrences from his childhood in Calcutta. Blechynden asked him if he liked his father's profession; he 'pretends he does very much'. Therefore, Blechynden gave him Arthur's indentures to copy in his own name and sent for his trunks. The indentures were executed the next day. The following week, James started Bengali classes with Gopey's son Saum Churn Mozendar. An introduction to John Eliot at the Police Office was not a success: he was received 'very coldly'. The next month, nonetheless, when James was newly returned from the survey with Arthur, Blechynden set him to work examining and measuring bridges—having shown him how—in place of Arthur, who was unwell. The work was beyond the jurisdiction of Calcutta and ought to have been undertaken by the suburban establishment, which contained at least two relevant staff members. But Eliot had asked for it to be done and Blechynden decided to oblige using James, who had no official position, in order that he might be able to mention it at an appropriate time.[19]

Gradually, relations with James became more difficult. They began to exhibit the familiar tensions of a grown-up son returning home to conduct his social life in or from his father's house. Even in 1813, when not quite seventeen, he took to riding out with John Stewart and returning late for dinner. Though one might have thought Stewart a useful connection (he was the son of Alexander, an advocate, justice of the peace, and member of the Committee of Improvement), Blechynden was 'not partial' to the association, especially in the evening, fearing that Stewart would lead James to some 'bad place'.[20] A couple of years passed and James, just nineteen, offended by going with other friends to visit a Timothy Williams at Chinsurah, an indelicacy to Arthur and his pregnant wife because it was the very time that they were celebrating their son's first birthday. Returning after some days, James continued the association, which Blechynden also did not like, by going with Williams to a nautch. They gave thirty rupees to the dancing girls and then Williams, not thinking that enough, sent them fifty in his family's name. Blechynden sourly commented that Williams ought to pay his debts if he had so much cash. Soon James was avoiding being alone with his father and quarrelling with visitors. Blechynden had the doctor MacWhister look at an ulcer on James's leg, asking him if it was anything 'disreputable'.

One Sunday, James went into Calcutta from the gardens, saying he was going to church—his father did not believe him but could hardly forbid it—and then returned with a friend, admitting that he had not been to church at all. He stayed up until one or two in the morning, drinking and singing with friends (including John Stewart) and disturbing the women of the house. Blechynden could not hear this, but the thought of it was 'very shocking'. James's friends also took to riding races with each other on Blechynden's horses, without permission, injuring themselves and so risking his horses. James himself was badly injured later that year, his skull fractured and the end of a finger bitten off by a horse. He required the attention of both Shoolbred and MacWhister to dress his head wound, but 'thanks to the lord', his recovery was 'wonderful'.[21]

In October 1816, James 'scaled' the gate, 'deserted the family mansion and his kindred, and broke his indentures as an apprentice'. Blechynden was then 'as little disposed to act the relenting father' as James appeared to be to 'exhibit the penitent son'. He would have to take the consequences, as it was 'an imperious duty upon a parent to make a wide distinction between dutiful & undutiful children'. James might be certain his father would do so, Blechynden wrote. He had decided that James was idle as well as vain. He was 'apparently unwilling to put himself forward or fit himself for some situation in life, as though he alone were exempt ... from earning his bread'. His father would have to teach him 'a different lesson'. A few months later, he made an alteration in his will. When a letter arrived from James, Blechynden returned it unopened. Friends who were staying, Captain Price of the *Arabella* and twenty-year-old J. Roberts, took to arguing about James at Blechynden's dinner table. Roberts told Price that he was spending his days surveying with James until ten at night. Price responded that he knew nothing of surveying and it could not be done at that hour. Roberts got angry and called Price a 'damn'd rascal' and 'son of a bitch'.[22]

James's fault was 'libertinism'. A few months after James's recovery from his head wound, Blechynden heard from Arthur, who had had it from an indiscreet friend of James's, that his brother had written to a Miss Lee, daughter of a Lombard Street banker, inviting her to come to Calcutta to marry him. Blechynden was surprised 'at his vanity & assurance'. He could not have been sixteen when he 'pretended to fall in love' with this young lady, and now, before he was twenty or had 'a farthing he can call his own', he proposed to marry a woman of fortune. He was also treating his father in a cavalier manner by attempting to give him a daughter-in-law without asking his consent. It may have been this revelation that led to James's flight from his father's home and his apprenticeship.

Next, Blechynden heard that, having apparently recovered from Miss Lee, James was about to be married to a Miss Trotter, reputedly a very nice girl. James was 'the same as dead and buried' to him, said Blechynden, but added that he was too young to marry and even if he were old enough, his father would not agree while his eldest daughter remained unmarried. Also, he would pity the wife of one so 'volatile'. James wrote a letter to Arthur, asking him to deliver it to their father, as it was of the 'utmost consequence'. Blechynden told Arthur that it was too late. James (by this time) had had three months and three days to come to his senses. Blechynden drew up an answer for Arthur to send. More than a year passed; the estrangement was not resolved. The underlying problem was now James's relations with another girl, Miss Villebague, daughter of H. Villebague of Serampore, latterly Deputy Collector of Government Customs and Town Duties for Calcutta. Later it was reported that the couple did not like each other very much, but the girl was pregnant.

James had somehow managed to secure appointment as Surveyor to the Collector of Burdwan, Charles Trower. Fergusson,[23] for whom James was also surveying, told Blechynden that he must forgive his son. John Stewart's father interested himself on James's behalf and said that he would support any application from him, as would many others; but nothing could be done while James was not 'countenanced' by his father. James's conduct, said Fergusson, was 'not so bad as represented'. He offered some commonplace humbug in justification. James had been very ill used, Fergusson said, and in fact had benefited the girl (Miss Villebague), for if she had not fallen in with James, 'she would have gone upon the town such is her inclination'. Fergusson had very much wanted to see Blechynden about this and had thought of writing to him, he said. Blechynden asked if he would mind doing so: the letter would justify the reconciliation he was apparently now considering, should he ever be accused of 'countenancing the libertinism' of his son. When a friend, Mrs Betts,[24] told Arthur's wife Fanny that she thought Blechynden had been cruel to James in refusing to let him home after he expressed sorrow for his conduct, Fanny explained to her the 'variety and nature' of James's offences: 'so far from amending he became worse and worse'; the folly that caused the breach was only the last in a series. Mrs Betts was astonished. She changed her mind about James's being hard done by.

Fergusson's letter arrived on Christmas Eve, 1818. He expressed his concern about James, saying that his conduct amounted to nothing more than 'an indiscretion which either of us in our youth might have fallen into'. Seduction, he added, had been quite out of the case. He would not interfere but for the good opinion he had formed of James and the sincere regard he had for Blechynden. Arthur read this too, but said nothing. Blechynden replied on Christmas Day that he was sure Fergusson would not have interested himself on James's account had he not felt his father 'might rely on the promises of better conduct in future', which he presumed James had made. It was 'kind, considerate and humane' on Fergusson's part and he would show the reliance he placed on him by acceding to his wishes. His skill as an advocate was shown by his choosing to write at the season of goodwill to all men. Blechynden trusted James would be grateful to him. The exchange put Blechynden into good spirits.

On New Year's Day he cited Matthew 18:22 (replying to Peter's question, '[H]ow oft shall my brother sin against me, and I forgive him? Till seven times?', 'Jesus saith unto him, I say not unto thee, Until seven times: but, Until seventy times seven'). James had neither called nor written, but still his father started putting work his way, claiming that James had more time than he did. For his part, James started sending to Blechynden for peons to assist him, which he had not done before. Finally, after more than two weeks, he wrote to his 'Dear Father', saying he had heard that, after repeated intercession, Fergusson had prevailed on him to forgive him. He asked when he could visit, at the 'earliest opportunity', expressing his 'deep contrition for the past' and promising good conduct in the future. Unimpressed by this lack of urgency, Blechynden merely folded the letter like a chit and sent it back with the note: 'Luke ch.15 v.18' (the prodigal son: 'I will arise and go to my father, and will say unto him, Father, I have sinned against heaven, and before thee'). These staccato Biblical references were no doubt intended to leave James in no doubt of where he should seek guidance for his conduct. Next day, in marched James at breakfast time. Blechynden read him a lecture and warned that this was the last aberration he would pardon. James explained that Fergusson had been downriver and he had not seen him until a day or two ago. He looked thin, sickly, and dejected. It was at this stage that Blechynden heard the rumour that Miss Villebague was with child, which seemed to him just 'another torment'. Arthur set James to drawing. In the coming days, he remained 'glum and uneasy' and distracted Arthur more than he helped him.

James had lost his post as Surveyor to the Collector. The story was that the Company was reforming Trower's office and would allow him only one surveyor, and required that it be a certain Osborn, recommended by Gordon Forbes, former Commissioner at Chandernagore and Chinsurah, and a friend of Villebague. Blechynden suspected that James had been ousted either to induce him to marry Villebague's daughter or for revenge. Osborn took up his position, according to James, only to neglect it, spending his time laying out gardens and planting trees in Garden Reach, 'currying favour with the great'. James next thought that he might go to

Dacca to take charge of the lands and concerns of Colly Sunker Ghosaul, entirely forgetting (wrote Blechynden) how much time he had still to serve of his apprenticeship. Blechynden found James dilatory in his work, especially over a plan he was preparing for the Asiatic Society: in the end, Arthur had to colour it in. James failed to help Gopey make out the bills for the previous month when asked. Still 'sauntering about', not working, he next wanted his father to get him appointed to take charge of the bunds at Tamluk, which Blechynden could not do, as the post was held by a nephew of his friend Betts.[25]

James was not without support, however, notably from Fergusson. He also went to see Mr Stewart about a position at Rs 200 a month, which Stewart thought would not be sufficient. He said he was very pleased to hear that James was reconciled with his father: it was a great thing in his favour, he added, and launched into praise of Blechynden. Stewart suggested that when James had earlier applied to be reinstated in his post with the Collector, Dowdeswell had refused because (Stewart implied) there were very 'heinous charges' against him, namely seduction. James stated the particulars, as he had to others, and said that he could bring papers to prove what he said. Stewart gave him a rigorous cross-examination and ended by remarking that what James had said presented matters in a very different light. Might he repeat it to Dowdeswell, he asked. Of course, James replied. Stewart added that if Dowdeswell were convinced, he (Stewart) might assist James publicly. Otherwise it would be in private, as he could not appear to oppose Dowdeswell. It was, he went on, 'a great pity to see a young man genteelly brought up out [of] employment'. Upbringing, we may note, was thus trumping illegitimacy, Indian birth, and mixed race. It did not seem to matter, once it was explained away and justified, that the relationship with Miss Villebague continued.

To Blechynden's mind, James spoiled the effect of this interview by asking 'modestly' for a *promise* of support, as if he doubted Stewart's word. Many, thought Blechynden, would have turned on their heel at such a question, but Stewart merely said that he could not promise anything until he was sure of being able to fulfil the promise. James said that he had heard Mr Villebague was likely to lose his post at Howrah, and asked if he could have that. Stewart had heard of no such thing. When James persisted and asked if he could give him a chit for Sir Charles D'Oyly, the Collector, which would secure the position for him, Stewart replied by asking what he could say. He was anxious to serve James, but not at the expense of others; he wished to be just to all, and did not like to see old men put out to make room for young ones. It was a wonder, noted Blechynden, that he did not add: especially 'one situated as he is with regard to you'. He probably thought it. James was nothing if not forthright. Unlike his father, for example, he later spoke out against a colleague whom he considered to be at fault and who was then suspended. Blechynden could only think that the man must surely have friends who could respond by attacking James.[26]

Next, James was sent by Blaquiere to divide some disputed land, the magistrate telling him that he had just to make a division and Blaquiere would enforce it. Blechynden remarked that that was a question of 'civil rights'. He warned James to be careful and James replied, naively, that he would not make any report until he had been paid. That was not what he meant, said Blechynden. James had to be careful of his reputation and work as conscientiously as if he were about to die or the parties to appeal to the Chief Justice, Blechynden explained. The case was one both Blechynden and Arthur had refused. Arthur had replied that there might have been a confusion with his brother James, as he himself knew nothing of the dispute. It was a worry that James had been called in by Blaquiere, who was a friend of Villebague and might be employing James so as to lay the blame on him for any problems with the division. Arthur warned James accordingly. James reported that Blaquiere asked him if he was not the Surveyor to the Lottery Committee, and when told that that was Arthur, had said, '[O]h aye—you are the Surveyor to the Collector'. James had said that he used to be. This made Blechynden suspect that at the least Blaquiere was trying to embarrass James, because he was sure he knew perfectly well who was who. He then told James that he had found that the division of the land was supposed to be into five and twelve-seventeenths, which James should work out and leave the rest to Blaquiere. James provided the magistrate next day with a traced copy of his plan, but not the original.

This advice to James reflected a more general concern about his reliability and character, also once again in evidence at his father's house (though James now had his own rooms). One day, he arrived inebriated and late and brought an equally drunk and uninvited friend to dinner, a Captain Jones, with whom he continued to drink and have conversation 'not always of the most polished kind', judging from the looks of the ladies, until he fell asleep with his head on the table. Two cups of coffee revived him enough to play cards. He and Jones stayed until half-past eleven, long after Blechynden had gone to bed. The Captain had moved on to half pay, in return for which he had received £1,000, and was going back to Britain. He seemed, according to Arthur, much taken with James.

James could also make trouble within the family. At another dinner, he spent his time whispering to Sarah or talking loudly to his cousin Tom Blechynden, once or twice calling him, in 'a familiar way', a 'blackguard'— not language to be used when ladies were present. Arthur later explained to his father, very reluctantly, that when James whispered to Sarah, he was sneering at Arthur and his wife Fanny. He kept rolling ripe mangoes across the table so that they fell in Fanny's lap (a reference to her being pregnant). He was making coarse jokes with Tom, criticizing the quality of his father's beer, and seemed to have been trying to pick a quarrel with other guests. He got drunk with a stranger he had brought to dinner (another captain, who remained quiet and apparently sober), and even went out on to the terrace and made water in front of a maid into her betel box, which she could not snatch up in time. 'He is,' commented Blechynden, 'a sad thorn in my side & I know not what will become of him.'

A flavour of James's character may also be seen in his attitude to servants. At the dinner just described, he was scolding Arthur's servants as if he wanted to annoy their master; they ran off for fear that he was going to beat them. On another occasion, Blechynden's *dooria* complained that James had flogged him. Blechynden said nothing to his son but sighed to himself, thinking that nothing seemed to tame him. A little later, James complained of the insolence of a *ketmutgar*, Babu, whom he had instructed to bring over to his house anything left over from Blechynden's breakfast. Babu asked what the dooria would eat. James said that Babu was also drunk; James wanted to 'give him a good castigation'. Blechynden said that he must not. James had already beaten the dooria, he said, which he should not do again. James retorted that the dooria had been impertinent. James told him to procure him a *metrany*, who, when she came, would not stay at night. The dooria said that she had children at home and also was afraid of cats. James thought this a 'quizzing answer' and threatened to beat the dooria, who said that if James did, he would complain to Blechynden. At that point, James threw a brick at him. As for the ketmutgar, however, it happened that Babu was already in trouble with his master for an unexplained absence. When he reappeared, he did seem drunk and Blechynden gave him three or four stripes on that account.[27]

Professionally, James was not to be held back long. Soon, he sold one of his theodolites for Rs 500 to a Lieutenant Wroughton, who offered him Rs 200 a month and his food to accompany him on an official survey of the Bogrutty River (the Bhagirathi, in Bengal). Blechynden recommended that James accept, but first, out of politeness, consult Stewart. James said that he anyway needed a letter from him for the Surveyor-General,

Colonel Colin Mackenzie. Stewart advised him to accept, in the hope that the assignment would lead to something better. Mackenzie wanted to see some surveys on which he had worked and Blechynden gave James seven, which Mackenzie admired. He too advised James to accept and to be sure that 'proper mention was made of his assistance' in Wroughton's report. He added that if anything came up in his office, he would ask Stewart to write to inform him.

Matters were concluded swiftly. Wroughton, a 'tall good looking young man', came to Blechynden to ask if he could borrow a large drawing board so as to get as much of the river as possible on to one sheet. Blechynden said that the size of paper would be the limiting factor, but, anxious not to throw any obstacles in James's way, cleared his largest board, effectively a table top, for Wroughton to inspect. He decided that it was too unwieldy and instead borrowed Blechynden's largest drawing table. Blechynden also had out Rennell's atlas for him to trace the rivers—the survey was to start only a little beyond Hooghly—and the two surveyors had a general conversation about surveying rivers, problems with the sandbanks that formed, and so on. Blechynden then warned James not to be too familiar with Wroughton and to remember that he was his employer, paying him from his own pocket. James had a draft for Rs 500, which he made over to Arthur in return for cash, presumably (Blechynden thought) to maintain Miss Villebague while he was away.[28]

There continued to be reports of James's social misdemeanours; but also, the New Year brought an effusive letter from him to his father, trying to counteract his 'present impressions' by claiming 'every pulse' in his 'now painfully agitated heart' throbbed 'with pure lively & unvanquishable gratitude' to his father for an 'incalculable gift of benefits'. He owed his father for his 'paternal benevolence', his 'kindness like the refreshing dews of Heaven that drop upon a desert land', it continued. Blechynden treated this 'gulbarnum' as it would seem to have deserved. It cut no ice with him and he went back to his reading—the poem of *Don Juan*.[29]

Next he heard that James was paying court to a Miss Radfield while 'his heart was another's'. James denied the latter. Eventually, on 20 July 1820, he married Sarah (Sally) Radfield Thackeray, illegitimate daughter of Richmond Thackeray, sometime Secretary to the Board of Revenue and Collector of 24 Parganas. Blechynden was consulted and gave consent, as was necessary to 'extricate' James from 'the horrid connexion he had formed'. Sarah Blechynden wrote to Sally, saying that she must not expect invitations between brothers and sisters but they should take meals together, as it would save money. Blechynden seems also to have taken responsibility for providing or, more likely, paying over to Sally's mother Charlotte Rudd a monthly pension of twenty rupees. Later, while Sally and James were stationed at Cuttack—an unhealthy post—Blechynden had a lock of his hair cut off to be sent to Sally. James eventually accumulated sixteen years' service on surveys. In 1836, he was granted a pension of one-third pay on account of his 'destitute condition and loss of health', attributed to a fever contracted on public duty in Assam.[30]

# 7

# Brides and Prejudice

[M]arriage ... was the only honourable provision for well-educated young women of small fortune ... .

But how little of permanent happiness could belong to a couple who were only brought together because their passions were stronger than their virtue....

           – Jane Austen, *Pride and Prejudice*[1]

## HONOURABLE PROVISION

Charlotte had been expected to arrive on the *Sovereign* in July 1812 and Blechynden heartily wished all three of his children were coming together. However, not only was James still at school but Sarah had been retained in England so that she could keep Blechynden's house when he came there—how provoking this was! She had 'made up her mind' to stay with Mrs Theobald, he discovered in August 1812. He could have spared Charlotte a year or two longer, Blechynden reflected, as she was young, but Sarah had no time to lose. Who would marry her when he was dead and could not be of service to her husband? Who would marry 'one of her colour without interest & without youth to tempt them'? She had made her choice, he commented crossly, and he might make his own, after what he had to call her 'defection'. When she did not even arrive with James on the *Essex* in 1813, Blechynden declared that she would 'bitterly regret this undutifulness'—he had sent her home to be educated, not kidnapped.

In the middle of 1812, Blechynden's town house was being altered and repaired for Charlotte's arrival (and possibly that of Sarah and James). He began looking for beds, bought a swinging dressing mirror, and found a separate house for his bibi Isabella. Arthur reflected that they would have to cut their expenditure to allow for the extra costs about to be incurred. His calculations seemed to show that the Blechyndens were living beyond their means. Their total monthly outgoings were Rs 1,089, excluding exceptional items, such as doctor's bills, buying a saddle and lottery tickets, and several donations, that brought the total to Rs 1,240. Spending had increased by forty rupees a month over the previous year. Money received from making and registering surveys did not amount to more than seventy-seven rupees. The result was that Blechynden's official pay did not cover his expenses in India, let alone remittances to England for the other children. The shortfall was made up from occasional rents and the profit on various works, which was also the only source of savings. Arthur thought that they needed to sell houses they were not using and to economize on costs. His calculation was misleading, however: it underestimated the additional sources of income.

Charlotte's name headed the list of passengers on the *Sovereign* in August 1812. She was 'almost everything' Blechynden could wish for. She was accompanied by an initially glum Josephine Frances de Carrion, the sister-in-law of Tiretta. With these arrivals, a different social life developed. Blechynden now kept a coach and 'the girls' would go out in it with young lady friends, such as the two Miss Brittridges (Ann and Elizabeth), who would also come to dinner and whom they would visit. Or the buggy would be used—it was better for Charlotte—and Blechynden and Miss de Carrion would take the coach.[2]

Some time after her return, Josephine de Carrion showed Blechynden Mr Theobald's account with her, in which she had taken nearly £90 of Blechynden's money to pay Mrs Theobald and transferred the balance to herself. He said he had always expected this, had said as much to Arthur 'from their first arrival', and 'begged her to consider the debt as cancelled'. This slightly mysterious entry implies that Josephine had returned to India under Blechynden's aegis, possibly after the death of her brother-in-law Tiretta, or following on from connections Blechynden had provided to her when she first left Calcutta for Europe. There may also have been a new context for these financial discussions. Arthur and Josephine Frances de Carrion, called Fanny by the family, were married on 7 December 1813.

No record exists in the surviving diaries of the circumstances. It was suggestive, however, that quite early on, Josephine was upset at not travelling to the gardens in the buggy with Arthur and declared (on that account, Blechynden suspected) that she preferred a buggy to a coach—he could have saved his money, he thought.[3] Fanny and Charlotte may also be assumed to have been close, not only from having travelled together, but because there was a double wedding. Charlotte too was married on

7 December 1813, to John Henry Warner, born in Dublin in 1783 and a Captain in the Bengal Native Infantry. This seems to have been a satisfactory connection, though Warner—a surveyor or engineer—faced a 'melancholy' situation in his career and spent much time away, sometimes accompanied by Charlotte. Any lack of news from them would alarm Blechynden and contributed to the objection he later expressed to husbands having military employment.[4]

Fanny was soon pregnant. Blechynden spoke to her kindly after hearing that she was apprehensive, believing her sister had died in childbirth. Fanny admitted that she had some fears but said that they had been greatly exaggerated in the telling. An acquaintance, Mrs Lyell, had tried to reassure her by saying that having a baby was 'so far from being painful that she did not care if she had one every day'. More realistically, Blechynden told Fanny that Mrs Tiretta had not died until three days after giving birth, having been kept in a sealed room with a charcoal fire in July—so that the elder Dr Hare had declared that she had effectively been murdered.[5] Blechynden entreated Fanny to Christian resignation, made some 'innocent jokes', and brought her into very good spirits. The baby, named Richard after his grandfather, was born on 7 October 1814. The usual childhood dramas were recorded once again: bad trouble with his teeth, his gums being lanced, and vaccination. On 23 October 1815, Fanny gave birth to her second son, Arthur Henry. In early February 1816, she was feared to have had a miscarriage: she passed blood after a fall on the Dum Dum Road. She was again ill and confined to her room for fear of miscarriage in October of that year. Another child, Charles Edward, was born on 19 November 1819.[6]

There is little evidence about the family life of Arthur and Fanny. They joined Blechynden's dinners and house parties, but at some stage moved into a separate house in sight of Blechynden's. Fanny had to remind her father-in-law that it was Arthur's birthday when he forgot, in 1816. Blechynden was annoyed at the impertinence of Tommy Betts, son of his friends,[7] when he claimed that Arthur neglected his wife. A few months later, however, Blechynden himself commented 'what folly' it was when Arthur did not return home until 3 AM after a late afternoon dinner with four men, including Blechynden, who had left early. Fanny was given to tears during the family dramas of these years, but also seems to have exercised a calming influence. Once, in 1821, she was very glum at dinner and Blechynden wrote a note on his slate asking Arthur what was the matter. He wrote back: he had just asked Fanny the same question. Blechynden, though he had thought it might have been the presence at dinner of someone Fanny could not bear, drew a bottle on the slate. Arthur nodded and shrugged. He must have told this to Fanny, for later she abraided Blechynden for having drawn the bottle and he reflected that Arthur could not bring himself to lecture her without 'lugging in' his name; he would be on his guard. These incidents imply that Arthur's attitudes were similar to his father's in the domestic as in the professional sphere.[8]

## AN UNDUTIFUL DAUGHTER

Sarah eventually returned to India during 1815. Blechynden later threatened to sue for defamation a certain Mendes, who apparently told Sarah at the Cape that she would be subject to her father's French mistress when she arrived in Calcutta, which made her very unhappy for the remainder of her voyage until she arrived and found this 'mistress' to be none other than her old acquaintance and new sister-in-law, Fanny. Sarah had not pined over much, perhaps. In January 1816, she received a letter from a former companion who was again on board ship, lamenting that she was not present for their festivities and prophesying that in six months she would no longer be *Miss* Blechynden.

Family parties now continued with Sarah, even musical evenings—one in which Sarah played the piano and a guest (called Scott) the flute, though piano playing tended to send Blechynden to bed. At one time, the whole family except Blechynden went on a pleasure outing to Chinsurah, Sarah being one of those badgering her father until he agreed to this excursion. They had an unpleasant boat trip that they were all glad Blechynden had missed, but eventually returned much improved by the change of air. The downside of this enlarged social life was that Blechynden—so he complained—was being 'eaten & drunk' out of house and home by the hospitality he provided. With a family of eight, he was living beyond his official salary and breaking in on his savings when he still had three daughters unmarried.[9]

At the same time, the female members of the household also engaged in 'continual squabbles and bickerings about trifles'. On top of problems over his and Arthur's official position and other harassment, Blechynden felt 'domestic strife' had almost driven him mad. Sarah's alienation was compounded by the trouble over James. At an early stage in the estrangement of father and son, Sarah brought Blechynden the same letter that Arthur had had, saying that Warner had asked her to do so. Blechynden said he had seen it and had nothing to say. James was staying with Warner. Sarah and Charlotte went there to meet him. He showed them the note from

Arthur, which Sarah said was 'very unkindly written'. She asked Fanny if it was from Arthur or at her father's dictation; Fanny did not know. When asked, Arthur would not say. Sarah was more glum than usual at dinner, so much so that Blechynden was driven to bed to avoid seeing her. Her being miserable and then occasionally high-spirited seems to have been a major part of the problem in the household. It is not hard to imagine why.

In September 1817, an old friend, Ned Brightman, approached Blechynden and told him that Ino G. Duncan, a sailor, wished to become a member of his family. Blechynden said that he was opposed to giving a daughter to a soldier, let alone a sailor. Brightman said that he agreed. Duncan wanted him to find him some work ashore. He had not managed to do so and feared that Duncan had no property of his own. To this discouraging recommendation Blechynden replied that he thought as much. The fact was that at this time, the whole town was 'full of country officers *starving*' or at least unable to find work. A fortnight after Brightman's approach, Blechynden received a letter through Sarah, in which Duncan asked for her hand. He admitted that he had been unable to find a situation on shore, but would take a voyage if necessary and hope to be more fortunate on his return. Blechynden believed that he would be unable to get a ship either. He concluded, though Sarah was agreeable to the match, that it would be 'an improvident father indeed' who would yield to her wishes and contribute to her 'wretchedness'. The following year, his attitude hardened even further: 'on no account' would he give another daughter to a soldier or sailor. 'All the family suffered so much,' he recalled, 'while Warner was in the field and in general they [soldiers and sailors] are so long absent from their wives they might be said to be no husband to them or their wives to them' and there was 'no knowing to what a woman may be driven for want of what St. Paul calls due benevolence'.

Sarah began to rebel more openly at her situation and her father's attitudes. She went riding one evening with a Dr Arnott, whom they barely knew, and ended up at a Mrs Harman's at Alipore, not returning home until eleven o'clock. Blechynden thought this thoughtlessness 'like all the rest of her conduct'. However, he agreed that she should go with the Betts to the Botanical Gardens the next day. A few days later, Sarah came into the house followed by Arnott, having arrived in his buggy instead of Blechynden's carriage, he later found. They went into Sarah's dressing room and pushed the door partly closed. Blechynden saw Arnott raise his hand to throw it around Sarah's neck. Her father went in; Sarah slipped away to her bedroom. Blechynden reproached Arnott for his 'indecent behaviour'. He stammered out an excuse, but shook Blechynden's hand very familiarly as he left. Blechynden speculated on what could have been said in the buggy to explain Arnott's indelicacy.

A letter came to Sarah, which she showed her father, a 'rig-ma-role' from Arnott excusing himself from dinner and apologizing to Sarah for his conduct: he 'could not resist [a] sudden effervescence of spirits'; he wished to lighten Blechynden's burdens, not increase them. When Arnott next called, he was received very coldly. Both Fanny and Arthur reproached him for his impropriety and told him that Blechynden had wondered what could have been said while he was riding in the buggy with Sarah. Arnott insisted that there had been nothing improper: they had talked about how Blechynden brought up his children and the pain he must feel at James's defection. Though dubious, Blechynden agreed that Arnott could be invited to dinner—it was Fanny's birthday—noting that Arthur 'appeared very composedly to have made up his mind to that already'.[10]

## A SUITOR DENIED

By late 1818, Arnott had been replaced by another suitor, an Irishman, Lieutenant Foster Fyans, of the 67th King's Regiment.[11] Sarah was still annoying her father, infringing on his notions of what was proper. She invited an Ensign of the 67th to dinner and Blechynden blamed Fyans. Arthur said that Sarah herself had issued the invitation at a ball, and Blechynden turned his irritation on her: 'very ladylike, very delicate', he thought, to do so without his consent; 'what must the man himself think of such an invitation', he wondered. Fyans annoyed him too, when about to go with his regiment to Bombay, by sending his *hookabadar* to enter Blechynden's service. Blechynden told the man that he was already provided for. Then, worse, Arthur reported that he thought Fyans had formed an attachment to Sarah. Blechynden said that he was surprised at that, given that he had made plain his objection to sailors and soldiers, especially King's officers who were reduced to half pay in peacetime. All he wanted for Sarah was a man with certain income—Rs 250 to Rs 300 would be enough—who lived near Calcutta so that he could see her from time to time. Because of Fyans's effrontery in not appreciating this preference, he refused to accept a letter from him and asked Arthur to write to explain why. Tom Blechynden overheard Arthur telling his father that he had done so, and informed Sarah. 'This is the gratitude I get for educating him,' fumed Blechynden.

Fyans replied by asking Arthur to deliver his letter nonetheless: he was going to Bombay but was seeking a transfer back to Calcutta. Blechynden was adamant in refusing the letter and sought other reasons to back up his view: Charlotte was married to a captain and so his eldest daughter could hardly marry a lieutenant; he would carry her far from him; he was a stranger to them; they did not know his family or what he had to live on apart from his half pay. It was also odd that Fyans had told Arthur not to mention anything to a fellow officer, Hennessy, who had brought him to Blechynden's house originally. Why not, if he was an old friend? When Hennessy next came to dinner, there was a great deal of whispering between him and Fanny, and Blechynden hoped to hear later what it was about. (It does not seem to have been anything of consequence.)

Next day, Sarah appeared with a letter that she wanted her father to read. She admitted it was from Fyans. How could a man they had known hardly a month write to her, asked Blechynden. He refused to read this letter because it was addressed to Sarah. He noticed that it was an octavo sheet, in a scribbling hand, with lines crossed over like a Europe letter to save paper: a 'very impolite way of sending a love letter'. He admonished Sarah for receiving it, given that she knew his aversion to soldiers or sailors. She could have any other suitor: clergy, lawyers, doctors, civilians, merchants, even Company military officers, but not King's officers, sailors, or, finding another objectionable category, indigo planters. Blechynden went out shooting, 'his mind unhinged'. The family went to Dum Dum to hear music. On their return, there were tears. Next day, Blechynden went to console himself with his bibi Isabella, now in her own house.[12]

Fyans invited Arthur to breakfast with him. Blechynden agreed that he should go, telling him to put an end to the suit. Sarah found an excuse to spend the following day with a female acquaintance, saying it was her birthday. This was obviously 'a fudge' to avoid staying at home, considering it was Harriet's birthday too. She was in England, but Blechynden wrote a letter to her and Emma, drank to her health at dinner, and expressed his usual hope: 'may God make her a good and virtuous woman'. Arthur reported that at their breakfast, Fyans had started by saying that he was attached to Sarah. Arthur had advised him to give her up because of Blechynden's attitude. Fyans said that he knew his views but hoped his letter might alter Blechynden's mind. He would relinquish his commission for Sarah if he could find a civil situation; Blechynden perhaps might be able to help. Arthur was discouraging on that score also, and cited the fact that his father had been unable to find a position for Tom. Also, Blechynden was not rich: his income was smaller than his expenses. Fyans said that he had thought him too generous and hospitable to be rich, and again asked Arthur to speak to his father on his behalf. Arthur said that it would not do any good: he agreed with his father, remembering how they suffered from having a brother-in-law in the Company's army.

Fyans then said that he admired Blechynden's concern for his children, but when an attachment was formed, it was not easily subdued. It had not been sudden but progressive. Though he had only his commission at present and would not speculate on what might come to him, both his parents being alive, he had no debts and could live happily with Sarah. She understood how to manage and had not shown herself to be extravagant. Arthur told him not to hold out any hope. Fyans said that he regretted his poverty. Arthur commented that it would not help his case to suggest a pecuniary motive. Fyans replied that Arthur misunderstood: he meant that if he had been rich, he could 'command interest' and so quit the army and remove the objection to his suit. He did have a letter that he wanted Arthur to read and that he would enclose in another letter to Blechynden. It was from Lord Norbury (the 'hanging judge', another Irishman, John Toler, 1745–1831). Arthur urged Fyans not to send it. Their breakfast ended with Fyans expressing his keen appreciation of the family and of Blechynden's hospitality.[13]

A couple of days later Blechynden opened a letter placed in his palankeen box, but finding it was from Fyans, put it down unread. Quite upset, he went to shoot birds. A day later, he read the letter, which enclosed another: 'Surely my dear Sir it is not your intention to mortify my feelings or treat me with that indifference none but a worthless character deserves. I depend much on your kind and generous heart.' Accordingly, Blechynden at last read the original letter that was enclosed. It referred to Fyans's 'slow realization of sincere & unalterable attachment'. He had Miss Blechynden's consent to address her father. He set out his financial circumstances frankly. Blechynden replied that the letter pained him. He did not receive it originally because informed of its contents. Arthur should have warned Fyans from the first. He did not need the letter from Norbury, as whatever he had seen of Fyans in their short acquaintance showed him to be 'perfectly gentlemanly and satisfactory'. He had no personal objection to him, but only to his profession. He mentioned what he had gone through in having one daughter married to a captain who was in the field. Nothing would induce him to go through that again. He wished Fyans success in his life. Somewhat encouraged by this, which he considered a 'very kind letter' despite the refusal it contained, Fyans approached Betts and asked him if he could intercede on his behalf. Clearly urged on by his wife, Betts made a special trip with her to the gardens, in the sun, in order to approach Blechynden; he was not impressed by their charitable exertions and repeated his arguments. He silenced Mrs Betts by telling her that if Charlotte were widowed, he would have her back; but if Sarah married Fyans, he would not receive her again.

Fyans was still in Calcutta early in 1819 and had not given up. Blechynden reiterated: 'I love my daughter too well to send her to Bombay ... Kandiesh ... England ... West Indies to die of the yellow fever!' Sarah complained that everyone thought Fyans a very good match for her. Her father replied that a lieutenant on half pay was not a good match. The result was 'Tantrums'. Soon Sarah and Fanny fell out, causing Fanny to be very glum at dinner, her eyes filling with tears. Blechynden thought Sarah's 'ebullitions' unpardonable: she seemed miserable if she was at peace with her family members. Another letter came from Fyans and was returned unopened. Sarah took to driving to town and spending time with Mrs Betts, taking the carriage without permission. Its next trip, fulminated Blechynden, would be to the auction room. Meanwhile, there was charity for strangers. A poor man at the gate was given alms, a horse blanket for warmth, and two doses against cholera. Another beggar wanting shelter was 'much rejoiced' to be told to go to the charity school or the stables.

Blechynden's sleep was disturbed by Sarah's 'insolent deportment' and the suspicion that she was meeting Fyans at Mrs Betts. A Mrs Frome invited her to spend some days with her; Blechynden was sure this was a ploy to meet Fyans. He told Sarah that she had to stay at home to be with a girl who was visiting before she returned to school. He asked Tommy Betts if Fyans came to their house (he said not) and hoped that Tom would mention this to his father so he would know of Blechynden's objections: when people were not to be married, the less they met, the better. Yet another letter came from Fyans, postmarked Barrackpore, obviously sent through Charlotte, who had also written to Sarah. Fyans said that he regretted the artifice, forced on him in contradiction of the 'open and undisguised' conduct he was taught was 'safe and honourable'. He had hoped the 'powerful appeal from a child to a father' would have softened Blechynden and made him yield 'to the force of Nature', seeing how closely his daughter's happiness was connected with Fyans's. He was soon to leave Calcutta and had to try a last appeal. Blechynden's approval of a union between him and Sarah would ever stamp his 'kindness as a father ... and prove Sir your liberality and confidence towards a stranger'.

Blechynden was immoveable. He was, he noted, not blind to Sarah's imperfections or to 'the feelings of my own sex when a visionary passion is gratified'. He could not believe Great Britain would keep an army of 67,000 men in peacetime whilst the 'nation is ground with taxes'. It would be disbanded. Fyans would be forced to eke out life on half pay with a wife and perhaps children. Sarah would always be as miserable as Charlotte was. Blechynden resealed Fyan's letter and got Arthur to return it with 'as polite an intimation' as possible of his father's determination. Sarah had taken refuge once again with Mrs Betts, from whom Blechynden suspected she 'embibed no submission'.[14]

## DÉNOUEMENTS

Sarah had a kind of revenge on her father in lasting disruptions of family life. A few days later, she and Miss Betts did not appear for dinner at the gardens. Blechynden heard that they had taken the carriage to visit Mrs Betts, without a 'by your leave'.[15] He found it 'very mortifying' to be treated 'in this contemptuous way'. Sarah did not return home until after nine o'clock in the evening. On another occasion, she went out, kept away all day, and then stayed on to take part in a musical evening. Blechynden wrote to Warner about Charlotte's involvement, and Sarah complained that her next letter from her sister was 'very different' from the past and contained 'but one endearing expression'. Blechynden hoped that this was either spontaneously in response to Sarah's own 'philipick' (presumably a bitter complaint against her father) or, more likely, as a result of something said by Warner. It was probably not the latter, however, as Blechynden next received a 'very improper letter' from Warner—'to call it no worse'—that quite 'unhinged' him.[16]

A man came to the gardens with a note for Sarah that turned out to be a bill of forty rupees for a gentleman's fine engraved gold seal, from F. Dormieux, the jeweller. Blechynden supposed it was the fruit of her trip into Calcutta the day before. She was trying to avoid her father, but eventually he cornered her and asked what had happened to the seal. She said she had given it to a friend and, after being asked three times, admitted the friend was Fyans. Where was her pride and female delicacy, Blechynden asked; and '[w] ith all the brass in the world she replied "if I receive a present, am I not to give one in return?"'. There was no 'if' in the case, he replied: 'she ought not to receive a present from any one without her parent's consent'. Sarah went off to her room. Blechynden then tried to confine her to the gardens, forbidding the carriage to be taken out, but she got away in a palankeen with a friend who had been staying, a Miss Jones, who was part of the Betts household.

Fanny burst into tears when asked about this. It transpired that Arthur had ordered that no horse should go out without permission, except for the buggy horses, but not that Sarah be kept at home. It was not polite on her part, thought Blechynden, nor on the part of Miss Jones, who should have said farewell if she was leaving. Later, Betts came to say that Sarah was at his house, and after Blechynden told him that it was without his permission, shrugged and then walked off with Arthur, talking to him for a long time. Arthur later said that he had asked Betts if Fyans visited and he said that he had never seen him in his house. Blechynden felt this was no proof.[17]

When James returned next day, Blechynden told him that he had been to the court for a habeas corpus for Sarah, who had absconded. He blamed James for the example he had set. James was dumbfounded. Tommy Betts arrived. Blechynden took him aside and asked him to tell his father that he was glad Sarah was with such a respectable man but that she had left without permission and his orders were that she should return. She would be welcome to go back in future if they invited her. Tommy had told Arthur that he was afraid there was going to be a breach between the families.

After quite a delay—some debate, Blechynden suspected—a letter came from Sarah, requesting the carriage so that she could return and complaining that she had had to leave in a palankeen as the coachman had refused to take them when Miss Jones wished to leave. This was quickly followed by a letter from Betts, saying that his son Tom had passed on Blechynden's message, but adding that Mrs Betts had asked that Sarah be allowed to spend a few days with them and hoped Blechynden would be able to spare her. There was only one buggy in town and it was too late to send the carriage, and so a palankeen was dispatched to bring Sarah back to the gardens. On this occasion, Blechynden made her no reproaches whatsoever. When she asked for the carriage to take her to the Betts's next day, he ordered it and told her that she would have had it before if she had asked instead of sending him insolent letters. He wrote to Betts explaining what had happened and had a civil reply.

Somewhat later, Sarah asked if Mrs Frome, the wife of an army captain, could live with them until she moved to Ceylon. Blechynden agreed and remained at the gardens while Sally and Mrs Frome stayed in town. When he visited, he found the whole of the lower part of the house, the upper hall, and the room where he used to sleep so cluttered up with furniture that it was almost impossible to move. This, he hoped, would show Sarah what a soldier's wife had to bear. Worse, Captain Frome was head over heels in debt and was intending to sell everything to prevent its being seized by his creditors. Blechynden was not overly pleased to have his house used for 'such a transaction'. He commented to Arthur that if a captain who enjoyed the patronage of the Duke of York could not manage on his income, how would a lieutenant fare? Arthur confirmed that he had heard Fyans was indeed about to be put on half pay. Blechynden decided that he had been so eager to get a wife in order 'to assist in making the pot boil'.

Yet another letter arrived from Fyans, full of sorrow and regret. He was leaving Bengal, merited kinder treatment, was convinced Blechynden meant well by his daughter, but believed her welfare would be best served by their marriage; he had the good opinion of Blechynden's friends; and so on. He promised to return to Calcutta in some months and would hope for a good reception. Blechynden was 'prodigiously' vexed and started picking apart Fyans's words. Fyans referred to himself as 'honourable' and to be 'not taking an advantage'. Did he mean Sarah was 'so infatuated' that 'she would have surrendered directly and disgraced herself' had he but asked? Did he take her for a Miss Villebague? Referring to his friends' wishes was also 'pretty bold'. The Betts had been 'weak enough to intermeddle in family matters' and Mrs Frome had 'made some small flippant observations on the rank of King's officers'. They were hardly the sum of Blechynden's best friends. Fyans would never enter Blechynden's doors again. Blechynden spent a bad night, working himself into a rage about the phrase 'taking an advantage'. A little after this, he noted that James's friend Captain Jones (who also served in the 67th) spoke slightingly of Fyans and did not seem to like him.[18]

For Arthur's birthday in 1819 ('God bless him'), Sarah extravagantly bought a 'profusion of ice', half of which was wasted, and before that served a salted round of beef that no one could eat. (It cost four rupees and the *consomah* could have bought a whole ox for three rupees and then corned it.) Blechynden did not understand this 'fete', as they had never made such a fuss before. He suspected Sarah was trying either to curry favour with Fanny or to mark her contempt of Blechynden's other children. If it was anything, it was perhaps the latter. Two days later, Sarah went off in the chariot without asking, although Fanny had already arranged to have it in order to go to Mrs Betts. Two days after that, Sarah took the carriage to go into Calcutta with Mrs Frome, again not having mentioned the plan beforehand. She did this on purpose, Blechynden decided, as if she wanted to see how far he would submit to insults, the extent of his patience.

By February 1819, despite Fyans's persistence, Blechynden seemed to think that Sarah was looking elsewhere. For a dinner party attended by Betts, Mr (the Earl of) Warwick, and John Stewart, she wore her petticoats 'indecently short', displaying 'crossfolds of ribbon sandal fashion'. Her father remarked that 'she is much mistaken in our sex if she supposes that a snare'. But Sarah did retain feelings for Fyans. Blechynden's household remained extremely uncomfortable. One dinner passed 'very pleasantly' with James not speaking to Arthur and Fanny, and Sarah equally silent towards their cousin Tom. No one consulted his feelings, Blechynden complained. Several times, Sarah went to stay with Charlotte and Warner in Bandel, Malda, and Bueliah. It was a relief. Warner had been ill (taking mercury: Blechynden, who disapproved, said he would become a walking barometer). Warner got it in his head that Blechynden objected to these visits because he had not had a letter from him. Blechynden thought Warner ought to just come and spend a week with him to see how harassed he was.

He knew for a fact, from a letter James had incautiously let his father see, that Sarah was carrying on a clandestine correspondence with Fyans. 'How miserable the last year has been to me!' Blechynden exclaimed at the start of 1820; it was 'the most mentally afflictive' of his entire life, because of professional troubles but also his 'undutiful children'. Sarah did not forgive: not a letter could she write to other members of the family without 'having a fling at her father'. At the New Year in 1821, when Blechynden expressed his hope that the hearts of his estranged children would be turned back to their duty, Sarah merely coldly nodded at him, and shortly afterwards asked if he had had a letter from Fyans. As this not only ignored his ban on communication from him but meant that she was admitting her secret correspondence, he reproached her with 'undutifulness & indelicacy' and she 'went off in a huff'. Blechynden's ultimate response was to copy all Fyans's letters and set Gopey to reproduce them and Blechynden's replies, intending to send everything to the Commander-in-Chief.[19]

Sarah's housekeeping again gave grounds for complaint—rotten meat, broken china, and the bottle store having to be completely cleaned and fumigated with gunpowder and vinegar. Blechynden thought that she ought to 'learn the duty of a wife' by taking proper care of her father's property instead of 'whiny-pinying' about her soldier. Some female acquaintances seemed to Arthur to be officiously reminding her of her grievances, and now she was forever whispering with Tom. No one in his family 'seemed to know the meaning of word gratitude', complained Blechynden. Arthur welcomed the possibility of another guest in the hope of diverting Sarah, who annoyed him continually about Fyans, which meant everyone was uneasy. One day, Sarah went for a ride in a buggy with a man called Pringle and then seemed more cheerful, 'gay as a lark', blaming him for the way he was driving his horse, and also, with another female guest (not said to be very ladylike), tickling Tom about the ribs, according to Fanny. Sarah was 'too old to be a hoyden' was Blechynden's sour conclusion. But next day, she started quarrelling with him directly about Fyans once again, so much so that he had to escape into the garden, where anger and the heat gave him a headache. He was so annoyed that he completely forgot it was little Richard's birthday until Fanny reminded him to drink to his health.

Tom too started disappearing, not turning up until after 1 PM, 'pretending' that he had been walking. One day, Sarah received a chit, the contents of which she did not divulge to her father but apparently read to Tom. She first went to her room and then, giving Tom significant glances, went out on to the terrace. After a pause, he followed her. Blechynden went after them and said that Arthur had warned them against this continual whispering together: what was this 'eternal private confabing' about? They would have to be separated and Tom should look to provide himself with lodgings somewhere else. Tom was very taken aback, and after standing for some time, went off to his room. Sarah returned, smiling to Fanny, and after a time took her away—making her lamentations, Blechynden supposed. Tom did not appear for dinner. Over the next few days, he contrived to dine out. Sarah once again spent her time with various friends.

Finally, Sarah gave her father a letter from Fyans, from Kishenagur, dated 28 October 1821. He said that, not having received any communication from Blechynden as he had hoped since his return to Bengal, he was abandoning his suit after three years. He trusted Blechynden would forgive the uneasiness he had caused him. Fyans still felt an attachment to his daughter; it would cause him pain and mortification, but he could not marry without her father's consent. Though she was the 'most excellent and amiable' of women, he would not trouble Blechynden again. Wretched but sincere, he assured him that throughout he had behaved as a gentleman. Blechynden, who was not very well, admitted this was a relief. However, he had to have a last complaint: Fyans's secret correspondence with Sarah did not seem to him to fall within the definition of gentlemanly conduct.

At the new year of 1822, just a month before Blechynden's death, Arthur wished him many happy new years, Fanny embraced him, Sarah nodded at him, looking glum, and Tom took no notice of him at all. Sarah was shortening his days, he said, and as for Tom: 'education, board, lodging & raiment' were not worth thanking him for, it seemed. Tom's 'laziness & ingratitude' had 'nearly exhausted' his patience.[20]

With the benefit of hindsight, it is not obvious either that Blechynden's prejudice against Fyans was rational or that the pain it produced was worthwhile, given its effect on the Blechynden family and quite possibly on Fyans himself. Though Fyans did eventually travel far away in pursuit of a distinguished career, he remained a long time in India, and having courted Sarah for three years in his twenties, did not marry until he was aged fifty-two or fifty-three. For her part, after her father's death, Sarah returned to England, married Robert Graham Dobinson at St Pancras Old Church, London, on 4 June 1828, and had at least three children, named Robert, Sarah, and James. Robert Blechynden Dobinson, her oldest boy, died in Victoria, Australia, in February 1880. Though he bore his mother's family name, he may have been unaware of the share in his and his children's British and Australian heritage due to his Indian maternal grandmother, loved and remembered by his grandfather.[21] After as well as before Richard Blechynden's death, the Blechynden line was 're-legitimized' and 're-Anglicized'.

# 8

# Educated and English*

No man's knowledge here can go beyond his experience.
All men are liable to error; and most men are, in many points, by passion or interest, under temptation to it.

—John Locke[1]

## PRIDE

A father's strictures and the miserable state of his family life were, it is important to remember, expressions of care in Blechynden's mind. He was anxious for his children, and in that respect typical. A cameo performance of fatherly care, attitudes to paternal involvement, and an Englishman's reliability was provided by one Bernard Stacking, who came to talk to Powell about his son. Powell, a friend and occasional lodger of Blechynden, was just about to leave on one of his voyages; Stacking's son was presumably one of the ship's company. 'The feelings of a father are very natural,' wrote Blechynden. After Powell went out of the room, Stacking squeezed Blechynden's hand and wept. Blechynden said to him that he should be comforted. A Frenchman might have made a thousand promises about his son and would fulfil none of them, but Powell, making no promises, *would* take care of the boy. Blechynden also agreed to reinforce this with Powell by putting in a good word for Stacking's son.[2]

Beyond such conventional concern, however, Blechynden imposed higher standards on his children than on himself if one considers his

* Some sections of this chapter have been adapted from 'Children, Emotion, Identity and Empire: Views from the Blechynden's Calcutta Diaries (1790–1822)', *Modern Asian Studies*, vol. 40 (1), pp. 175–206 (2006) © Cambridge University Press, reproduced with permission.

concubines, though not otherwise. More than that, he insisted on such standards, sometimes above the norm, *because* of his own shortcomings and also because of the challenges provided by India and by changing mores. Of the last of these, Sarah no doubt gave evidence, though her rebellions were limited and symbolic: she was no Lydia Bennet, at least in her father's lifetime. Meanwhile, Blechynden's travails over the marriages of his daughters and the employment of his sons showed a keen and specific sense of responsibility for the children's future. He hoped they would behave 'well', and when he thought they did not, would be censorious and inflexible, as also towards his acquaintances.

In general, his reactions could be pragmatic, inconsistent, or emotional. He was swayed by financial considerations, seeking the security and comfort he thought appropriate to his and his children's station in life. But above all, standards of ethical conduct (as with Sarah and with James) shaped his actions and hopes. Arthur's professionalism had a moral dimension; James's (and Tom's) shortcomings were regarded as defects of character that would limit their chances of worldly success. These calculations were also culturally specific. Ethnicity and illegitimacy counted for little or nothing in Blechynden's consideration; the attributes of class and nationality were what mattered to him.

Loyalty to family, expressed by Blechynden through gritted teeth towards Marmaduke and Tom or by the Theobalds to two generations of Blechynden's family, was an expression of belonging, of identity, that (in Blechynden's stated philosophy) was also the basis of patriotism. So it was that Arthur made himself English, married a European woman,[3] and produced children who also seem to have married Europeans, as their children did. Arthur's children too were sent to England for their education. Charlotte married an Irishman; Sarah's suitors were all European. What had changed? Blechynden could joke about skin colour. On 'white ants', he remarked that some might be 'uncles' (not aunts), there were so many of them. Mrs Samuel Jones replied that she had heard everything was 'white' now at Blechynden's, a sly reference to his bibi, then European. Blechynden replied: no, Adam and Eve (James and Charlotte) were still brown. He feared that their illegitimacy would stop his daughters marrying—especially Sarah, after being gored by a dog—but mentioned Sarah's mixed race just once, when very annoyed that her delayed return to India was damaging her prospects. Then Fyans, a gentlemanly officer in a King's regiment, was refused and thought unsuitable to be her husband purely because of the insecurity of his profession. Blechynden proclaimed his expectations were modest when he wanted Sarah to have a husband of settled habits, cheerful, with some sense of religion, and at least Rs 300 a month, and not someone with riches or a title.[4]

Blechynden himself, for all his protestations, was now richer than before. But the real difference was the unspoken assumption that for the daughters, not only their education in England but their marriages would make them English, by assimilation: the husbands provided the added contribution that for the boys came from professional and ethical conduct. Charlotte and Sarah did not differ appreciably from their half-sisters, whose parents were possibly both European. In England, the latter also would be expected to become more like their father in class terms and in behaviour. After Blechynden's death, when Arthur was head of the family, Emma was married to a lieutenant, John Theosophus Lane, in 1826 and Harriet the year before to Alexander Davidson Rice.[5] James's bride was of mixed race, as he was, but generally the Blechyndens of his and the next generation overlooked their mixed parentage and admitted only one English, middle-class heritage. Their's was a melting pot, but also monoglot.

Some others in India acquired, or chose to adopt, a new hybrid identity, Anglo-Indian or Eurasian, that acknowledged a mixed background while also insisting on cultural affinity with their Christian, European side. Some mixed-race children undoubtedly 'became' Indian in the eyes of the English, if not the Indians. But the Blechyndens were on a journey shared by many of their 'fellow countrymen'; it repeated a trick that had been successful for centuries. It was also occurring at an interesting moment: as national loyalties and cultural affinities were being redefined in the aftermath of the union of England and Scotland, following the desertion of the American colonies, and amidst the upheavals of the French Revolution and the Napoleonic wars.

What was true of marriage was equally implicit, as said, in the sons' employment. James was 'genteely raised' and deserved a gentleman's situation. Having finessed the shortcomings of his youthful exuberance and arguably his character, he did indeed manage to find employment as a surveyor. Blechynden strove to have Arthur assist and succeed himself, but on merit, after serving an apprenticeship. The Blechyndens had a reputation for hard work, against what was perhaps not a high standard. (One military surveyor declared tetchily that Blechynden and his sons might 'kill themselves if they please', but he was damned if he would survey, in January, after seven o'clock in the morning.) Most important, however, even in employment, were probity and the avoidance of vice. His father did not need to warn Arthur to be careful, but he tried to give lessons to James.

Professional life had to be matched with either an impeccable or rather a deniable private life: the two were scarcely separable, as was shown when the 'libertine' James lost his first post. Arthur was the more successful of the two sons in this regard, in his father's eyes. For example, Blechynden hated the thought of a teenaged Arthur going to a nautch, but, after attending, Arthur declared himself disgusted. Arthur's own account makes it plain where he placed himself. He went, as a foreigner, to Rogan Ram Ghose to learn Bengali[6] and observed, as a foreigner, what he described as the three exogamous 'casts' of India: the Brahmans, Hindus, and Moormen, divided into many sects that would not eat or drink with each other. He was 'stunned' by the noise of drums at a Bengali holiday. Seeing Indian soldiers exercising smartly, he remarked, 'I am afraid some day they will be able to drive us out of the country.'

Arthur's strictures on India as an outsider were more about manners than essences. He reflected that being an architect, a profession good for mind and body, was not as agreeable as he had expected 'in a country like this where the customs and manners of the natives are so widely different from those of Europeans'. He found Indians unscrupulous, idle, and in need of constant supervision. True, he had been at first amazed at the people's resilience in the heat and had suffered very much himself. But such Indian problems were something to be overcome: he soon became 'habituated' so that he was no longer affected, even in an exceptionally hot and dry year, with temperatures over 120°F.

Acclimatizing to England, not India, was the key. Manners mattered and fell short also among country-born Europeans. Isabella's mother's abrupt conduct when Arthur first met her (described in *Sex and Sensibility*) 'proved her to be of no gentle family'. Finding Isabella herself ungracious at being given a present by his father, he remarked, 'Such are the precious manners of this Country! Thank God I was not brought up here.' When Isabella decided that she should leave and was upset at the thought of abandoning her daughter Harriet, Arthur exclaimed at the 'wretched education of this country' and thanked his father for having 'civilized' him by sending him to England.

He had brought back, presumably, most of the 115 books he owned when aged eighteen, and some linguistic markers of changes in Britain by his time: he wrote 'plaster' and his father 'plaister'; he 'dressed' while his father 'shifted'; unlike his father, for Arthur 'it's' meant 'it is'. More fundamentally, as soon as he settled in India, he began to attend church, unlike his father. He declared his 'grand rule in life' to be Leviticus 19:15, which he quoted in Latin: not committing evil but judging righteously, without discriminating between the poor or the powerful. He would not depart, he vowed, from the 'smooth paths of honour and justice for the rugged unsafe roads of vice'. Here his father *was* an example to him because, despite his heavy losses and debts, great obligations, and small salary, he 'kept firm to his well-known honesty and integrity' while he repaired his fortune. Another ideal may be judged from Arthur's remembering a school friend, Daniel Stevens, who wrote to him as a 'true John Bull, open and liberal', one who 'would scorn to do a mean thing'.[7]

Arthur was to be better than Calcutta and than his father, especially after Blechynden had accidentally flaunted his weakness when Arthur walked in on the bibi Isabella on his unannounced return to India. Fortunately, the costly and Christian education stood the test of exposure to Calcutta standards, and even equipped Arthur to become a kind of adviser to both parties and even a go-between in the long, torrid unravelling of the relationship. It brought him even closer to his father, as a confidant as well as a son, something again that was common enough at the time. Blechynden had only one recorded argument with Arthur, when a summons arrived for the non-payment of an account for materials. Arthur had (he said) repeatedly tried to pay the account. Blechynden was ill, stressed, and in a foul mood. He said Arthur was 'insolence personified', which was very hurtful to Arthur. Eventually, he wrote, as his father refused to listen to him. Blechynden put the letter down unread. He finally did read it, but still informed Arthur that he 'had acted the part of an idiot': how could he trust him with any business in future? Given his 'angry humour', Arthur barely defended himself, thinking privately that he had not acted as his father claimed. A few months later, he wrote once again in his diary of his gratitude to his father for all he was learning from him and hoped that he might be as clever and useful a man as he was.

Basically, all was well, especially with Arthur, because he proved himself firmly English and as principled as and perhaps even more priggish than his father. There were temptations: once when he was sound asleep, he was disturbed by a woman gently pressing his body, trying to arouse him, whispering that everyone was asleep, and trying to get into his bed. When he pushed her away and called for the bearer, she threatened to claim that he had 'been guilty of the crime' she was endeavouring to provoke. He gave her a violent push and called the *dhye*, who was sleepy and told him to go to bed. He asked for a light, which was not to be had, and so he bolted his doors, checked under his bed with a stick, and finally got back to sleep. The intruder—the second he had had to repel—was a *metrany* who, he assumed, was trying to get money from him. He had never taken any liberties with her that justified her coming to him and 'thank God', he exclaimed, 'I was able to resist my passion'. It was no wonder, he added, that young men were ruined 'in this infernal country where women endeavour to seduce the men'.[8]

It was of great significance that Arthur's diary began with a summary of his life, placing himself in the world, which entirely failed to mention his mother or to acknowledge his mixed ancestry. He resorted to innumerable excuses and downright refusal when Isabella tried to involve him in annual ceremonies, when lights were lit and food provided at his mother's graveside. He was surely encouraged by his father's assertion that insistence on these observances was decidedly unchristian in Isabella.[9] The trick had been carried out and Arthur was an Englishman to himself, if not unequivocally to Calcutta. He attributed his character to his father and his education in England, and constantly reminded himself of the merits and benefits of both. It was a double English inheritance, but also honed by his experiences in Calcutta after his return. He emphasized 'industry and honesty', and a somewhat vague humanism. Witnessing a hook-swinging ceremony in Calcutta, he remarked, with a seventeen-year-old's conviction, that it was a sight to disgust someone 'just come from England' who would 'hardly believe that a civilized nation could invent these tortures for the sake of pleasing God'. Indians claimed superiority, he said, but their 'pre-eminence' is 'only in their speech, for their acts disgrace human nature'.[10]

## MAKING INDIVIDUALS

Experience showed Blechynden that probity was no guarantee of worldly success; infamy was more efficacious. But he would not countenance any shortfall in his sons' or daughters' conduct that would undermine their reputation. The reason was he thought honesty, superiority, and acts that *graced* human nature vital to the project of making his children English. Let us explore what that meant. We need to retrace our steps and ask again what had been the point of sending the children to England. It was not only for pragmatic reasons, preparing them for future employment; or rather, in so far as it *was* that, the chosen professions indicated something more, and the same consideration made proper behaviour and suitable marriages so important. The children had English names and an English baptism. They were sent 'home' to 'enlarge' their ideas, to make them English by occupation and by culture. Could it be done? Blechynden thought so. Why else send half-Indian, Indian-reared children to England at an early age, condemning them to learn Bengali as a foreign language on their return? Such thinking had three main aspects: the notion of the self, the nature of identity, and the issue of race. In each case, the location, Calcutta, also mattered.[11]

Blechynden believed in the self as a product of education and experience, as proposed in Locke's *Essay on Human Understanding*. In thinking that an Englishman could be made, it seems that he also followed Locke in his ideas of human development[12] without noting explicitly that he was doing so. In Blechynden's own life, self-awareness was manifestly something for which he did not always have the vocabulary but which he nonetheless achieved as one part of a broader prospectus. He considered himself a man of rationality and science. He made measurements—for example, astronomical observations to correct clocks and watches—and he also conducted experiments, such as when dosing sick animals. While undertaking translations for the French traveller Pierre Sonnerat, he criticized him heartily for ridiculing the whole Newtonian system.[13] He respected Belidor, his guide to hydraulic engineering, as much as Palladio, his model for architecture. As remarked, he owned a set of Buffon's natural history.[14]

Perhaps he did not distinguish between the principles of engineering and aesthetics. Perhaps he did not concern himself at all with debates about taxonomy. But certainly Blechynden lived in an age when humanism and the scientific revolution affected the way people thought. On one hand, humanism, especially in rediscovering the classical, spoke to a constant inherent universal. The discovery of Indo-European by Sir William Jones, so admired by Blechynden, might be considered to embody that principle. On the other hand, the scientific revolution ultimately sought practical knowledge that would control and change the world, not understand it philosophically. Whereas Aristotelian syllogisms depended on the prior acceptance of a first premise that is taken to be universal (from common experience), modern science after the seventeenth century looked to individualized experiments in order to form and limit general rules.

This shift in emphasis between deductive and inductive science, as others have remarked, also affected the popular sense of self. To regard human nature as being derived from or subject to experience was, as Peter Burke argues, one (and not the only) kind of self-consciousness.[15] It was associated in Europe with the Renaissance, with authorship, portraiture, autobiography, and particularly travel. The problem of the Others encountered on journeys was of course writ large for Europeans who travelled and lived in India, even though they sought to make India familiar to them in many ways and to subordinate it to their own system of ideas. Experiment, exploration, and empire all required *unfamiliarity*, which reinforced the need to develop inductive methods, to reach out towards universal rules by explaining what was not known, rather than by generalizing from experience. The change is often linked also to the development of centralized states and to material culture: printed books, mirrors, personal artefacts, and so on. These too were the everyday experience of people in Calcutta as it became the seat of a bureaucratic, regulated government and one of the major urban centres of the world.

In this context, by keeping a diary, Blechynden was engaged in an observation of himself. As has often been remarked, a diary was a mark of introspection, of what David Riesman called the separation of the 'behaving and scrutinizing self'.[16] Blechynden was consciously, indeed artfully, preserving and reflecting on his life as narrative. When he encouraged Arthur to keep a diary, clearly he regarded the process as both therapeutic and improving. Keeping a record required reflection and judgement, and this ordered experience constituted the person. Gandhi referred to his autobiography and his life as an experiment, but some such idea of the self has a much longer history. As the Duke pronounced in *Measure for Measure*, 'Spirits are not finely touched but to fine issues'—which means not only that virtues need to be expressed in actions, but also that it is actions that create them. The idea of the 'test' as both a measure and a maker of character is central to that play and in much of Shakespeare, and was also an eighteenth-century commonplace. In Mozart's operas, for example, it is most obvious in Schikaneder's quasi-Masonic rituals for *Magic Flute*, but it is also apparent in the self-revealing flirtations of Da Ponte's *Cosi Fan Tutte* or the ordeal contrived for the Count in his *Figaro*; Don Giovanni's refusal to learn is his undoing. Within such plots, the self is being constructed in Locke's sense. In Cartesian terms, this is the difference between human awareness as intrinsic to a thinking being and as *derived actively* through the continuous process of thinking. In the latter case, memory is vital to recover the self from moments of self-awareness: hence the importance of the diary. Rousseau, whose notion of human nature in *Émile* is arguably just the mirror image of Locke's, set out the position at the start of his *Confessions*: 'This is what I have done, what I have thought, what I was.' By being sent to England, Blechynden's children were being tried and given the best chance to make themselves.[17]

## IDENTITY IN TRANSITION

Turning to the nature of identity and its creation or change, we see that the transitional nature of the times provided a special opportunity. Though there were special cases in terms of rights or treatment (Jews or English Catholics, say), European monarchs and states had long defined their subjects on the basis of *jus soli*, identity by place of birth. For the convenience of the state, all residents owed it allegiance. By the late eighteenth century, on one hand, the concept of 'country-born' for Europeans and mixed-race individuals born in India had extended the principle of place of birth, building on the related idea that culture and capacity could not be fully realized beyond the homeland; hence the vital importance of the English experience. On the other hand, the notion of the subject was also being stretched to cover those living in all territories owing allegiance to the Crown, an imperial concept that began with the American colonies and other plantings of the flag overseas. It was applied also to the union of England and Scotland; but not, for example, when earlier rulers had more than one dominion, such as England and Normandy or Gascony, say, or Spain and the Netherlands. As the state became indivisible (rather than a figurehead with many different local titles), it required and produced a common citizenship.

And then, in France, with the 1790 constitution and the civil code of 1803, another form of belonging had been devised, of *jus sanguini*. It offered a legal expression for cultural affinity. Notions of being English by blood already existed, of course, but they had had to be fairly flexible, as once again for 'British' after 1707. Blechynden's children were subjects of the king by birth, but their bloodline and class had to be established by forgetting their mothers. Their cultural identities had then to be reinforced and demonstrated through their life history, rather like all those other 'naturalized' English from the Normans to the Huguenots.[18]

At the turn of the nineteenth century, there was everything to play for as Blechynden's children sought to establish their status. Officials were struggling too: on one hand, placing restrictions on the employment of the country-born, and on the other hand, demanding the allegiance of all residents of 'British' territory. Arthur's return to Calcutta was without restriction, given his parentage, whereas young Richard Blechynden Brittridge, because he was not the son of a native woman, was allowed to rejoin his parents in India only on giving his bond of £500 that he would go back to England in the event of their return or death. Plainly, the rules of identity were in flux; and, as we have already noted, when norms were unclear and standards various, a greater role was demanded of friendship, moral conduct, and reputation.

We can take that point further. In a court case in 1804, involving measurements of landed property after the removal of a wall, a violent attack was made by the counsel on Blechynden's character and integrity. Sir John Anstruther, summing up, backed by his two colleagues Royds and Russell, made such a 'elogium', such a forthright defence of Blechynden that it became the talk of Calcutta. Its subject had missed hearing it, having forgotten to use his hearing trumpet, and thought instead that he was being condemned and would lose the case. Blechynden's diary, written after the event, once again narrates the story so as to play up the drama, suspense, and surprise.[19] Some people, not knowing Blechynden, were ready to believe the worst of him, especially as the magistrates to whom he reported were notoriously a 'set of extortioners and oppressors'. Others put the record straight from their own knowledge and by quoting the judges' verdict. Blechynden continued to be upset at the language and accusations of counsel, and was not at all appeased by being told that lawyers merely said what they were paid to say. When an acquaintance who (he heard) had believed the criticism came to sit beside him after the ladies left at a large dinner, he told him that he preferred to sit beside 'gentlemen'. That would show him, he thought.

In the adversarial court system of Calcutta, with its loose rules of evidence and procedure, the lawyer evidently tried to secure a verdict by unsubstantiated assertions—in fact improbable claims, as Blechynden was supposed to have corruptly favoured someone who shouted at and abused him, in preference to a client who paid him to make measurements. In turn, the judges clearly reached their judgement by bringing their own knowledge to bear rather than on the basis of evidence they had heard. At stake (apart from a lost cause and costs) was reputation, a challenge to who Blechynden was, which his reputation answered. In this respect, identity was not proven, as at the start of a trial, before a witness statement, or by hearing testimony; it was recognized. In such a court, then, and typically in Calcutta at this time, the person was not an objective and fixed entity, measured by standard markers such as name, date of birth, and nationality; but the product of a subjective acceptance that had to be continually re-established. The person was accepted by recognition, just as (in myth) a reincarnated god was, or a returned but unrecognized hero. Acceptance could even be effectively suspended, as in cases of insanity. This was the context for creating identities and defining them. It was a moment to be seized, not a permanent fixture.

Of course, trust and reputation will always be vital. But, as time went on, the realm of the objective, continuous person was expanded—for example, by definitive office, profession, qualifications, or record—while that of the subjective, experiential kind would contract, being a matter of personal and domestic more than of public concern. Another way of saying this is that it was both easier and more necessary for identities to be *established* in a partially regulated and objectified world. In such circumstances, it mattered greatly (returning to Locke) that experience made the man.[20]

Blechynden, believing this, traced to his childhood his own habits of early rising, for example. He always got up the instant he awoke, usually after about six hours' sleep, not only because lying in bed in a hot climate was debilitating, but also because he thought sleep a defect in nature that sadly diminished the time for active life and because, once awake, he considered it evident that 'nature is satisfied with the refreshment she has had'. As a child, he remembered, his mother would put him to bed as a punishment, even in the middle of the day: 'The *intention* was possibly to keep me out of mischief, but the *consequence* has been that of making a very early riser of me, from a dislike of bed.' The 'force of early impressions' was borne out also by remarks he recalled by 'the celebrated Dr Hugh Smith'. He had said in Blechynden's hearing, when he was very young, that the medical profession was 'very troublesome and irksome'. He would rather be a shoeblack, and as a boy, actually intended to be one. He took up medicine, Smith said, only because he fell in love with one Sally Brown, who would not have him unless he became a doctor. He signed on as apprentice to his father and qualified as a physician, though Sally Brown died. However, he declared, 'there is not one upon Tower Hill that should have put such a polish upon a shoe' as he would have had he been a shoeblack. This remark kept young Richard Blechynden awake half the night. It made such an impression upon him that he attributed to it his determination, ever since, 'that I never put a thing out of my hand but in the *best way* I can do it'. If he had any little merit (which he really did not pretend to have), he certainly owed it 'to Dr Smith's speech', he wrote.[21]

## NURTURE AND IDENTITY

As a consequence of this emphasis on experience or nurture, Blechynden constructed his view of childhood around notions of shelter and direction. If example and education were to form personality, childhood had to be a protected space: a construction typical of his time. It was desirable anywhere, but imperative amidst the dangerous corruptions of India, corruptions reflecting the famed barbarity of the East (transmuted from an earlier discourse of monsters, so Dorothy Figueira claims),[22] but more particularly the barbarousness of Europeans in the East. Such contamination proved the influence of experience on personality and also justified fears for the young. Blechynden was appalled at stories of indecency being relayed in front Mrs Tiretta's younger sister (much later Fanny Blechynden) and, on also being told that she was 'in love' with *him,* retorted that she should be sent to school and taught music, dance, and accounts. He was aghast when an acquaintance, John Da Costa, asked for a copy of John Cleland's *Woman of Pleasure,* which since its appearance in 1749, had been the most celebrated pornographic text produced in England. He was aghast because Da Costa said that it was 'the best book that could be put into the hands of a young person just arriving at puberty'. Blechynden railed against such a risk to morals and health; he believed that a father should 'stifle vicious sentiments as long as possible'.[23]

If his ambitions for his own children were essentially moral, it meant that they were to be brought up understanding principles that would show them how to behave—first towards their parents and siblings; then, by analogy, towards their fellow citizens; and then towards all of creation. Blechynden recorded one tale revealing some of what this meant and did not mean. The justice Levi Ball, then an officer in the army, had an elder brother who married an heiress with £20,000. Their mother possessed an annuity of £400. The elder brother promised that if she made it over to him, he would pay her £500 instead. It proved a swindle, for he paid her nothing. Levi Ball therefore sold his commission to give the money to his mother. He also promised his sister £200 if she was really in love with a young man whose father would not consent to the match because she had no fortune. This was 'acting like a son and a brother', in Blechynden's verdict. Similarly, after the death of the merchant Deverinne, his wife, whom Blechynden had gloomily predicted might follow her husband on to the funeral pyre, remained mistress of their house. Blechynden congratulated her sons on this treatment of their mother: it brought honour upon their father.

There was a right and a wrong way to create a proper moral sense. Edward Tiretta's way was wrong, for example. When his young daughter Angelique threw his favourite puppy to the ground and killed it, Tiretta was annoyed. Blechynden remarked that he had warned him against permitting her to pull sparrows to pieces as if they were inanimate things: if such cruelties were not curbed, killing puppies was to be expected. Tiretta himself set a bad example when he tested his gun by firing at a cat. He missed, but Blechynden thought the 'poor harmless Catt was an intended sacrifice to the Brejoo Tallow bridge', disputes over which had angered Tiretta. A few weeks after the puppy died, Tiretta quarrelled with his house guest Dr Burlini, who allegedly slapped Angelique for pulling another little dog about. Burlini asked Tiretta for the dog and was told that it had been given to the child to prevent her being struck on its account in future! Another furious scene soon followed, after the ayahs claimed that Burlini had hit the child again. Burlini would not give up the argument with Tiretta, even when told that if he did not find himself 'comfortably situated', he could go elsewhere. Later, when Tiretta shot at a tame adjutant bird, wounding it on the wing, he refused to kill the creature or, at first, to remove the injured wing, saying that it would heal. Blechynden thought it a useful bird, eating refuse, carrion, and frogs, and commented that he was often surprised at Tiretta's cruelty and at his 'permitting his child to have young sparrows and crows to play with and torment'. Blechynden and James Mackay (the Assessor of Houses) read Tiretta a lecture.[24]

For his part and on similar reasoning, Blechynden disapproved of cruelty *to* children—for example, in his view of the educational dangers of beating. It was to Mr Purchase's school at six rupees a month that Arthur was first entered as a day boy, aged four and a half. A few days later, he was reluctant to return. Blechynden wrote at once to Purchase to warn him that Arthur 'must not be corrected as it might have a very disgraceful effect on his riper years from the aversion he might take to his book'.[25] Add doubts over the usefulness of learning by fear, and this instruction was an echo of Locke's *Treatise on Education*, published in repeated editions from 1693. Despite the apparently growing popularity of pornography featuring flagellation, educational practice was becoming somewhat less brutal than before during the eighteenth century, as reflected in James Nelson's mid-century guide to child-rearing.[26] So too, when he heard his little daughter Charlotte crying, Blechynden went to see what was wrong, saw the nurse whipping her, and ordered that she be dismissed as soon as a replacement could be found. Again, he remonstrated with Isabella over her cruelty to their child Harriet, when she came to Blechynden one day with her face swollen and bleeding, complaining that her mother had beaten her. Isabella came to fetch her away and Blechynden asked what Harriet had done. She would not read her book, it seemed. Isabella had stabbed her twice in the cheek with a pen. Harriet's right cheek was bruised from Isabella's fist and there were lacerations inside the child's mouth where it had been struck against her teeth by the blow. Blechynden reproved Isabella gently—'too gently'—for 'this barbarity'. She replied that he had better get Harriet out of the house or she would kill her. He reflected that it would not be Harriet who would leave and told Isabella not to try to teach her any more. Harriet was then three years and six months old.

Blechynden himself would administer a beating to reinforce a point, as when his papers were scribbled on or when Charlotte nearly drowned James. His chief concern was to avoid associating learning with punishment. Once, working outside Calcutta, he investigated some piercing screams and found two boys, each hoisted upside down by one leg to the beams of a hut as a punishment (he found) for playing truant. He ordered them to be let down and would have had their master strung up likewise, that he might see how agreeable it was; but he had 'made himself scarce'. Behind all this was an expectation that education should inculcate principles and behaviour that were judicious, humane, and self-disciplined.[27]

## IDENTITY AND RACE

Finally, we come to the issue of race. The question of acquired versus intrinsic character is at the heart of the encounter of Indian and European. Mark Harrison has written about the relationship between climate and race.[28] He suggests that the development of the nineteenth-century sense of ethnicity depended on what he calls deep analysis as opposed to surface distinctions. Deep categorization depended upon intrinsic, unchanging biological characteristics, specific features that are the basis of the natural categorizations derived from Linnaeus. (Of course, they might also be *generally* formative, after Aristotle; in flux, following Buffon; or interactive, as in set theory.) Harrison suggests that for many, the starting point—appropriate equally to Christian and to Enlightenment thought— was an assumption of common humanity that differed through reactions to circumstance, a surface distinction. But if, say, an enervating climate predisposed the people of hot countries to stagnation and fatalism, would a European last long in the tropics without being corrupted? Could standards be preserved, living in the heart of darkness? (To be fair to Conrad, that reference is not entirely apt, in that his narrator Marlow specifically equates the darkness with a lack of civilization rather than with place, and his tale is at best ironic or equivocal about the benefits of an efficient imperialism, a point to which I shall return.) Nonetheless, as Harrison explains, in order to justify a tropical European empire, it was necessary to have a different theory explaining how Europeans would retain their supposed superiority. Accordingly, it was decided that it was not the bracing climate of the North which made them enterprising, but their inherited character; thus the East and the South could be conquered and reformed. As it developed, this idea would threaten the Blechynden children's transformation. Some came to argue that mixing races promised if not infertility (Buffon again), then even more extreme degeneration than was to be found in supposedly lower races or species of humans.[29]

Explanations of difference evolved over perhaps a couple of hundred years and did not emerge fully as a doctrine of race until the middle of the nineteenth century. In other words, Arthur's Englishness (the best documented example) took advantage of a window of opportunity that would never close but would be narrowed. For his part, Richard Blechynden was constantly aware of difference, but not just between Europe and India: it was also within categories of people according to behaviour and beliefs. He distinguished between Frenchmen of the ancien régime on the one hand and French democrats and free thinkers, whom he despised and distrusted, on the other. But if Frenchmen could change their nature by their actions, it was also possible for a boy born in Calcutta to be translated into a true Englishman, defined by mores and conduct. Blechynden had his own theory of patriotism too: that it was a natural attachment expressed as a series of circles of interest and partiality building out from one's immediate family.[30] His plan for Arthur and the others was to catch them within that net by making the circles concentric: kinship with an English father would be reinforced by ties with English relatives and thus with all the English.

## CLASS, CHARACTER, AND EQUITY

Importantly, at the start of the nineteenth century, class and status could still trump race—or at least mixed race—and also illegitimacy, as an extension of the power of family. Colonel Alexander Kyd, for example, was the father of two Anglo-Indian brothers who were close friends of the Blechyndens. They developed the famous Kidderpore dockyards, constructed by their father and partly improved by Blechynden.[31] When the boys first arrived back in Calcutta from England, having trained as shipwrights, it was arranged that one (James) would go to Waddell's shipyard and the other (Robert) to Archer's, which was one-third owned by the auctioneer Dring. Blechynden thought Robert would be better with Gillett & Edwards. He said so both to Robert Downie, who had arranged the placements, and to Jonathan Gillett, pointing out that Colonel Kyd's influence might otherwise be enjoyed by one of his competitors. This argument underlined, obviously, the position of the Eurasian offspring of an important man. The Colonel, it was said, had no objection to his sons 'working as hard as any of the Europeans' in the shipyard, but would not let them *associate* with such people. He did not require a salary for his sons, expecting that in time they would come in for a share of the business.

In the event, no change was made to the arrangements, but Robert Kyd later left Archer's, probably because of Archer's 'shocking temper' and for his habit of reserving, in any articles, the right to turn out a co-partner at the discretion of the partners. At this point, Blechynden again suggested a move to Gillett's, but Colonel Kyd preferred to place Robert too with Waddell. The Kyd brothers became Waddell's partners and their shipbuilding flourished. A little later, the brothers became stalwarts of the Anglo-Indian (Eurasian) community of Calcutta, rather than being absorbed into a European elite.[32]

The point here is not about equality or even fairness between recognizably different types of people. In the celebrated tale of Captain Stedman and the mixed-race slave girl Joanna in Surinam, she claimed that if he were to treat her with too much respect, he would 'degrade himself' with all his friends and relations. She refused to accompany him when he left Surinam; but she also declared that though a slave, she hoped she had a soul not inferior to that of a European. For his part, Stedman went through a ceremony of marriage with her. He borrowed heavily to buy her and their son's freedom and that of a boy servant. He acted on the view that humans 'only differ in colour, but are certainly all created by the same hand'. The moral, therefore, was not about universalism or oneness but about justice: 'if it has not pleased fortune to make us equal in rank and authority, let us at least use the superiority we possess with moderation...'.[33] The ambiguities in such attitudes were used by Christians to accommodate both the tower of Babel and warring tribes in the Old Testament *and* the equality before God of all believers in the New. (Islam too accepted this principle, as did some heterodox elements of Hinduism.)

Stronger than these ideas, however, in the late eighteenth and early nineteenth centuries, were the stereotypes of, say, lazy natives and upright Englishmen. Indian and European too were already meaningful labels. Yet there was still room for the humanity of the individual alongside the hierarchy of types, for many categories remained inchoate and inconsistent. It was for that reason, I suggest, that Lockean self-creation mattered and that Arthur, a boy of mixed race, could be transformed by education and partly by class. He could be John Halifax, Gentleman, *avant la lettre*— made by manners and not blood.[34] In Mrs Craik's novel, Halifax was orphaned but Saxon in appearance and allegedly the son of a gentleman. Yet 'he was indebted to no forefathers for a family history, the chronicle commenced with himself, and was altogether of his own making. No romantic antecedents ever turned up, his lineage remained uninvestigated, and his pedigree began and ended with his own honest name'. Moreover, at the end of the novel, he died peacefully on 1 August 1834, the very day when 'honest old England had lifted up her generous voice, had paid down cheerfully her twenty millions, and in all her colonies the Negro was free'. In short, John Halifax represented a self-made identity from experience and conduct amidst still-blurred intrinsic categories. He shared a just and noble Englishness and he exemplified the essential equality of all men, known by their deeds and not their blood.

The same was true in much neoclassical political economy, as when Ricardo defined 'rent' as unearned income.[35] That stance was apt while explorers and adventurers pursued trade and empire, and when individual local entrepreneurs were forging the British industrial revolution, as they would the American, to the same refrain of individualism. However, it was less fit for the age of the corporation, or its social equivalents, the community and the nation. Then the universalist ideal was increasingly clouded by racial stereotypes and distinctions, which relied once again on intrinsic qualities, as in Social Darwinism. By the 1830s, Arthur would have been an Anglo-Indian, put in a category with known characteristics.

It is not that self-improvement disappeared, but it came to be enacted within more complicated constraints. The muddle of Oliver Twist makes this plain: the workhouse boy steeped in crime turns out to have been a gentleman by birth. By contrast, in Great Expectations, Dickens seized on the ambiguities between the appearance and the reality of character, class, and ancestry (in regard to Pip, Joe, Magwitch, Estella, and so on). A more telling literary connection, however, may be that of Thackeray. After his Eurasian half-sister Sarah married James Blechynden, Thackeray himself benefited from Blechynden trust funds to pay off gambling debts in England. He admitted to feeling some guilt about Sarah after her death in 1841, and once had an Anglo-Indian niece to stay with him in England. But he seems never to have acknowledged or admitted the connection thereafter and it has been suggested that the references to mixed race in his works are marked by animosity.[36]

Deciding on the character of Eurasian people was clearly relevant to the transition between the autonomous individual and the type. Mixed race posed greater difficulties, the deeper or more intrinsic categorization became. Hybrids contradicted the sense of binary or unified categories, so that 'Anglo-Indian' or 'Eurasian' was needed and had to be given its own essential, defining qualities. In rejecting India and his Indian half, Arthur made of himself an autonomous individual, a process that was culturally specific and related to a particular value system.[37] Something of his attitudes came to characterize Anglo-Indians (Eurasians) even when it was no longer possible for them to merge into a single European society within India. Arthur could only be English by upbringing and conduct, according to the false syllogism: these are English qualities; Arthur has these qualities; therefore Arthur is English. The alternative proposition was: all Indians are unreliable; Arthur is part Indian; therefore Arthur cannot be wholly trusted. British officialdom came to see Anglo-Indians as suitable only to be subordinates, a standing that in practice (if not by label) was very different from that secured by such Calcutta luminaries as the Brightmans or the Kyds. The Supreme Court made an important distinction in 1822, ruling that illegitimate Eurasians could not be deemed British subjects for purposes of Company employment, a judgement against the Anglo-Indian Charles Reed. It was later challenged in England by John Ricketts, representing a new organization of Anglo-Indians. In 1830, the Company confirmed that they were to be considered (Indian) native Christians.[38] The small examples and particular cases discussed in this book, therefore, have a wider resonance, defining a possibility that seems to have been less complicated before about 1830 than it was afterwards. It might be thought that becoming English, as Arthur did, is not without interest to issues of identity for both diaspora and host communities to the present day.

# 9

# From the Everyday to the Imperial*

Train up a child in the way he should go; and when he is old, he will not
depart from it.

—Proverbs 22.28.

It is not time or opportunity that is to determine intimacy; it is disposition
alone.

—Jane Austen, *Sense and Sensibility*[1]

This book tells the story of Blechynden and his children during his lifetime.
Further information on the children and their families is now available on
the web.[2] The character of the girls would have been pleasing to their father
if it could have been said of them all, as it was of (Jane) Harriet, who died
young after childbirth, 'as a wife, sister and friend, she was most exemplary
and has left the memorial of her virtues deeply engraven in the hearts of
those who have known and loved her from her infancy, who must ever
mourn her early and sudden removal' (from her tombstone in the North
Park Street Cemetery, Calcutta).

The available story of the next generation of Blechyndens belongs mainly
to Arthur's children. They were respectable and prosperous. Arthur's will
revealed the extent of his fortune, referring as it did to his 'several landed
properties Viz. my Garden House at BellaCouchee my Dwelling House
No. 100 in Jaun Bazar Street my Timber Yard and working sheds in Jaun
Bazar Street situate to the West of the foregoing property my Brick Field
at Baletollah and Chuckerbere and the Garden Land at Cooleah on the

* Some sections of this chapter have been adapted from 'Children, Emotion,
Identity and Empire: Views from the Blechynden's Calcutta Diaries (1790–
1822)', *Modern Asian Studies*, vol. 40 (1), pp. 175–206 (2006) © Cambridge
University Press, reproduced with permission.

Southern Bank of the Beiliaghaut Canal'. One of Arthur's sons, Arthur Henry (1815–1894), was twenty-eight and Deputy Secretary of the Agricultural and Horticultural Society (he served it for fifty years) when he married Theodosia Eliza Francis, aged eighteen years, on 16 March 1844 at the Old Church, Calcutta. Another son, Charles Edward (1819–1914), was a merchant, railway inspector, and silk contractor when joint executor of the will of Thomas Blechynden in 1845.

Charles Edward evidently became the custodian of Blechynden's diary and presumably that of Arthur as well. Charles was the father of Kathleen Blechynden, author of *Calcutta Old and New*, a book that made unattributed use of the diary. Kathleen, a long-term resident of the Isle of Wight, was not only respectable but literary: her great-grandfather might have envied her settled and retiring life. The diary was then in the possession of Kathleen's brother, also called Richard (1857–1940), who bequeathed it to his executors 'Upon Trust for the British Museum, The Bodleian Library, India Office or such other body of similar standing as my Executors in their absolute discretion shall select and who may be willing to accept it'. It seems he may have read it, for he added cautiously, 'And I direct that on no account shall such Diary be published until the expiration of such period as my Executors shall in their absolute discretion consider reasonable.' He then included a threat to the very existence of the diary, perhaps to encourage those destined to receive it: 'And I further declare that in the event of my Executors being unable to find a Public Body of similar good standing willing to accept the said Diary within twelve months after my death then and in such case the entire Diary without reservation shall be burnt and destroyed.' Finally, he showed how much importance he attributed to the bequest by continuing: 'And further until the said Diary shall have been disposed of as aforesaid and an Affadavit by my Executors setting out how it has been disposed of filed in the Central Office of the High Court of Justice none of the legacies or bequests under this my Will shall be payable.' As the British Library accepted this bequest, fortunately, we are now able to trace not only the practical ambitions of Blechynden for his children, but also their underlying motivation and the character of his ideals, which (to an extent) his children and their children were able to fulfil.

## DIARIES AND THE SELF

The Blechyndens' diaries invite us to consider changing or constant concepts of the self. The nineteenth-century *Diary of a Nobody* was a satire precisely because biography, like history, was for heroes. The *Autobiography of an Unknown Indian* was written by one certain of the importance of his views on major events.[3] Quite the opposite is the standpoint of a private diary, even though it almost always assumes a reader. A diarist's record—the struggle to recall, order, and understand events—treats the personal as important not only because (to quote Roger Smith)[4] it was a 'moral and spiritual narrative', a record of the control and development of the self, but also ultimately because it was 'uniquely and irreducibly' the diarist's own—a criterion that is subversive of the priorities of history, though not of those of philosophy or literature. Richard Blechynden's diary provides many examples of ways in which information was sought and selected, criteria of explanation and justification, and modes of memory.[5]

Many associate such diaries with the emergence of a characteristically modern and Western identity, and more generally assume that self-perception differs between cultures. Blechynden's diaries adopt a narrative form to represent the experience of a self that is both constant and evolving, concerned with proper motives and moral actions. Excellence was attained during life, not judged after it, as in Aristotleian ethics or in those parts of Christian thinking focused on eternity.[6] Blechynden's views on children and education echoed this. He was also forever lamenting (and demonstrating) that sensibility was more powerful than sense. It seems Enlightenment philosophers provided much of his psychological vocabulary, rather in the manner that race theory pervaded the later nineteenth century or psychoanalysis the twentieth. The implication is that post-Enlightenment identities are traceable to, among others things, Descartes's idea of the conscious individual, Locke's arguments about consciousness and memory, and Hume's theories of perception and natural sympathy.[7] If such a new 'self' developed, it justified itself by the results of actions (as Bentham put it) not motives.[8]

The diaries join sentiment and self, as the title of this book suggests. Among philosophers, as far back as Aristotle's faculties of the soul (in *On the Soul* and *Parva Naturalia*), emotions were regarded as constituent of personality and coming in various forms: violent and passive; related to external stimuli, but most of all to internal appetites and conditions, as in the theory of humours. In the seventeenth century, emotions were equated with 'passions', following Descartes' *Passions of the Soul* (1649), or with 'sentiment' after Pascal's *Pensées* (1670). It was a question whether personality was fixed or responsive and evolving. We have seen how Blechynden negotiated this quandary. In the eighteenth century, Hume and many others explored and elaborately categorized 'passions', 'sentiment', and 'sensibility'. Hume paid attention to the sympathy experienced for the feelings of others. Emotions, including disorders such as melancholy or enthusiasm (religious mania), were now thought both to have bodily origins and to be contagious by example or influence. By the nineteenth century, moreover, the pursuit of happiness was regarded as a proper and necessary goal of human society.

Two changes seem to have been involved. First, it might be left to virtue and aesthetics—rather than denial or discipline—to moderate self-interest, as if (as Shaftesbury said, in 1711) morality derived from feelings rather than reason. It followed that 'sentiment' and 'sensibility' came to mean fine feeling and tenderness, and to imply generosity and gentility. Secondly, the ideas that external stimuli—for example, art—ought to be designed to promote emotional control and that internal discipline should shape conduct and the external world were supplemented or even supplanted by the contrary notions that external stimuli ought to excite the emotions and that the best self-expression would aspire to the heroic and the sublime. Thus, 'sentiment' and other cognate terms came to be imbued with new meanings, both negatively (as when explaining female 'hysteria') and positively, in public and private benevolence.

These ideas have been much discussed in regard to eighteenth-century literature, especially Richardson and Sterne. John Mullan analysed such 'sentimental' fiction as reflecting how sociability was thought to depend on the communication of feelings, sentiment forming social bonds. Ann Van Sant noted the mixed nature of sentiment (like sensibility, both physical and psychological) and its links to delicacy and to sympathy. In her examples, she found that the visibility of others' feelings inspired philanthropy and— relevant perhaps to roles of Blechynden's friends and servants—suffering invited both observation and engagement, a 'tension between curiosity and pity'. Barker-Benfield remarked that because sensibility was thought to originate in the senses, sentiment in the eighteenth century became associated especially with internal and external stimuli. Hence sentiment, though particularly associated with women acting in defence of their 'honour' or hopelessly susceptible to their emotions, also created a demand for manners and morality in men and children.[9]

'Sensibility' or 'sentiment' with such meanings as these was clearly a product of leisure or at least economic sufficiency and was expressive of civility. In large measure, it was either philosophical or literary in its lasting manifestations. But it cannot be denied a part in defining the British imperial 'burden': the supposed need for sympathy towards, but improvement of, the colonized. Turning to Blechynden's account, we see that he experienced sentiment—as understood in his day—both in his sympathies, not least for servants, and in his passions for his work, his children, and (in *Sex and Sensibility*) his sexual partners. And yet he always regarded himself as resisting the worst and welcoming the best in order to improve. The same conduct he urged on his servants, his friends, his children, and the Company's government. He created his identity, therefore, not out of all sentiment, but from a selection of sentiments. His feelings certainly defined him, but through his passion for justice and duty and against venality and negligence. Here was sentiment modified by sense and sense reinforced by sentiment. Like Bentham—a political philosopher who made so much of a feeling, happiness—Blechynden was very concerned about orderly and rational systems. Ruskin would later say that government and cooperation are the laws of life; anarchy and competition the laws of death. That is, as Blechynden might have put it, there are laws of self-respect and laws of selfishness.[10]

Roger Smith notices that seventeenth-century diaries reflected an individual's exploration 'of her or his own subjectivity … in a culture that valued such sensibility and refinement'.[11] In making such contextualizations, there is a danger of confusing the obvious linkage of society and self, both open to a variety of influences, with a necessary relationship between a particular environment and a primordial identity. I argue that a diary is a social as well as a personal record, but not that it must conform with a homogeneous prevailing ethos. Rousseau's *Confessions* (covering his life from 1715 to 1765) were deliberately at variance with expected morality—thus they laid claim to 'honesty'. Blechynden set up propriety and ethics as universal truths while also recording the continual derogation from them in Calcutta and in himself.

## ENCOUNTERS AND DOMESTICITY

The conclusion of *Sex and Sensibility* defends the historical importance of ordinariness and insignificance. The assumption of this book is that social attitudes are expressed and revealed in domestic trivia. Importantly, for example, the Blechynden diaries seem to challenge stereotypes of ethnicity. It is often said that formal autobiography depended on Western notions of historical causation and the exemplary life, while the Indian sense of self emphasizes community rather than individuality. Doubt might be cast on both ideas from Indian and Islamic antecedents. There is little evidence of the latter in my tales of Blechynden's servants and (in the other volume) of concubines. Perhaps communal identities depend on more certain concepts of status and more stable sets of relationships than experienced by many people in early colonial Calcutta.

The Blechynden diaries do record interaction between West and East and may sometimes reveal 'implicit understandings'.[12] Greg Dening invented another, much-quoted metaphor for such encounters: he called them 'crossing the beach', the process whereby a foreigner enters the island of another culture, one which he cannot decode.[13] How fitting is the metaphor? I question if different cultures are really islands, even in the Pacific, and 'other' to the foreigner because they are separate as well as distinct. I wonder if the encounter, the crossing of the beach, is always a 'dramatic' moment, as Dening puts it? Richard Helgerson, writing of Columbus's account of his voyage to the Caribbean and other similar books, claims that in them, 'Europe first saw the other, but ... also first saw itself interacting with that other', saw itself indeed 'as an other—... other, that is, than it ... had thought itself'. Expansion led Europeans to reconstitute themselves as trading nations. But of course, if understanding is limited and if there are problems of translation in many senses, then the resulting confusions and ill feeling may mean that others are denigrated as inferior or bestial.[14] This would be a dramatic response to the expansion of European power. Seeing the non-European world made Europeans form their own identities while incidentally foisting identities on others: orientalism, racism, nationalism, all children of exploration and of Europe's extension across the world; like other forms of modern 'knowledge', imposed by the powerful on the weak. Is it so?

One point to notice is that the encounter was not really sudden. Leaving aside the classical world and Arab contacts, even before the fifteenth century, the European world map was already being filled in. Tales of 'imaginary monsters' slowly gave way to eye-witness reports.[15] Blechynden was acutely aware of the difference between himself and the Spanish and Portuguese when travelling in their countries as a prisoner of war. He refused to pay for his prison billet, having no money but also (he said) 'more English blood than prudence'. The difference was partly Catholicism, as we would expect, but not only that. It related also to what Blechynden called 'Philosophical or Natural History'; to assessments of Iberian cities, architecture, landscape, food, and manners; to impressions of a different culture. The differences were so obvious to Blechynden that in his youthful *Journal* (1780), he said that he would refrain from cataloguing them. Blechynden in Spain already felt that he was an Englishman; in Calcutta, the otherness of the Portuguese or the French was as commonly in his thoughts as the strangeness of Indians.

More generally, the British denigrations of fellow Europeans as superstitious, idolatrous, idle, feckless, and unfree—all the things the British supposedly were not—were rehearsals for the assessments of more distant peoples such as those of India. The perceived problems of others (disunity, despotism, famine) were thought to be the opposite of Britain's experience. They were attributed to the enemy, France, and only later to the colony, India.[16] Alienation did not depend upon experience within any particular or wide geographical spread. It could rest on unfamiliarity in the next county, the next valley, the next family, or the next person. Hence denigrations of others do not originate with power, as is sometimes supposed. In some senses, they reflect powerlessness: inability to penetrate mysteries. Power articulates them as public systems of belief and gives them practical consequences.

Indians in Bengal also were witnessing an ever greater panoply of otherness and had been doing so for generations. One might cite Mughals, non-Bengali Hindus (present as zamindars and princely exiles), 'tribals', Malays, Portuguese, Greeks, Danes, Germans, Italians, Americans, Africans (most of these mentioned by Blechynden), plus those also listed by the eighteenth-century traveller Dean Mahomet: 'The greatest concourse of English, French, Dutch, Armenians, Abbyssinians, and Jews ... besides merchants, manufacturers, and tradesmen, from the most remote parts of India'. That 'Indians' are set as a group against non-Indians may be significant, though Dean Mahomet could be a special case, because he was writing in Europe.[17] Arguably, therefore, what happened as Europeans explored the world was not so much that identities—the self and the other—acquired their particular form and hierarchy, but that they became more complex and generalized. It was less to do with encounters than with nation states, institutions, and technologies; with information and ideas.

The idea of an encounter depends upon the depiction of cultures as closed. Perhaps, on the contrary, islands of all kinds have had such a hold on the imagination—from Prospero's to Shangri-La—precisely because they are different from the norm, because they are *artificially* isolated and distinctive. Blechynden seems to tell us that there was no pre-existing or fixed sense of categories. After a dinner in December 1793, he recorded how one Mr Corbett had made them 'all laugh very heartily at his descriptions of England and the customs there—and how most surprised they were at his East India fashions'. Blechynden was not securely 'English', though he thought he was, and he certainly did not encounter some fixed category of Indian.

The encounter was incomplete and it was conducted through local intermediaries who helped shape it. C.A. Bayly has written of an indigenous information order—the British manipulated it and were influenced by it, and it also adapted itself to changing conditions. Alternatively, the encounter was avoided altogether. Blechynden continued to spend most of his time in a milieu familiar to him; often, he ignored or misunderstood anything that seemed strange. As one study of early Calcutta said: 'it seems to have been a miniature London ... The East is entirely absent' from the record; 'so far as this city itself was concerned... All those old letters and documents speak in the same tone and of the same things that one would expect to find in similar letters written in England.' However, this last point also overstates the case. Lovers of the city will reluctantly agree with a 1928 guide: 'few things on earth ... can compare, as a method of torture, with the moist heat of Calcutta from May to August', for 'Calcutta has Three Seasons'—hot, wet, and cold—which 'may be reclassified into only two, Bearable and Unbearable. The cold season is the former and the rest the latter'. The weather alone prevented even the grandiloquent Calcutta 'white town', or later the ersatz-Surrey hill stations, from truly being 'forever English'.[18]

Blechynden subscribed to the prevailing view that Calcutta's climate was 'ungenial' [sic] to a European's 'Constitution'. Yet in general, he conveyed remarkably little sense of Calcutta's 'oddity'. In Elizabethan Britain as well, some well-travelled merchants, without noticing it, used measures and weights whose names had been imported and were unknown to the English language. So too was much of the polyglot vocabulary of words and life in eighteenth-century Calcutta.[19] Blechynden counted in lakhs and measured in feet and inches. The marvellous *Hobson-Jobson*, a compendium of Anglo-Indian usage, later encapsulated the familiarity of this strangeness. The Englishman made himself at home in the new city and land, and became not quite aware of which parts of it were new. The Indians did the same, though of course the familiarity was never with exactly the same city for any two classes or communities.

Calcutta represented the emergence not just of a single authority in the state, but also of separate, objective, generalized, and secular hegemonies in law, science, and the marketplace. Yet it was no mere 'facsimile' of modernity (to paraphrase a recent South African study).[20] Nor was there a sudden jump from one 'order of things' to another. What Foucault called heterotopia coexisted with modern orthodoxies.[21] One reason was that Calcutta soon became familiar both to the would-be colonizers and to the so-called colonized. I do not just mean the facility in foreign languages and concepts achieved by Orientalists such as William Jones or Bengali intellectuals such as Rammohan Roy. I mean the extent to which Indian experiences were accommodated by Europeans. On one hand, Edward Said has remarked: 'Far from being unitary ..., cultures ... assume more "foreign" elements than they consciously exclude.'[22] On the other hand, Bishop Heber explained, musing that the indelicacy of naked Indian figures was obscured by their different skin colour, 'So much are we children of association and habit, and so instinctively and immediately do our feelings adapt themselves to a total change of circumstances! it is the partial and inconsistent change only which affects us.'[23]

Sometimes, too, contempt implies a familiarity that bred it. Another element in European condescension was appreciation of the 'picturesque', perhaps with dubious overtones. Towards the end of the nineteenth century, the vicereine Marchioness of Dufferin and Ava, arriving in India, was amused at having in her private chamber, instead of 'one neat housemaid', some 'seven or eight men in various stages of dress [from smart tunics with gold braid to a mere cotton rag], each putting a hand to some little thing to be done'. She applauded her husband's perpetual artistic delight 'over the muscles exhibited by those who wear few garments', such as 'bronze athlete' waterbearers or the 'small boys, lightly clad', whom he proposed to employ for fetching balls on his new tennis court. The numbers involved and this frisson of impropriety both remind us of the extent of intercultural contact even at the most rarified social levels, even after a European *cordon sanitaire* was said to be in place, especially for elite European women. Meanwhile, the Marchioness's keen eye for dress extended to a regret at any adoption of European clothes by the girls of the Zenana Mission. This was romanticism, not respect. The vicereine's reaction to the charming Maharani of Kuch Behar was that, *though in 'native dress'*, she 'must be very intelligent—she has so quickly and completely got into European ways'.[24] On one hand, there was arrogance. It required, on the other hand, contact and observation.

The colonial state is sometimes seen as a distinct type, opposed to the modern state as much as to the nation state and epitomized by alienation, exploitation, and oppression. Eloquent personal testimonies still speak to a harsh social and political divide between Indians and Europeans.[25] But it was a divorce between people profoundly influenced by their cohabitation. Indian voices imply arenas from which Europeans were absent and excluded—in housing, food, ritual, and medicine; in social, sexual, and family relations; and in attitudes. However, they suggest excluded spaces, not wholly disconnected spheres or classes. They also indicate points of contact and influence.

## MISRULE AND ENGLISHNESS

At the start of the second part of this book, I noted that aspects of the preceding chapters revealed the impact on Europeans' identity of their positive and negative relations with Indian servants and of a narrative of Indian misdemeanours. Subsequent chapters reinforced what had already been said on the influence of *European* corruption on empire and identity. If the legacy of imperfections and system for Indians was one important subject, another was the way the same imperfections and system impinged on Europeans. Finally, therefore, I return to the question of the Blechyndens' Englishness.[26] In what did it consist? It was a specific set of characteristics, behaviour, and attitudes. It tells us something about the Calcutta of Blechynden's day and about British self-perception.

For Blechynden, 'English' and 'British' were largely interchangeable (though of course still distinct for others, especially the Scots, who were so important in Calcutta).[27] The standards that made his family English were, in part, also the markers of the Britishness that justified imperialism. Blechynden's attitudes display these markers, for example, in the duties of friendship or the education of children, especially the 're-creation' of Arthur. We saw them too in *Sex and Sensibility* when Blechynden's awareness of the impropriety of his sexual relations worked through his sensibility to the construction of rules of conduct, even in regard to bibis. The same connection between transgression, regulation, and good conduct also featured in many other arenas. It led to the hope of improvement, before that became a byword of Victorian altruism and self-interest. Let us turn to these broader contexts.

As already noted, the East India Company was developing its own notions of public service from the 1760s to the 1840s. Peter Marshall documented both the making of what he called *East Indian Fortunes* and the attempts to regularize Bengal administration.[28] Contrary to common opinion and despite the excesses of interest groups and of many individuals, Company servants recognized from their first exercise of political power that the Company needed to take a long view rather than a quick profit. Amidst public and private greed, they conceded that it had a duty of care to its Indian subjects. The famous indictments by Burke and the attempted impeachment of Warren Hastings were party-political skirmishes rather than the introduction of a great new principle. Hastings agreed with Burke that government bore responsibilities and, despite a ruthless pursuit of private and Company profit, he also supported very many initiatives that were unlikely to pay directly but which accorded with post-Enlightenment theories on government in society. His or his contemporaries' concerns with landed property, legal rights, education, and scholarly or geographical explorations all fitted some idea or other of the proper conduct of states. They reflected an increasingly competitive image of enlightened rule—so Prussia one day, England and France the next, and tomorrow Bengal.

Historians began to recognize this with the reintroduction of ideology into what had been largely Namierite accounts of East India Company politics. Noted also, at the institutional level, were the Company's increasing regularity of process, its concern for legality, and its more systematic records.[29] The Company began to profess rationality and benevolence. It sought to govern on the basis of information and analysis, as in the surveys, measurements, and reports required of the Blechyndens. Thus it generated expectations, including ethical conduct and an esprit de corps. In practice, the Company's structure, procedures, and terms of employment were still quite some way from the ideal of a modern government or corporation; but they had started to approach that ideal, in order to meet the challenges of administering vast territories and to rehabilitate the Company with the British elite.

There developed, in effect, a demand for public efficiency. New definitions of corruption appeared. In rhetoric, if not practice, it was now increasingly seen to be 'corrupt' for anyone holding public office to use it for private profit or advantage.[30] There arose too a renewed professionalism, whether in general or in specialist services. Even in advance of the demand for formal qualifications, many official and civil tasks were being reserved, at least in theory, to those with proven competence in them. From clerks to surgeons, more of the employees of the state and the servants of the public were being publicly trained—that is, made fit to do their 'duty'. Abroad, the experience of facing the unfamiliar added impetus to this demand for expertise. Empire made it desirable to possess knowledge rather than to rely only on native informants; and that meant policing the possessors.

The usual assertion is that these changes provided arguments to excuse the known injustices and abuses of empire. It may be, however, that the relationship between the abuses and the arguments was more direct. Announcing its virtue while falling far short operationally actually reinforced the Company's aspirations, because the shortfall encouraged further rules and better processes. Examples of Europeans 'corrupted' by India helped *generate* technical and bureaucratic improvements as well as the rhetoric of duty and responsibility then deployed to justify empire—in some cases by Indians as well as the British. Some of the imperial ideas of European superiority and duty the Blechyndens clearly internalized, either in the face of obvious corruption or because of it. That last counter-intuitive proposition is worth testing through the specific example they provide.[31]

At this time, public and private interests remained blurred, despite the reforms of Hastings, Cornwallis, and Shore and the imperialism of Wellesley. Many individuals in the Company's employ still profited on their own account, both honestly and dishonestly, from undertaking the Company's work. As surveyors also responsible for roads and drains, the Blechyndens were well placed to observe how Company materials and workers were deployed in the private houses and gardens of influential officials, including judges. Richard Blechynden suffered when the costs of Calcutta's improved Circular Road were grossly inflated in order to conceal the private profits made from the supply of materials for building Wellesley's excessively expensive Government House. The Police Office, responsible inter alia for public works and road maintenance, seems to have been particularly irregular. As Arthur wrote in his diary in 1807, the magistrates were 'so slow in their operations, and so lazy and negligent in their duty' that business could hardly be carried on, works were continually delayed, sure justice was not to be obtained, and bribery was rife. In May 1809, the accounts for December 1808 had still not been made out, though payments were continuing in a haphazard way once approved by the Auditor-General, whose requests for explanations, however, tended to go unanswered.[32] The chief agents of this inefficiency were two of the justices, Martyn and Blaquiere.[33] Martyn had long been notorious for his private life as well as the capriciousness and partiality of his legal judgements. Blaquiere was said to be the 'corruptest man in the whole Settlement'. At one count he held fourteen offices, but was still grasping for profit.[34]

Arthur's testimony is useful because he was reflecting on the environment for the first time as an adult. His father's attitudes were very similar, however, even though we cannot recover them at the same stage, just after his arrival in India. The experience was a lesson in proper conduct, on *not* acting as some Englishmen did in India. Arthur and his father had plenty of complaints about Indian judgement, reliability, and workmanship, but it was European corruption that most held their attention. The years of

Arthur's apprenticeship saw a struggle of power and principle, in the course of which he and his father redefined their own standards and character. A brief account will demonstrate the point. The cases were experienced by the Blechyndens but exemplify a more general crisis in public life.

In the early years of the century, the justices began to withdraw aspects of work from their Superintendent of Roads, Blechynden. They entered into contracts for the maintenance of particular streets and for the supply of materials, labourers, and transportation. They professed to be trying to remedy problems of cost and supply and to be relieving the Superintendent of tasks he was too busy to perform. They were acting, they claimed, in the public interest. Various battles ensued over supplies and appointments. Posts were abruptly withdrawn from Blechynden's men (road peons, scavengers, and so on), who were replaced by new people who would answer only to the justices or their agents, though the Superintendent remained technically responsible for them and their work. Blaquiere's men took to insulting Blechynden's servants, jeering that their master's job had been taken away from him. His position became virtually untenable, while the roads deteriorated and floods threatened because of unrepaired drains. Blechynden was held to account while being denied the means to provide remedies.

Power was arrogated in particular by a Constable Hessen, a Dutchman supposed to be employed to assist the Superintendent. Hessen obstructed Blechynden at every turn, refusing his requisitions for supplies. He was a 'creature' of Blaquiere's. He was also clerk to a public market, where he collected dues and ground rents. He was said to make appointments to posts carrying a stipend of four rupees a month in return for bribes of at least twenty rupees; he refused one offer of four monthly instalments of eight rupees. He took control of the Company's carts, which he could use for private purposes, and of the certification of the numbers of workers and the quantities and quality of materials that he or his associates had supplied. He was thought to be pocketing ten or twenty rupees a day just from unclaimed property recovered from the streets and supposed to be sold for the public purse. He was certainly obtaining income from those who were making encroachments on the public roads, the prevention of which was a major preoccupation of the Superintendent. Blechynden found his men resisted by an insolent insistence that some illegal building or other had been sanctioned by Hessen. The constable himself received fifty rupees a month for allowing illegal trading on part of the Circular Road. More lowly employees too took advantage: the scavengers (or street cleaners) became notorious for their demands, for 'tricks upon tricks', impositions sometimes so glaring that investigation could not be avoided. But always, according to the Clerk to the Police Office, Blaquiere ensured that the inquiries were dropped.

The confusion no doubt owed much to the indolence and the other occupations of the magistrates. But it was also convenient for them. The contract system was instituted in the face of Blechynden's repeated recommendation that direct working and a single line of authority be instituted, a reform again suggested by others and again not implemented in 1811. The magistrates' motive was plain: the contracts that were issued were in effect with Martyn and Blaquiere themselves. Martyn's agents included one Sunkur Mundal, who supplied bullocks of very poor quality and made 'a good deal of profit' for Martyn. Others of his associates supplied labour. The workers' pay was kept months in arrears until they refused to work, while the daily returns recorded more workers than were employed. From the resulting margins, the contractor paid Martyn.

Blaquiere supplied the bricks and gravel for the roads, a corrupt connection that caused comment but no action from his superiors. He had promised an improvement in quality, but what he supplied was worse than before, often so bad as to be unusable. In time, his men also took over the maintenance: at first, as said, for particular roads—a contract for Kidderpore Road, for example, given to one Kinker Banarjeah. This man later revealed many of Blaquiere's secrets to the Blechyndens in revenge for being excluded from new arrangements with Hessen and fobbed off with a retainer of fifty rupees a month, a fraction of his former profits. Later, when Blaquiere discharged Blechynden's men and replaced them with his own, his takeover of general road maintenance opened up further possibilities for fraud, as earlier for Martyn. As said, there was no independent check on any of the measurements. In July 1812, Arthur made a rough assessment of the materials stored at the riverside landing places and concluded that only a small fraction of the quantities being charged for even existed in the town.

Blaquiere's abuses allegedly extended wherever he had influence. As a justice of the peace, he was said—by the Anglo-Indian Charles Reed, who threatened to expose him—to have conspired to protect one of his associates from punishment, in a typically elaborate scheme to thwart the Sadr Diwani Adalat. That court had forced Blaquiere to convict one of his associates, whom he then incited to take out a complaint against himself with the Supreme Court for false imprisonment. Similarly, at the Alipore gaol, the European Chief Warder reported to Blechynden that he could do nothing against Blaquiere's people, led by a Bengali 'who does everything as he pleases', consorting with the leading prisoner, monopolizing all the gaol's supplies, and giving his orders daily to the other guards, sitting on a carpet 'like a chief'. Many prisoners were dying from neglect, while the gaol's surgeon, Dr Young, merely took his salary and came occasionally to the Bengali warder's house, with 'great hauteur', to write the death certificates.[35]

Blechynden naturally rallied his friends to try to remedy the situation in which he found himself. He dropped hints and snippets of information in what he hoped were receptive ears at Government House. His strongest threat was to create a storm by writing officially to the Governor-General. But there were risks. His complaints could rebound on himself. Just as Blaquiere and Martyn manipulated the law and their office to protect their men, so too, they could be supported by highly placed Company officials, often their schoolmates or friends, possibly those with whom they had shared a voyage from England. Both men were repeatedly confirmed in their offices in the face of barely concealed scandals. Blaquiere, who enjoyed a long life, was celebrated by his later contemporary, the Rev. James Long, as the 'oldest [European] resident' of Calcutta, a kind of father of the Company's town.[36] As in many more recent situations that resemble early Calcutta (in that respect), corruption relied on lack of effective scrutiny from within as well as from a suffering public.

Recording the abuses in his diary, Arthur expressed private indignation: his father's interest was in jeopardy and he himself was being denied office as his deputy. He still expected a post to be created for him as his father's son and through influence. On the other hand, as befitted this transitional period, he justified his expectations by claiming that he was well qualified after a formal apprenticeship and that a need had been demonstrated through his having undertaken the work unpaid. In his criticisms of the magistrates, moreover, he also appealed to the public interest. He sought probity, as professed in the Company's own declarations and as promoted by activists and critics such as Charles Reed. Both Blechyndens repeatedly expressed a confidence that justice would be done and that villainy would not pay in the end. The terms of Arthur's indignation are significant. 'It is lamentable', he noted, 'to reflect that such iniquities are suffered to pervade almost every department' of the Police Office. Referring to Blaquiere, '[h]ow much longer', he asked, 'will the strong arm of friendship continue to support his abominable system calculated solely to benefit a Magistrate and his creatures'? 'How improper of him,' he wrote on another occasion, 'to make his duty subservient to his interest 'How infamous!' he exclaimed of Martyn's conduct, 'How degrading to the character of a British Justice of the Peace!'[47] Two things are plain: the problem was unBritish conduct, as Dadabhai Naoroji would later argue, and the remedy was regular administration. Autocracy would reform itself through its own atttitudes and institutions, if it were to be reformed at all.

There was no even progress (the baleful effects of failure have appeared often in this book) but regularity was presented and increasingly internalized as an ideal. Around this same time, John Eliot, nicknamed Tipperah Jack, Judge and Magistrate of 24 Parganas and Superintendent of Alipore Gaol, was appointed as a justice in the Police Office and also to the Committee for Improvement. In Blechynden's view, he was overbearing and insolent. The worst of his behaviour was probably to be seen in the deplorable conditions still continuing at the Alipore Gaol, reported to Blechynden as he inspected its collapsed water reservoir. Eliot did not visit the place for months, but he was continually remitting prisoners. This was because he tried to undertake too much, had no time to carry out his duties, and was constantly in arrears of work. Also his judicial practice was no bettter than that already observed in others. He committed defendants to prison without investigation or any trial worthy of the name, usually without hearing a word from them in their defence. He awarded indeterminate sentences that were grossly inappropriate or for a non-offence: a bear handler imprisoned indefinitely, for example, because Eliot's horse shied at his bear, which was shot. To cope with the inrush of prisoners overwhelming the covered prison, Eliot established a compound surrounded by sticks—a concentration camp before the name—in which 500 were confined, exposed to the sun and rain, wholly isolated from the outside world. Those who fell ill were taken to the hospital; if they died, as they commonly did, their bodies were thrown in the nullah; no relatives would be informed. The man, Nash, ostensibly in charge of the gaol and appalled at the conditions, was entirely intimidated by Eliot and fearful of losing his post at the slightest pretext. So no word of this abuse, apparently, reached the ear of the government.

Eliot's philosophy was that 'nothing is done in this town or country but by the point of the bayonet'. He was thus the very caricature of a bigoted imperialist, but he was also a 'blind zealot' who would 'set all parties at loggerheads'. At first, he was for wholesale reform of the management of roads and conservancy, and putting everything entirely under Blechynden. Then he interfered with and countermanded Blechynden's work on roads, drains, and bridges, so that many people urged Blechynden to make a formal complaint. Eliot proposed to require lanes to separate the houses and huts being rebuilt after a fire, a policy Blechynden supported but which he also argued had to be introduced by due process: this was

Calcutta, not the mofussil, and Eliot would 'get into a scrape' if he acted illegally and without taking advice from his several lawyer colleagues. Eliot wanted to pull down buildings to improve the drains and to build new roads using a large government advance, paid back from the lottery. Blechynden replied that he would bring lawsuit after lawsuit upon himself. Eliot then wanted to 'check the interference of the supreme court'. Blechynden said that people could not be divested of their property on his *ipse dixit*.

Eliot horsewhipped passers-by trying to cross a nullah where work was in progress, including a havildar (sergeant) leading a guard of sepoys. Luckily for Eliot, the havildar refrained from retaliating, but was thought bound to complain to his officers. Eliot threatened to flog the scavengers (their management by then taken away from Blechynden) if they put in any more petitions to the Governor-General. Blechynden remarked that petitioning was the right of any British subject. Eliot confined fourteen fishermen and banned from Calcutta the small—he said 'stinking'—fish eaten by the poor, so that no fish at all were available ('with the usual stretch of power inherent in Blackey'), leading to petitions to the government from the fish-sellers. In 24 Parganas, Eliot was said to be ignoring court orders to discharge persons being held, and some months earlier was said to have had more than 300 complaints brought against him before the Court of Circuit. He summarily executed a whole group of thirteen men, four of whom he believed had been involved in killing one of his *paiks* (attendants). Blechynden was amazed that Eliot boasted of this behaviour in front of witnesses, as if he were an absolute monarch.[38]

The pattern of action and reaction gives us a context in which to interpret Eliot's behaviour. What do we see in each of these cases? On one side is the arbitrary conduct of an energetic but unscrupulous individual. On the other side are responses generated by his conduct, implying or demanding greater regularity from government. In short, a rhetoric of public service and accountability existed and was even fired up by the experience of abuses of power. The rhetoric was firmly believed in, against the odds, by at least two men in Calcutta: Richard and Arthur Blechynden. It was promoted, as said, by the Company's rules and sanctions, inflected as they were with ideas of due process and individual responsibility that formed the bedrock for concepts of justice and propriety.

A kind of parallel to the Eliot examples was provided by a sad incident in 1810. The reins on Blechynden's buggy broke in the hands of his Eurasian coachman William Grey; the coach horse (Holkar) bolted; and a woman was run over by the buggy. Grey and the 'little ketmutgar' Muttiollah, who

was with him, were both imprisoned. Blechynden went to Martyn to secure
the release of his buggy and servants, but the servants did not appear and
remained confined. Blechynden also visited the hospital to check on the
injured woman: she was unconscious, with a head wound and broken leg,
and later died. Grey was then imprisoned for about six weeks. In addition,
Martyn fined everyone in sight ten rupees. For the coachman, this was one
month's pay, though the event was an accident. For the *ketmutgar*, it was
two and a half months' pay, though he had only been sitting in the buggy.
For a grasscutter, who had happened to be running behind the buggy, it
was three months' pay. Blechynden's bibi Isabella became involved, going
to the Police Office without Blechynden's knowledge, sitting through the
hearing, and then paying the fines, making it seem (Blechynden objected)
that he had sent his girl to strike a bargain, as if he was a wretch and she
humane.

This story joins the many other examples of arbitrary justice that we
have encountered. Martyn claimed that he acted to oblige Blechynden,
who (though not above inflicting collective punishments on his servants)
was displeased that Martyn judged him 'by his own standards'. The point
was that there should have been an inquest and a verdict of accidental
death, in which case the family would have appealed to Blechynden for
compensation. Martyn thought it more convenient to punish the innocent
employees. If he intended the fines as recompense, the sum was miserably
small. Blechynden, denied 'due process', still accepted 'responsibility' and
sent money to the woman's family.[39]

Typically, there was altruism in this but no hint of an acceptance of
democratic or equal rights. The Blechyndens' high-mindedness was about
process. It had nothing to do with calls for 'liberty', whether in Putney,
North America, or France. An echo of those arguments influenced the
emphasis that the Company placed on responsible conduct by its 'private',
unaccountable government in India. In response to Burke and other critics,
it was forced to espouse a social and ethical code. In motivation, however,
the ideals were linked less to accountability than to the development of
public policy, official duties, and definitive law. The Blechyndens' take
shows how this contributed to the definitions of what Englishness and
Britishness meant. The definitions emerged out of the political exigencies
of eighteenth-century Britain and from various conditions, as discussed by
others,[40] but clearly had distinctive counterparts in India. Arguably, Indian
experience gave a particular edge to the conjunction of ideas.

Blechynden repeatedly bemoaned—without ever resisting—the lack
of standards that led him and most of his fellows to consort with women

who were not their wives. At the same time, in public, he meticulously observed the various protocols that protected the outward forms of propriety. Similarly, the East India Company, facing its Parliamentary critics, professed upright conduct in order to justify its governmental role and to control the worst excesses of its servants. Regulation and censorship were the more necessary in such a corrupt and grasping environment, which led to the development of complex codes of practice and the start of slow expansions of the state's role. Also, for support or quiescence from their subjects, governments rely upon prestige, benefits, and force, which operate mutually, but differ in expense. The cheapest way of achieving prestige, for the Company if not individual officers, was by a profession of fairness. The Company thus communicated an everyday morality, internalized by the many Arthur Blechyndens of the empire and by many Indians too, that became part of a discourse of rights. They even provided an argument for an acceptance of empire and indeed of curbs upon English liberty and especially on the poor. And this was partly because Company morality did not reflect any consistent contrast between British and Indian standards of honesty and service, as the cases of Martyn and Blaquiere demonstrate. Practice was often very different from rhetoric. But then, in defining national characteristics, what is said often matters more than what is done. Hypocrisy, self-delusion, and identity are frequent bedfellows.

These points imply another way of approaching these issues, very often appropriate to the stories told in this book—namely, by considering the nature and operation of law. Where Benthamite reformers would seek certainty, there was much ambiguity here and on many different levels. The jurisdiction of English, Hindu, and Muslim law was being defined, as at the same time was the remit not only of different English systems (civil, criminal, ecclesiastical, equity, military, and so on), but also of the state as a whole. There was, for example, an overlap between public and private enforcement and between enforcement and reformation. When Blechynden punished one of his workers for a common assault in the street, he denied the state its monopoly of force. When he also read the culprit a lecture on morality and dismissed him from his job, he confused other categories of values, space, and authority (public and private, criminal and civil) that later would be thought more distinct. Conversely, when he threatened an adulterer with the magistrates or even the Supreme Court, whether Irish as with W. T. Jones (discussed in *Sex and Sensibility*) or Indian in the case of his *dooria* Mangoo, he showed that he expected officialdom and the criminalization of conduct to reach more widely than they subsequently would. A similar confusion applied, of course, in the rule making, punishment, social leadership, and charity of an English squire and justice of the peace. In place of the more dispersed and collective authority of craft guilds and town corporations, it was also translated into the new capitalist, bourgeois order in the towns, in the employer's initially total, unquestioned authority over his workers.

On the other hand, as in those cases also, familiar bifurcations were developing, making for a growth of the state and its responsibilities. The answer to corruption and oppression was institutional: for example, laws of evidence that outlawed the worst abuses in Calcutta's petty courts. Another was reform of attitudes and expectations, as embraced by Blechynden. By such means, the state came to be regarded as having a duty to define, regulate, and protect, and it expected exclusive powers within defined limits. The development was a consequence of ideas, of more modern and urban forms of living and production, and, in Calcutta, of the exigencies of colonial rule. Just as a factory invited attention to its needs and abuses by concentrating production and defining workers, work, and the workplace, so too a colonial city focused interest on the responsibilities and imperfections of its administration. Both processes were conducted under the scrutiny of science, measurement, and print. The anarchy of early Calcutta represented a stage on the way to greater order in the same way that, by the end of the nineteenth century, altruism and self-interest were beginning to promote international rules for labour conditions, currency, or prisoners of war; and that, in response to a globalized free-for-all of greed, another international order was being sought in the early twenty-first century—with limited success—for capital markets, product safety, and environmental impact.

These genealogies are related to but different from those for social reform. My argument is that anarchy and corruption led to 'improvement', with more general and systemic impact than the equally moral impulses towards specific social and political remedies. The latter—for example, the abolition of sati or slavery—though contemporaneous and a crucial part of the same story, depended mainly on committed publicists and activists who shifted opinion on three distinct principles: on guilt, justice, and human equivalance (in rights, qualities, and potential). Opponents of sati or slavery evoked all three, with husbands' or slave-owners' 'rights' discounted on absolute or comparative moral grounds. Ethically speaking, a new administrative emphasis on probity, propriety, and imperial duty required only a concern for justice and then arguments of efficiency or utility. Indeed, they banished European guilt and implied Indian inferiority.

This underlines the denial that democracy or even public accountability motivated Indian or imperial reform, whatever the balance of influences in Britain. A certainty about European superiority bolstered all the new policies and doctrines in Calcutta. There was scientific universalism still that allowed the prospect of future advance for all societies, but it was never imagined that all societies were equal in the present. Arthur Blechynden could become 'English' only by repudiating—indeed, denigrating—his Indian half. Colonial rulers too could only justify themselves within their own principles of sovereignty, law, and political ethics by asserting that India was base and in need of the reformation they could provide. Examples of 'corruption' stimulated among its witnesses and victims new standards of public service, related to ideas of state responsibility. These ideals were constructed in opposition to what were thought to be Indian conditions and character. They were also shaped by continuing fears that Indian conditions were corrupting, not only for Indians but also for Europeans.

The law and the mores that Blechynden evoked and that these changes expressed were overwhelmingly English, or at least European, regardless of their recipients and contexts. Outside vague limits of social custom and religious practice, there was scant regard in the operation of law for the pecularities of the different cultures to which they were applied. On the other hand, there was more scope for accommodation and co-option in practice. The rules were supposed to be universal, moreover, in *potential*, and so contributed 'improvement' and 'protection' as justifications for colonial rule: Indians should and could benefit from better governance; everyone deserved some basic 'rights'. Later, scientific racism dulled the optimism of this goal, but never in practice removed its influence on policy—neither for so-called 'lower' classes, nor for so-called 'inferior' peoples.

John Malcolm, celebrated Indian civil servant and protégé of Governor-General Wellesley, elevated all this around the same time into a prospectus for British rule in his *Sketch of the Political History of India*.[41] He attributed British conquest to the self-defence of the Company's territories against its neighbours and to the 'rapacity and ambition of ... [its] own servants'. Not for him the excuse advanced by slightly later historians of rescuing India from anarchy. Malcolm then advocated goals and methods that were at the same time conservative and quasi-liberal. The Company needed, he wrote, the 'unshaken firmness and dignified spirit of an absolute, but tempered rule, [combined] with the most unceasing attention to the religious prejudices and civil rights of our Indian subjects, whose condition it must be our continual study to improve, in the conviction that our Government ... cannot be permanent, but by their means'. Securing British territories through political non-interference had proved 'unwise and impracticable', and the force of an effective army was necessary. (Its Indian personnel and their families also should be rewarded.) On one hand, a civil code of regulations and laws 'founded in a spirit of attention to the usages and religion of the different tribes of India' would attach to British rule those devoted to peaceful occupations. On the other hand, though European settlement was not to be encouraged, European example would help 'advance the natives of India in every branch of useful knowledge'. In short, India was to be ruled so as to 'introduce civilization'—for example, through the liberal arts and public works—and also to advance the happiness and prosperity of Indians, rather than in the exclusive interest of Britain.

Implicitly, all this was also constructing an imperial Englishman—his sense of duty, his probity, his civilizing mission. It was just what Richard Blechynden appealed to and what Arthur was making of himself. This reinforces Anthony Pagden's comment: '[T]he British insistence that their empire was essentially dedicated to improving the condition, the "liberty", both political and economic, of all with whom it came into contact, was not a mere sentimental reflection nor a simple ideological camouflage— although it also served both those functions. It was an essential component of English and later, with still greater emphasis, British identity.'[42]

Conrad, another self-constructed Englishman, put it more ambiva- lently, linking classical and modern empires as in the eighteenth century, and also the contrasting values of the East and the West: 'I was thinking of very old times, when the Romans first came here ...', said Marlow, on a ship off the south-east coast of England, '... We live in the flicker—may it last as long as the old earth keeps rolling! But darkness was here yes- terday.' He commented on how the Romans would have been appalled and fascinated by the primitive abominations of ancient Britain, but then went on:

... lifting one arm from the elbow, the palm of the hand outwards, so that, with his legs folded before him, he had the pose of a Buddha ....—'Mind, none of us would feel exactly like this. What saves us is efficiency—devotion to efficiency.... The conquest of the earth, which mostly means taking it away from those who have a different complexion or slightly flatter noses than ourselves, is not a pretty thing when you look into it too much. What redeems it is the idea only... and an unselfish belief in the idea—something you can set up, and bow down before, and offer a sacrifice to ...'.[43]

The same idea was being framed in India around the turn of the nineteenth century, and served an imperial purpose. In a celebrated essay, Bernard Cohn once concluded that British officials recruited to serve in India at an early age began with an 'idealized adolescent view of their own society and culture' that 'tended to become fossilized'.[44] Without exactly contradicting Cohn, this book makes the reverse observation. Blechynden as a moral actor, and Arthur, as an adolescent, adopted ideals and an identity that were being actively projected in India to justify foreign rule and to limit and manage autocratic government. They were translated back to England by others, to join and reinforce similar notions of different origin.

The personal and public stories merge in Blechynden and in a poem by James Thomson that he transcribed in his diary:

Ah, little think the gay licentious proud
Whom pleasure, power, & affluence surround
They, who their thoughtless hours in giddy mirth
And Wanton, often Cruel, riot waste,
Ah, little think they, while they dance along
How many feel, this very moment, death
And all the sad variety of Pain:
How many sink in the devouring flood,
Or more devouring flame. How many bleed,
By shameful variance betwixt Man & Man.
How many pine in want, and dungeon glooms,
Shut from the common air, & common use
Of their own limbs. How many drink the cup
Of baleful grief, or eat the bitter bread
Of misery. Sore pierced by wint'ry winds,
How many shrink into the sordid Hut
Of cheerless poverty. How many shake
With all the fiercer tortures of the mind
Unbounded passion, madness, guilt, remorse,
Whence tumbled headlong from the height of life,
They furnish matter for the tragic Muse.
Even in the Vale, where wisdom loves to dwell,
With friendship, peace & contemplation joined
How many, racked with honest passions, droop
In deep retired distress. How many stand
Around the death bed of their dearest friends
And point the parting anguish. Thought fond man
Of these, and all the thousand nameless ills,
That one incessant struggle render life,

One scene of Toil, of suff'ring and of fate,
Vice in his high Career would stand appall'd.
And heedless rambling Impulse learn to think;
The conscious heart of Charity would warm,
And her wide wish Benevolence dilate,
The social tear would rise, the social sigh;
And into clear perfection, gradual bliss,
Refining still, the social passions work.[45]

It was apt, and it is easy to see what Blechynden recognized in the poem. In his life in India, he *was* surrounded by affluence and careless display and by pain and death. He could readily see the 'shameful variance betwixt Man and Man'. He experienced pleasure and poverty, passion and remorse, friendship and loss. He was aware of his own moral imperfections and frailty, exemplified by his relations with his bibis. He felt he had often struggled incessantly without reward, thwarted by others' greed or incompetence. He took lessons from this experience and among his responses were, indeed, thoughts of charity and a search for perfection. Vice chose to 'stand appall'd' in empire and in nineteenth-century Britain, both of which displayed enterprise, innovation, probity, civic altruism, and sentimentality. Vice (appetite, callousness, and exploitation) also continued to 'dance along' thoughtlessly, cynically, thereby linking Britain and its empire.

# Glossary

Listed are non-English words used more than once. Modern transliterations, given if they differ from the form used, are from Hindi unless stated (A=Arabic; P= Persian).

*ayah*: lady's maid, nursemaid, nanny
*bheesti* (*bihishti*): water carrier
*bibi*: lady (an honorific title), also applied to Europeans' concubines of any race
*budgerow* (*bajra*): river barge
*chaprasi*: office messenger, orderly
*chattahwallah* (*chhata wala*): umbrella carrier
*chaukidar*: private watchman or (in Calcutta and villages) local policeman
*classie* (*khalasi*): surveying assistant or chain man (also a sailor)
*consomah* (*khansaman*): house steward or butler, usually Muslim
*cutcherry* (*kachahri*): administrative office or court house
*daffadar* (P. *daf'adar*): a petty officer or foreman
*daroga* (*darogha*): (Indian) head of an office, manager
*dhobi*: washerman
*dooria* (*doriya*): dog keeper
*durwan* (*darban*): doorkeeper, porter of a compound
*dhye* (*dai*)*: wet nurse; female servant, usually for women and children
*ghat*: landing place, quay

---

* According to Buchanan–Hamilton (Francis Buchanan, *An Account of the District of Purnea in 1809–1810*, ed. V.H. Jackson, Patna 1928, p. 256), Hindi *dai* meant 'midwife', as distinct from *dhay*, nursemaid, while in Bengal, *dhayi* were midwives and *dasi* or *chakrani* nursemaids. This is not the usage in Blechynden's diary.

*hircarrah (harkara)*: messenger
*hookabadar (hukkabardar)*: hookah bearer
*jemautdar (P. jama'dar)*: native officer, chief of a corps of men
*ketmutgar (khidmatgar)*: valet, serving man
*cranny (karani)*: English-writing clerk (by association of mixed race)
*lascar (laskar, khalasi)*: seaman; see 'classie'
*mali*: gardener
*mangee (manjhi)*: master or helmsman of an Indian boat
*mauselgee (mashalchi)*: torch bearer
*mater (mehtar)*: male sweeper
*metrany (mihtarani)*: female sweeper; female construction labourer; prostitute
*mistri*: foreman or skilled worker, artisan
*mohur*: a gold mohur was a coin worth about Rs 16
*munshi*: secretary or interpreter
*nautch (nach)*: an entertainment with dancing girls
*nullah (nala)*: drain, watercourse, canal
peon: guard, orderly, messenger, footman
*sekilgar (saikalgar)*: armourer, knife-grinder
sice (A. *sa'is*): groom
*sirdar* bearer (*sardar* [chief] bearer): Hindu house steward, butler, valet (Bengal)
*sircar (sarkar)*: controller and accountant for domestic and/or professional finances; agent, manager of work and workers, wages and purchases
*surky (surkhi)*: a hard mortar of crushed brick, lime, and water
*thana*: police post
*thanadar*: chief of a police post

# Notes

## NOTES TO CHAPTER 1

1. Jane Austen, *Mansfield Park* (1814), chapter 19.
2. RB, 9 May 1791. On Upjohn's merit as self-taught engraver: RB, 23 April 1794.
3. RB, April 1794. Tiretta and Blechynden quoted for a map based on a survey.
4. AB, 21 December 1806; RB, 18 April 1799. Eighteenth-century evidence: Alexander Hamilton, *A New Account of the East Indies* (1727), vol. 2, pp. 9–11; William McIntosh, *Travels in Europe, Asia and Africa* (London 1782), vol. 2, pp. 214–19; Mrs Kinderley's *Letters* dating from around 1770; Elizabeth Fay, *Original Letters from India of Mrs Eliza Fay* (Calcutta 1908), from 1780 to 1782. Also James Long, *Calcutta and its Neighbourhood: History of Calcutta and its People from 1690–1857* (ed. Sankar Sen Gupta; Calcutta 1974); H.E. Busteed, *Echoes from Old Calcutta being Chiefly Reminiscences of the Days of Warren Hastings, Francis and Impey* (Calcutta 1888; 2nd edn); A.K. Ray, *A Short History of Calcutta Town and Suburbs* (reprint from *Census of India 1901*, vol. VII, pt. I, ed. N.R. Ray; Calcutta 1982); Sumanta Banerjee, *The Parlour and the Streets: Elite and Popular Culture in Nineteenth Century Calcutta* (Calcutta 1989). Tercentenary publications: Sukanta Chaudhuri (ed.), *Calcutta: The Living City* (New Delhi 1990); Pratapaditya Pal (ed.), *Changing Visions, Lasting Images: Calcutta Through 300 Years* (Bombay 1990), citations by Jagmohan Mahajan, pp. 18 and 24. An authoritative overview of the Europeans: P.J. Marshall, 'The White Town of Calcutta under the Rule of the East India Company', *Indo-British Review*, vol. xxi, no. 2 (n.d. [1996]); also Anthony Webster, *The Richest East India Merchant: The Life and Business of John Palmer of Calcutta, 1767–1836* (Woodbridge 2007); Swati Chattopadhyay, *Representing Calcutta: Modernity, Nationalism and the Colonial Uncanny* (London 2005).

5.    Suresh Chandra Ghosh, *The Social Condition of the British Community in Bengal, 1757–1800* (Leiden 1970). Compare Anjana Singh, *Fort Cochin in Kerala, 1750–1830: The Social Condition of a Dutch Community in an Indian Milieu* (Leiden 2010), especially chapter 3, on greater separation within a hierarchical, European or mixed-race, largely Christian enclave; there was some engagement with India through concubines, servants, and slaves as well as by way of business, as in Calcutta.

6.    Charles Moore, *The Sheriffs of Fort William from 1775 to 1920* (Calcutta 1921), p. 9; *South Park Street Cemetery, Calcutta: Register of Graves and Standing Tombs—From 1767* (King's Langley 1997; 3rd edn), p. 22; Thacker, *Bengal Obituary* (London 1851). European: RB, 17 August 1798.

7.    Edmund Burke, *Reflections on the Revolution in France* (1790).

8.    RB, 7 May 1800. Informed that the Court of Directors had set their faces against Governors having their wives with them, Blechynden predicted: 'his Lordship will be apt to set his *breech*' against them.

9.    RB, 29 September 1797; 21, 25 September, 15, 17 October 1798. Mrs Deverinne discussed her menstruation as well as the size of her piles: 'an Englishwoman would die rather than thus bare her secret ailments'. Mrs Jones, I assume, was the second Mrs Samuel Jones, née Gardner; Blechynden visited her often. A roughly contemporary report on what must be another Mrs Jones (there are several to choose from) had her received as a lady at Cape Town, though she had been a serving maid, one of very good character. Blechynden commented: from 'the smallness & whiteness of her hand', at most this woman could have been the daughter of some 'favourite housekeeper or faithful ladies maid': RB, 25 September 1798. He would have known Mrs Samuel Jones's background. An acquaintance commented on the Samuel Joneses that she 'never saw so much pride and ignorance in one house' and apparently Blechynden was the only 'gentleman' who called: RB, 7 November 1800. In his will of 1808, Blechynden left 'the Topaz Ring I usually wear' to Mrs Jones, wife of Samuel Jones of Queen Square Holborn, formerly of the Calcutta Post Office, and a bible and book of common prayer (to be purchased) to her son Charles Richard Urquhart Jones (Blechynden's godson; 5, 9 December 1802).

10.    RB, 3 February 1795; Long, *Calcutta*, p. 113; Ray, *History*, pp. 146 *ff.*; Sumitra Sreemani, *Anatomy of a Colonial Town: Calcutta, 1756–1794* (Calcutta 1994), pp. 57 *ff.*

11.    Journal (1780) and before he joined the *Deptford* bound for India, Journal (1781).

12.    Journal (1780). Young Blechynden was placed under guard.

13.    RB, 20 November 1793. Dring, known for a trust to educate 'Anglo-Indians', had been eighteen years in India at this time; 7 October 1793.

14.    Philip Curtin, *Death by Migration: Europe's Encounter with the Tropical World in the Nineteenth Century* (Cambridge 1989), chapter 1, quantifies

the threat—particularly high in Calcutta even in comparison with Madras and Bombay, and many times that in Britain—even after the 1830s, when improvements were beginning.

15.   Ian Donaldson, 'The Importance of Dying Well', *Times Literary Supplement* no. 4950, 13 February 1998, on Michael Neill's book, *Issues of Death* (Oxford 1997).

16.   RB, 27 and 30 April 1794; Long, *Calcutta*, p.70; RB, 27 April 1794. Evidence for Jones's contemporary standing comes from Blechynden, via Kathleen Blechynden, *Calcutta Past and Present* (London 1905); Garland Cannon, *The Life and Mind of Oriental Jones: the Father of Modern Linguistics* (Cambridge 1990).

17.   Busteed, *Echoes*, pp.109–19; RB, 17, 23, and 29 September 1795. On Downie: RB, 23 May 1796. Mrs Leekes, once a chambermaid: RB, 20 April 1795. William Roper: first officer, *Carnatic* 1790–1, *Triton* 1792–3, captained *Royal Charlotte* 1795–1801; applied unsuccessfully to be Superintendent of the Salt Chokeys, 4 October 1795. Most of these officers, including Blechynden's friend John Wales, were based in Calcutta while posted to the Andamans station. After a dispute over reductions in their pay, most went back to Bombay (RB, 19 August, 4 October 1795, 1, 9, 23, 28 January 1796). Roper was suspected of sending an impertinent letter to the Marine Board in Wales' name, hoping Wales would be sent back to Bombay and he (Roper) would get command of *Cornwallis* (19 August 1795).

18.   RB, 9 and 27 October 1794; 24–5 March 1794; and 23 April 1794; 3 January 1795; 13 February 1795; 3 March 1795; 31 July 1795; and 1 August 1795. For 'unblushing fellow', see RB, 4 June 1798. Upjohn was said to be favoured by Cornish in preference to Blechynden for appointment as assistant to Tiretta in July 1797. Perhaps Hubert Cornish (1757–1823) regarded Upjohn as a fellow artist; he himself was a musician and celebrated watercolourist. From 1793–9, he served as private secretary to Sir John Shore, married to Cornish's sister, Charlotte. Cornish's power was apparent to Blechynden as early as 1794; from the *Alphabetical list of the honourable East India Company's Bengal civil servants from the year 1780, to the year 1838 ... to which is attached a list of the Governors-General of India from the year 1773 to the year 1838 with the dates of their appointments, also a list of the East India Directors from the year 1779 to the year 1838* (London 1839), he was not officially in Company service until made Private Assistant, 26 September 1795 to May 1797; he stayed with the Company till 1821.

19.   RB, 4 October 1797; 15 August 1798; and 13 September 1797. Jones, working in the Adjutant-General's office under Colonel Frith, was taken into the Paymaster General's office: RB, 8 November 1800. Frith cited his ingratitude: Jones refused an urgent letter, knowing it was from Frith, on the unexpected arrival of Frith's daughter in Calcutta. Jones said the rupee was

bad; another was sent but too late for the post. Sir Charles Blunt, Postmaster General, publicly bawled out Jones, making him send the letter at his own expense. Firth carried the (perfectly good) rupee, telling this story against Jones. Blechynden said Jones was forgetful of his origins. In 1801, he was about to lose his post and his house when an 'injudicious' appointment was made in his place, of one Batty, who knew nothing, said Blunt, while Jones had 'every routine at his fingertips'. Blechynden thought Jones 'feathered his own nest', with his chariot, buggy, and other signs of display, but wrote a letter to Lord Wellesley for him: RB, 24, 27, and 29 November 1801. Jones kept his position and retired on a pension: RB, 20 September 1804.

20.   RB, 3 and 7 September 1798.

21.   Sir William Chambers (1723–1796), Robert Adam's rival, first published his Palladian *Treatise on Civil Architecture* in 1759. Widely used by later architects, it combined neoclassical and Renaissance principles.

22.   The context includes the segregation of categories of knowledge and the rise of professionalism, the latter studied by sociologists (Talcot Parsons, Eliot Freidson, Karl Mannheim) as well as historians. M.S. Larsen, *The Rise of Professionalism: A Sociologicial Analysis* (Berkeley 1977), chapter 2, describes how professions built on early examples (divinity, law, and medicine) through professional associations and public education, as part of a movement away from employment by birth and status, and towards opportunities for control over both specialized knowledge and interpersonal situations (providing solutions for individuals). The downside, says Larsen, was overemphasis on narrow responsibilities, prestige, dignity, and conformity, not whole solutions and overall consequences. Professionalism affected government too: Calcutta bureaucracy's 'internal dynamics' compare with Oliver MacDonagh, *A Pattern of Government Growth, 1800–1860: the Passenger Acts and their Implementation* (London 1961).

23.   RB, 3, 5, and 7–8 January 1810; and 1 March 1810. Blechynden's Town Hall report: RB, 14 July 1810. Frostiness ensued with Garstin: RB, 20 October 1810. On Tiretta and Government House: RB, 29 September; 1, 2, and 8 October 1798.

24.   Buffon, in French, in twenty-four volumes: RB, 23 April 1793. Time: Blechynden frequently took observations for David Mills, the watchmaker, who corrected ships' clocks (for example, 7 September 1799 and 7 October 1797); Blechynden also prepared and sold almanacs for publication. Meteorology: RB, 11 January 1798. See also Partha Ghose, 'Scientific Studies in Calcutta. The Colonial Period', in Sukanta Chaudhuri (ed.), *Calcutta: The Living City* (New Delhi 1990), p.199; Busteed, *Echoes*, pp.109–11; Dava Sobel, *Longitude: The True Story of a Lone Genius who Solved the Greatest Scientific Problem of His Time* (London 1996). Ants: 16 November 1800, 14 July 1801.

25.   Hodgson: R.H. Phillimore, *Historical Records of the Survey of India, Vol. III: 1815–1830* (Dehra Dun 1954), p. 425. Wales: RB, 26 April 1805. Probate, Calcutta, 20 February 1822 (transcript thanks to Donald Jaques).

26.   Le Breen: RB, 9 May 1793 and 2 January 1794. Mysore: RB, 6 February 1793; mutiny: RB, 24 November 1793. In November 1793, the *Chronicle* press published a poem on the Mysore war by Lieutenant Lionel Berkeley: Shaw, *Bibliography*, p. 252.

27.   David Ludden, 'India's Development Regime', in Nicholas B. Dirks (ed.), *Colonialism and Culture* (Ann Arbor 1992), pp. 247–87. For transition from 'nabob' to 'sahib', an Indianized to an Anglicized persona: E.M. Collingwood, *Imperial Bodies: The Physical Experience of the Raj, c. 1800–1947* (Cambridge and Oxford 2001).

28.   RB, 11–12 February, 16 December 1798, 17 February 1799. Horse: from Deletang, that is, Amboise Pierre Antoine de l'Etang (1757–1840), who worked at the royal stables at Versailles, was banished after the French Revolution, came to India, and in Calcutta bought stables built by Blechynden (see below). Puppy: from Jacques Maxime Deverinne (d.1801), merchant (Deverinne & Sons) of Serampore, originally Chandernagore. Colt: to the Eurasian 'Ned' Brightman, in the Accountant-General's office (to 7 June 1800), then purser to Captain Lane on the *Commerce*; see Peter Robb, *Sex and Sensibility: Richard Blechynden's Calcutta Diaries, 1791–1822* (New Delhi 2011). Plants: from William Collier, probably a seafarer (his bibi was looked after when he went to Colombo). A. $W^m$ Collier was commander of the gun vessel *Swift* (1805).

29.   RB, 28 November 1795. Hayes, not identified, may be John Hayes, a Company servant.

30.   RB, 4–7, 10, and 15 November 1795. Barnett did not leave; the upper apartments were let so as to get rid of him (19 October 1796). On Collins and Callendar, see 6 October 1796, and Chapter 5, n10. A James Callendar captained the Bombay ships *Shah Ardesir* and *Sultan* between 1789 and 1795; he later fled his debts in Calcutta (7, 13, 19 October 1796, and 8 April 1797). An Alexander Munro was assistant agent for camels and grain.

31.   There is an obvious resemblance—modified by Calcutta conditions and most evident in formal associations (such as the Asiatic Society)—to the 'fashionable sociability' in Peter Clark, *British Clubs and Societies, 1580–1800: The Origins of an Associational World* (Oxford 2000).

32.   RB, 2–4 February 1805. Exactly two years earlier, Blechynden's children James and Charlotte had left for England (see Chapter 5).

33.   Webster, *Richest Merchant*, especially chapter 4; H.V. Bowen, *The Business of Empire: The East India Company and Imperial Britain* (Cambridge

2006); A. Tripathi, *Trade and Finance in the Bengal Presidency, 1793–1833* (2nd edn, Calcutta 1979).

34.   RB, 3 March 1796. His wife, very upset to find him there when she arrived from England, ended up residing in the prison though Tiretta had offered to let her eat with him while living in rented accommodation: RB, 1, 3–5, 9, and 13 March 1797. She died the same year: RB, 30 July 1797.

35.   Callendar: RB, 29 February 1796. Gardner: RB, 31 October 1796; 18–19 and 29 January 1797. T.P. Doncaster pursued speculative businesses, for example in salt, miscellaneous manufacture, and ship-owning. Mrs Gardner has not been positively identified, the puzzle increased by information about Mrs Samuel Jones, née Eliza Gardner, married in March 1798 (see Robb, *Sex and Sensibility*). John Gardner, attorney, died in 1787 and could have employed Blechynden. Edward Gardner, auctioneer, a possible employer, married in 1788 and is not recorded dying in India. Nor is John Philip Gardiner (of Procher, Redhead & Gardiner), Bank of Hindoostan proprietor. Only one other possible Gardner is recorded dying in India in the period: George, a Calcutta resident, died in 1785.

36.   RB, 9 December 1796. See also Chapter 8. Josephine's guardian was to be a Mrs White.

37.   Blechynden was involved in negotiations around the assignment to an Indian magnate of a large bond issued by Louis and Hyde on the security of a sugar concern. The lawyer Thomas Raban confirmed that a once a bond was assigned, no residual responsibility remained with the original holder unless specifically provided for in the assignment: RB, 16–17 February 1799.

38.   RB, 16 and 18 March 1793. Hari Prasad (a common name) has not been identified. Rees was a proprietor and notionally editor of the *Star* (17 January, 1 August 1795, 14 September 1796).

39.   RB, 17–18 April 1793; 14, 18, and 21 June 1793. Alexander Aberdein (d.1810) was one-time Deputy Commissary of Ordnance, a partner in an agency house, and secretary to the India Insurance Company. George French was later a partner of John Gilmore.

40.   William Pawson (1745–1802), Senior Merchant, served the East India Company from 1766; was dismissed on the abolition of the Provincial Councils in 1781 but permitted to draw his allowances until appointed to another office. Julius Soubise (1754–1798), a black West Indian, brought to England as a boy, learnt about horses under the patronage of the Duchess of Queensberry, and fled to India in 1777. My thanks to Ashley Cohen for identifying Soubise as this celebrated man.

41.   RB, 11, 18, and 22 September 1795; 7, 9, and 12–13 October 1795; 12 and 19 February 1796; 3, 5, 9, and 24–6 March 1796; 3 April 1796; 10

and 13–14 June 1796; 4 and 10 August 1796; 6, 10, and 12 December 1796. Pawson's stables were later sold by lottery and then sold on by the winner for Rs 5,000. They were offered to Blechynden, who could not raise the money, and were bought by Deletang: RB, 10 and 29 November 1797; 1, 4–6, 8, and 10 December 1797.

42.   P.J. Cain and A.G. Hopkins, *British Imperialism: Innovation and Expansion, 1688–1914* (Harlow, Essex 1993). I discuss economic roles of friendship in 'Mr Upjohn's Debts: Money and Friendship in Early Colonial Calcutta', *Modern Asian Studies* (forthcoming).

43.   The garden-house name presumably means 'belle couchée', lying beautifully or well-situated, or possibly sleeping well. There is a slight puzzle about it. Blechynden's and Doncaster's or Bruce's houses are referred to as being at Belle Couchée (for example, in Bruce's case, in lists of Calcutta residents). In a Calcutta suburbs map of 1817 the name 'Belgauchi' appears almost in the right place off the Dum Dum Road. In that map, however, there is an area immediately below Belgauchi marked 'Blychindel' that contains houses identified as belonging to Blechynden and Bruce. In the Lottery Commission map (1825), the house of 'Mr Blichenden' and 'Doctor Bruice's Diggy' are shown between districts labelled 'Doolal Sircar' and 'Dhankeen Ranree'. See Anil Kumar Kundu and Prithvish Nag, *Atlas of the City of Calcutta and its Environs* (Calcutta 1996), pp. 28, 32.

44.   The conversation lasted over two hours. For Doncaster and Gourt Money: RB, 9–11, 13, 15–16, 18, 22, and 24–5 June 1797; 3 and 9 July 1797; 10 September 1797; and 30 August 1797.

45.   Another example: Blechynden's writer Gopey lent Blechynden's whetstone to his friend, Powell. Fearing that Powell might be going to sea, Gopey called to retrieve it. He complained that Powell's servants abused him and refused to fetch the stone or to let him inside the door. Blechynden suspected that this story was just to cover up his having lent the stone and felt that Gopey should not have gone to Powell's without telling him. A chit came from Powell with the whetstone, complaining that Gopey had said Powell was a man of no consequence, just Blechynden's 'cranny' (*karani*, English-writing clerk, by association of mixed race). Gopey denied this hotly; he said that *he* was Blechynden's *cranny*. Blechynden accepted this, acknowledged Powell's chit, and explained when they met, in Gopey's presence: RB, 21 November and 4 December 1798. Powell did not sail until February 1799.

46.   Recent events should have shown how Blechynden would react. Earlier guests at the gardens had included John Grant from Beerbhoom, a friend of Arthur Hesilrige, met by Blechynden in January 1796, and based temporarily just north of Calcutta in Chitpore, refusing job offers, while financially distressed. He moved to Blechynden's garden house with his bibi, a baby, and an establishment of dhyes, washermen and servants 'as would

suit the first Civilian' of Calcutta, coming for a couple of days and remaining weeks. Their wet-nurse, a married woman, was said to be turning the house 'into a brothel' by consorting with Rufick, Doncaster's *mauselgee* or consomah, which 'strumming' was said to be spoiling her milk and making the child ill. Rufick, son of the mali Misry, climbed over the garden gate and was found with the nurse; when asked how he dared to be there, he abused and struck Blechynden's mali. Misry sent plaintains into town for the children as a 'peace offering'; Blechynden returned them. Blechynden ordered a milch goat for the baby; he suggested Grant dismiss the nurse and pay her wages directly to her husband in Beerbhoom. Blechynden later found her sleeping with Rufick on the verandah of Doncaster's, now C.K. Bruce's, house (see n47). Bruce felt he could not dismiss Rufick without offending Doncaster. Blechynden reproached the nurse with her behaviour, given that she had a husband, and told Doncaster what was happening. He was 'mightily indifferent'. Blechynden stressed what he thought the risk to the child's health and added that many hotheaded men would insist on satisfaction from a man who did not punish a servant about whom they had made a complaint. Grant was not that kind, but he deserved the attention due to a gentleman. Blechynden said that he would always complain to the master as he thought it most offensive to strike someone else's servant. Faced with this barrage of arguments, Doncaster agreed to flog Rufick and turn him away. Blechynden, never satisfied, objected to the double punishment. Doncaster returned to say that Rufick claimed 'not yet to have known woman' and many times to have left the bottle store where he slept because the nurse came to him there, offering him paan (betel). Doncaster believed him. He flogged another servant for climbing over Blechynden's gate, which Blechynden thought made him seem to be repeatedly complaining and of 'revengeful temper': RB, 19–21 May, 24 August, 1796, 4 May, 9–11, 15, 18, 22, and 24–5 June 1797.

47.   Grant spoke with good reason. The year before, in 1796, he was in Blechynden's garden house with his bibi and child when Doncaster had intended to stay there, having let his house to Bruce, who later would buy it (RB, 31 January and 8 February 1797). Blechynden offered to share his room, as it was eighteen feet square and neither of them had a concubine at the time, but Doncaster preferred to stay with Bruce and remit half his rent; Bruce agreed, though others thought it strange, even improper, to stay in a house after letting it. Grant had come to Blechynden for a couple of days and remained for weeks. Blechynden felt that he could not turn Grant out, but complained at disturbances (further to n46): Grant's bibi, furious at losing four rupees and wanting to hang herself, according to the durwan; or their wet nurse holding the child out to relieve itself on the hall steps close to the door instead of using a chamber pot or taking the child downstairs, creating a stench and attracting flies. Blechynden made objections to Grant while he was shaving, receiving no

reply and only a glance; Grant said nothing to the nurse. Blechynden decided that if it happened again, he would ask Grant to turn someone else's house into a pigsty: RB, 7, 25, 17, and 22–4 July 1796; 3, 9, and 15 August 1796. Grant later went to Cooch Behar with his brother, 4 November 1797, 31 January 1798.

48.    Breakfast and Collins's indelicate complaints (preferring roast meat or grilled goose): RB, 6 November 1796. Adultery: RB, 9 March 1799 and 14 April 1800.

49.    Lawrence Stone, *The Family, Sex and Marriage in England, 1500–1800* (1976; abridged edn, London 1979), pp.81–8; Stephen Taylor, *Caliban Shore* (London 2004); RB, 1 October 1816; AB, undated (1809).

50.    On Marmaduke and Sally, see Robb, *Sex and Sensibility*, chapter 7.

51.    RB, 6, 23, 26–7, and 31 October 1802; 11, 13–23, and 26 November 1802.

52.    RB, 1, 5, 8, 10, 23, 26–7, and 30 November 1802; 2 and 3 December 1802; and 28 October 1805.

53.    RB, 13 and 29 December 1802, and 8 January 1803. Sally was married on 10 January 1803.

54.    RB, 24 June 1803; 6–7 July 1803; 26 January 1805; and 2 and 8 February 1805. Sarah (Sally) Aungier died on 2 July 1803, aged twenty-two years and six months.

55.    RB, 12, 16–19, and 24 September 1805; and 27–9 October 1805.

56.    The immediate problem was a prolapsus of the anus, which Dr White said should be bathed in cold water, but from which he should recover as he grew: RB, 11 January 1806. Other illnesses: RB, 2 and 4–7 May 1806. Later, mercury ointment was being applied to Tom's stomach, for he could not keep food down; he seemed in great danger; eating nothing but fruit, he was persuaded to take a little bread with mangoes, and recovered: RB, 5–7 May 1808.

57.    RB, 1–2 November 1805; 4 and 7 January 1806; 7 October 1808; 4 and 7 January 1810; 13 July 1812; and 1 October 1818. Also AB, 12–13 July 1812; 1 October (second entry) 1818; 9–10 and 18 December 1818; 22 January 1819; and 3 January 1821.

58.    [Kyd], *A Short Account of Colonel Kyd, the founder of the Royal Botanic Garden, Calcutta* (Calcutta 1893), reprinted from vol. IV of the *Annals of the Garden*; RB, 23 July 1795.

## NOTES TO CHAPTER 2

1.    Jonathan Swift, *Gulliver's Travels* (1726), quoting the king of Brobdingnag, 'A Voyage to Brobdingnag', chapter VI.

2.    Pradip Sinha, 'Calcutta and the Currents of History, 1670–1912', in Sukanta Chaudhuri (ed.), *Calcutta: The Living City* (New Delhi 1990), p. 33;

also Keya Dasgupta, 'A City Away from Home: The Mapping of Calcutta' in Partha Chatterjee (ed.), *Texts of Power: Emerging Disciplines in Colonial Bengal* (New Delhi 1995), pp. 145–66. Rudrangshu Mukherjee, '"Forever England": British life in old Calcutta', in Chaudhuri (ed.), *Calcutta*: 'racial arrogance, passing into the sadistic or the impersonally inhuman, was the bond that linked the young writer' of the eighteenth century 'to the suave competition-wallah of the nineteenth'. Suresh Chandra Ghosh, *The Social Condition of the British Community in Bengal, 1757–1800* (Leiden 1970). See also Chapter 1, n. 5.

3.    Banerjee, *Parlour*, p. 23; Swati Chattopadhyay, 'Blurring Boundaries: the Limits of "White Town" in Colonial Calcutta', *Journal of the Society of Architectural Historians*, vol. 59, no. 2 (June 2006), pp. 154–79.

4.    G.H. Barlow was Secretary to Government, Acting Governor-General 1805–7. J.H. Harrington was Secretary, Board of Revenue, 1788 and 1799; from 1801, judge, Sadr Diwani Adalat. W.C. Blaquiere, Company's Persian Translator and Chief Interpreter, as well as Magistrate.

5.    RB, 10–11 April and 15–16 May 1799. Beaumais and Perrow: RB, 28 January 1799. Securing Calcutta: RB, 20–8 May 1799. Raban: RB, 3 June 1799. Perrow, unidentified, is presumably not an error for Perron (Pierre Cuillier, 1755–1834), as he was then serving Scindia and did not reach Calcutta until 1804. Later, a serious Hindu–Muslim riot occurred, with about thirty Muslims arrested: RB, 14 June 1799.

6.    *Hobson-Jobson* is coy about 'banchoot', used as a term of abuse, including casually by Europeans unaware of its 'odious meaning'; and cites the same cry against Europeans ('firingy', itself derogative) by Tipu's soldiers. Henry Yule and A.C. Burrell, *Hobson-Jobson: The Anglo-Indian Dictionary* (1886, 1902; Ware 1996).

7.    French: RB, 11, 14, and 16 April 1799. Muslims: RB, 9 and 18–19 April 1799, and 7 May 1799. Chait Singh was raja of Benares, deposed under Warren Hastings.

8.    K.N. Chaudhuri, 'From the Barbarian and the Civilised to the Dialectics of Colour: an Archaeology of Self-identities', in Peter Robb (ed.), *Society and Ideology: Essays in South Asian history presented to Professor K.A. Ballhatchet* (Delhi 1993).

9.    C.A. Bayly, *Imperial Meridian: The British Empire and the World, 1780–1830* (London 1989), p. 148. In a fine discussion, Sudipta Sen, *Distant Sovereignty: National Imperialism and the Origins of British India* (New York 2002), chapter 5 (also chapter 4), describes the 'decline of intimacy' and disruption of a 'relatively peaceful domestic frontier', linked to disease, Indian companions' exclusion from public society, disdain for Indians and Indian custom, and distrust between the rulers and the ruled.

10.    My discussion, couched differently from general interpretations of the evolution of racial prejudice, reflects the complex, contradictory positions

of an individual with mixed-race children. An excellent brief summary of debates on racial attitudes and national attributes, and their origins, is Kathleen Wilson, *The Island Race: Englishness, Empire and Gender in the Eighteenth Century* (London and New York 2003), pp. 8–15, concluding that attitudes were not static but 'made and unmade in historical circumstances and manipulated in the pursuit of power', meaning that biological determinist notions of race existed not just in the forms that emerged in Europe and America during the nineteenth century but also at many other times and places, with a *consistent* tendency for 'acquired cultural attributes' to be 'transformed into innate ones'. She also discussed the literature on colonial encounters, hybridity, and 'transculture' for people and commodities: pp.16–18. A richly illustrated account of European reactions to India from published contemporary sources is Ketaki Kushari Dyson, *A Various Universe: A Study of the Journals and Memoirs of British Men and Women in the Indian Subcontinent, 1765–1856* (New Delhi 2002, first edn 1978).

11.  Perhaps it was ever so: Clive Dewey, *The Passing of Barchester* (London 1991), has a not dissimilar account of a transitional patronage system in the nineteenth-century Church of England, with Dean Lyall at the centre of the web.

12.  RB, 21 February and 23 March 1793; 14 October 1794. The warehouse, for a Mr King, later led to litigation.

13.  RB, 6–7 November 1794; 26 February 1795; 9 March 1795; and 1 June 1795.

14.  Long, *Calcutta*, p. 103; Reginald Heber, *Narrative of a Journey through the Upper Provinces of India: From Calcutta to Bombay, 1824–1825, (with Notes upon Ceylon) an account of a Journey to Madras and the Southern Provinces, 1826, and Letters Written in India, Volume 1* (London 1828; 2nd edn), p. 20.

15.  RB, 12, 20, and 24 February 1795. On the stables: see Chapter 1.

16.  On writers: Long, *Calcutta*, pp. 147–8; on Cooper: RB, 10–12 February and 17 March 1795. The new printer was 'Mr Millar'. At the request of Cooper's elder brother, Blechynden interceded for Cooper but without success. As principal partner, Charles Rothman declined to reinstate him: his eye was ever on profit.

17.  Proverb: RB, 4 October 1791. Gofarrah: RB 27 January 1795; Elephant: RB, 2 February 1795.

18.  RB, 31 December 1800 and 10 January 1801.

19.  Andiram: RB 31 January 1796; 1, 4, 6, and 22 February 1796.

20.  RB, 30 January and 3 February 1800. The charity school, possibly acquired with his garden house, trained boys in arithmetic (RB, 1 January 1802) and practical skills.

21.   RB, 'Takoor Bharry' (shrine for a god = *thakur*): RB, 1 and 18 October 1796. On sati: RB, 4 December 1799 and 10 October 1801; on cremation: 11 October 1801. Doncaster built the temple, costing over Rs 500, in return for land for a kitchen garden: RB, 15 October 1796. The temple had images some months later: RB, 21 May 1797. On indifference to sati (opposite to most reports), compare W.H. Auden, 'Musée des Beaux Arts', on suffering taking place 'While someone else is eating or opening a window', or a 'dreadful martyrdom ... in some untidy spot/Where the dogs go on with their doggy life'. Campaigns, such as Rev. Marshman's, stressed male indifference to female suffering: Lynn Zastoupil, *Rammohun Roy and the Making of Victorian Britain* (Basingstoke 2010).

22.   RB, 4–5 December 1797.

23.   RB, 24 January and 2 February 1898. On the bibi ('Mrs' Griffith Jones): RB, 9 June 1800.

24.   RB, 1 July 1794; 10–11, 13, and 21 October 1794; 23 November 1794; and 14 December 1794.

25.   RB, 10 August 1796. Soubise later died after a fall from a horse: RB, 25 and 27 August 1798; and 7 September 1798; after which his 'wife' was said to have had a son by one Bush, having concealed her pregnancy from Pawson: RB, 3 August 1800. Pawson died in December 1802, owing Blechynden rent Mrs Soubise was not able to pay in full: RB, 18, 20–1, 23, and 25 December 1802.

26.   On cattle: RB, 16 October 1796 and 9 February 1797. Jones's experience: RB, 19 November 1799.

27.   RB, 1–2 April 1797; 26–8 May 1797; 20, 23–4, and 31 August 1800; and 1 June 1801. Visitors: Abul Qasim Khan (Mir Mangli), younger son of the Nizam of Bengal, 1770–93, Mubarak-ud-daula I; Mirza Jalil, Mubarak's brother-in-law; and Khan Sahib Khalilullah Khan, Mubarak's son-in-law. John Dowling (d. 1829) became Head Assistant, Commercial Accounts Department.

28.   RB, 21–2 and 30 January 1816; 4 February 1816; and 2 and 21 July 1817. Rammohan (1774–1833) served in Calcutta as a court pundit and as clerk to Thomas Woodforde in Murshidabad, then again with his long-standing patron John Rigby in Rangpur, presumably being back in Calcutta between the two appointments. The false horizon, a measuring device with a line to simulate the horizon, was an innovation of the period. The 'swing' may also be an instrument, perhaps a pendulum.

29.   RB, 23 January 1795. See John R. McLane, *Land and Local Kingship in Eighteenth-Century Bengal* (Cambridge 1993), esp. p. 255.

30.   On the impudence of Indians: RB, 11 May 1797. Buxoo's story: AB, 4 August 1798.

31.   Financial reasons kept Blechynden from joining, though for years he paid a subscription for Aaron Upjohn, part of the latter's debts. In better times, when Aguiton wanted Blechynden to become the Calcutta agent of the Philippine Society, Tiretta said that he should be an Asiatic Society member so as to present the Philippine Society's papers, which would need a special meeting. Others also stressed that he ought to belong and eventually he was proposed, elected, and paid his subscription. He could not always hear at the meetings he attended: RB, 30 June 1805; 8 and 11 January 1806; 3 April 1806; and 2 July 1806. Interestingly for the increasing specialization of knowledge, the Society later divided into physical and literary sessions, with members invited to join either (or both): RB, 14 September 1809.

32.   RB, 3 April 1811. Barretto's was a leading merchant house.

33.   RB, 20 November 1797 and 11–12 July 1801. On Hastings, see Mildred Archer and Ronald Lightbown, *India Observed, India as viewed by British Artists, 1760–1860* (Victoria and Albert Museum, London 1982), p. 16.

34.   RB, 7 October 1791; 15 June 1795; and 20 July 1795; on Durga puja, see also RB, 20 and 23 October.

35.   On the boys: RB, 25 January 1795. On Davy: RB, 25 February 1798. On his impartiality: RB, 2 April 1819.

36.   Thomas R. Metcalf, *Ideologies of the Raj* (Cambridge 1995), takes up the later story: for example, British goals of Indian well-being, not liberty; classifications of difference; and fears of degeneracy and disease.

37.   Paper presented at the School of Oriental and African Studies (SOAS), 26 January 1993. Dipesh Chakrabarty, *Provincializing Europe: Postcolonial Thought and Historical Difference* (Princeton 2000), posits two mutually influential kinds of history: 'universal narrative of capital' and 'diverse ways of being human' (p. 254). Harry Harootunian, *History's Disquiet: Modernity, Cultural Practice, and the Question of Everyday Life* (New York 2000), prefers experience's specificities to postcolonial theory's 'lifeless stereotypes' (pp. 50–3).

38.   Blechynden's workers and servants observed their own festivals. For example, when his writer Gopey was away, Tiretta's writer Peter (probably Indo-Portuguese) was at work: RB, 29 May 1798.

## NOTES TO CHAPTER 3

1.   Indrani Chatterjee, *Gender, Slavery and Law in Colonial India* (New Delhi 1999), p. 15.

2.   On Luso-Indians, see Holden Furber, *Rival Empires of Trade in the Orient, 1600–1800* (1976; Delhi 1990), pp. 322–4. Despite this description of their status and occupations earlier and elsewhere, disrespect for the 'Portuguese' (whether Eurasian or not) did exist in 1790s Calcutta.

3.   P.J. Marshall, 'The Company and the Coolies: Labour in Early Calcutta', in Pradip Sinha (ed.), *The Urban Experience: Calcutta: Essays in Honour of Professor Nisith R. Ray* (Calcutta 1987), pp. 23–38; Resolution by Richard Becher, William Frankland, and J.Z. Holwell, zamindars, to the President and Council, Proceedings, 21 May 1759, and Proceedings, 27 March 1760, 21 March 1763 (petition of Marshall Johnson, imprisoned for striking a servant), and 20 June 1766 (register of all servants). Also, on coolies, see Despatch to Court, 2 January 1752 (wage rise), Consultations, 6 January 1755 (advances), Proceedings, 7 April 1757 (pensions), 13 June 1757 (cheating by intermediaries), 28 April 1760 (daffadars, bildars, coolies, and payments at the fort), and 20 March 1760 (fraud), in J. Long, *Selections from Unpublished Records of Government for the Years 1748 to 1767 Inclusive: Relating Mainly to the Social Condition of Bengal with a Map of Calcutta in 1784*, vol. 1 (London 1869); also pp. xxvii and xxxii; Sreemani, *Anatomy*, pp. 158–60 (regulations of 1787).

4.   On Downie: RB, 31 July 1798. On slavery: Indrani Chatterjee and Richard M. Eaton (eds), *Slavery and South Asian History* (Bloomington 2006), esp. pp. 4–6, 19–28; and chapters 6–9. An excellent introduction is Margot Finn, 'Slaves Out of Context: Domestic Slavery and the Anglo-Indian Family', *Transactions of the Royal Historical Society (Sixth Series)*, vol. 19, 2009, pp. 181–203.

5.   See Finn, 'Slaves Out of Context', pp. 201–2; Ravi Ahuja, 'Making the Empire a Thinkable Whole: Master and Servant Law in Transterritorial Perspective', *International Review of Social History*, vol. 52, no. 2, 2007, pp. 287–94, on master–servant rules criminalizing workers' breaches of contract while providing only civil remedies against employers.

6.   RB, 2 October 1796 and 10 February 1800. The bearers had been paid regularly on the first of each month and had Saturdays and Sundays free to ply for hire. Blechynden decided that in future, they should not be paid before the fifteenth. The Englishman was Charles Weston, presumably the lottery purchaser of Tiretta's bazar. On Hafiz: AB, 15 July 1812.

7.   RB, 28–9 January 1798; 29 January 1803; and 3–4 February 1803. Marmaduke (b.1760), son of Blechynden's father's older brother, entered Company marine service as a captain's servant and rose to the rank of first mate. In 1803, he tried to seize his estranged partner, Sally (Chapter 5); Blechynden thought he ought to obtain something for a poor constable who lost his job after this assault.

8.   The name varied according to the holder's religion, a *ketmutgar* generally being Muslim and the sirdar bearer, according to *Hobson-Jobson*, a Hindu of the Kahar caste. 'Sirdar', commander, might have meant a head palankeen bearer; but in Bengal, the term was used for a valet or other manservant. Occasionally Blechynden had both a sirdar bearer and a ketmutgar, the former taking charge

of clothes, furniture, and petty cash with the latter waiting at table, serving as valet. Henry Yule and A.C. Burrell, *Hobson-Jobson: The Anglo-Indian Dictionary* (1886, 1902; Ware 1996).

9.   RB, 18 April and 9 February 1799. Thomas possibly came to exercise a horse, as for Wales, but not always. In 1800, Blechynden hired a boy, Doman, to ride with him in the mornings to exercise his horse Captain, until the boy caught smallpox: RB, 15 and 18 January 1800; 3 April 1800; 13 and 25 June 1800. On 'boy', see n37.

10.   RB, 17 February 1798.

11.   RB, 7 November 1794; 28 November 1797; on Ingun: RB, 10 November 1798.

12.   On Hurry: RB 11 and 29 July 1803; 1 and 25 October 1803. On Gopaul: RB, 9 February 1805. On Tilluck: RB, 10–11 March 1805. On the old bearer: RB, 15 September 1808. On Gopey: RB, 9 December 1818; 2 April 1819; 2 September 1819; 2 October 1819; 1–2 February 1820; 4 January 1821 (illness); and 1 March 1821.

13.   RB, 21 December 1792; 16 April 1793; 5–8, 11, and 19 February 1794; 24 July 1794; 13 August 1794; 8–9 September 1794.

14.   RB, 28 December 1792; 2 January 1793; 26 April 1793; and 18 May 1800.

15.   On horses: RB, 24 October 1796; 11 February 1797; 1 and 12 August 1797; and 2 November 1800. On the budgerow: RB, 18 February 1799. Earlier, Padre was lent to Doncaster for the cost of his feed: also RB, 17 March and 16 June 1797.

16.   RB, 26 October 1802; 18 and 21 April 1805.

17.   RB, 6–7 and 22 October 1800. Presentiment of disaster: RB, 27 and 29 September 1800.

18.   RB, 14 July 1798; 1 and 3 June 1800.

19.   RB, 6 December 1797, 15, 29 September 1799.

20.   RB, 14 May 1794; 22 July 1794; 27 September 1794; 20 December 1794; 25 January 1795; 19 July 1795; 26 July 1796; and 7 November 1796. The story of Tiretta's marriage is told in Peter Robb, *Sex and Sensibility: Richard Blechynden's Calcutta Diaries, 1791–1822* (New Delhi 2011), chapter 2. Reta was eventually dismissed: RB, 5 April 1802. On 'boy', see n37, on the meaning 'servant'. Thomas *was* clearly a boy or young man, and so probably were some others whom we will find described thus (Doman, Cato, the horse-riding Buxoo) and others not (for example, possibly, Alberto).

21.   RB, 19 and 21 April 1797; on Reta: RB, 7 March 1798.

22.   RB, 9, 10–11 September 1797, 27–8, 30 August, 2 September 1796.

23.   RB, 31 May 1794; 6 February 1795; 5 and 7–8 November 1796; 2 and 5 September 1797; toenail: RB, 14 June 1800.

24.   RB, 26 and 28 May 1794; 13 September 1794; 15–16 May 1795; and 1 August 1796. Rumjohnny died on 15 August: RB, 16 August 1795. Later, another Rumjohnny was in Blechynden's employ. According to *Hobson-Jobson*, Ramjohnny was a vulgar term applied to female prostitutes (*Rama-jani*, dancer) or a low class of servants frequenting the wharves to gain employment from newcomers. Here it would be the common Muslim name 'Ramazani' (also in *Hobson-Jobson*).

25.   The castes in question are probably the 'pure' Sudra Goala (cowherds) and Muchi (leather workers).

26.   RB, 3–4 and 6 July 1801; 13 July 1805; and 4 October 1818.

27.   RB, 26–7 and 30 January 1804; AB, 25 May 1811. James Hare, assistant surgeon, was well known and friendly with Blechynden. His son James, assistant marine surgeon and military orphan society surgeon (1805), also treated the Blechyndens.

28.   RB, 6 October 1795. On Punjabee: RB, 27–31 October 1805. On Davy: 5–7 February 1816.

29.   RB, 27 January 1795. Years later, Callindy died from snakebite and Blechynden gave five rupees for her burial: RB, 4 May 1804.

30.   Cassinaut, RB, 19 January 1805.

31.   RB, 5, 8–9, and 13 February 1798; 9 and 11 July 1798; 25 September 1798; and 19 January 1799. On another occasion, Martyn committed Tiretta's writer, Peter, to prison, without allowing him to speak a single word in his defence, for allegedly having thrown stones into another person's compound. Various attempts were made to get him released, partly because of the effect on Tiretta's work; Blechynden was penning letters to the justices: RB, 19 and 20 March 1798. For other interventions over Indian servants, adultery, wives, and husbands, see Robb, *Sex and Sensibility*.

32.   On the peon: RB, 4 May 1793. On Reed: RB, 2 February, 24 March 1798, 2 May 1799. In 1810, Reed was selling timber to Blechynden, but had debts to him, secured by a mortgage from his mother who lived near Calcutta.

33.   RB, 6–7 January 1795; 6 March 1802; 9 October 1803; and 25 September 1809.

34.   RB, 30–1 July 1800; 2 August 1800; and 11 January 1801.

35.   RB, 2–7 April 1804; 25–6 June 1805.

36.   RB, 9 February 1797; grain: 22 December 1798; On the Thursday absences: RB, 6 January 1803; 12 and 14 September 1813; 23 August 1813. On the peons: 17 January 1819. Baddinaut was employed by W.T. Jones (see Robb, *Sex and Sensibility*, chapter 6), then worked again for Blechynden till dismissed in 1813. Blechynden had to go himself to ensure the free flow of water, prevented by one Goroopersaud Bhose. His people refused to open

the dam and at first prevented Blechynden's malis from doing so. A peon or chaukidar named Seeboo puffed tobacco smoke in Blechynden's face when he explained that he should not stop a public current, that water ought to be as free as air. Blechynden knocked his pipe from his hand.

37.   On Emaundee, Hingun, Ameer: RB, 9, 11–12, and 25 April 1797; 8 and 12 June 1797; 16 June 1797; 24 and 25 August 1797. On Doman and Buxoo: RB, 19, 22, and 25 October 1800. On Deenoo: RB, 2 September 1801. On Rumjohnny: RB, 1 February 1805. On Ashraf: RB, 7 July 1805. *Hobson-Jobson* says that 'boy' for a palankeen bearer or a servant more generally, a south Indian usage, may derive from English or caste names (Telegu and Malayalam *boyi*, Tamil *bovi*, Hindi and Marathi *bhoi*). It is fairly unusual in Blechynden. Buxoo *was* probably a boy in age (he is not the man of that name in Robb, *Sex and Sensibility*, chapter 5). On Doman: also see n9. Another missing manservant, Boodoo, and Buxoo were drafted in to accompany Blechynden to Tamluk: RB, 17 February 1801.

38.   RB, 1 and 3–4 June 1805. See Robb, *Sex and Sensibility*, chapter 8.

39.   RB, 27–8 and 30 June 1799. On Reed: RB, 2 February 1798.

40.   Daffadar meant the supervisor of a small body of men; this one had been employed on Blechynden's public works as a bricklayer, rather than with the police or in the army, where the rank would also be found.

41.   RB, 15–16 February 1801; 14, 29, and 30 March 1801; 25 and 28 (wrongly headed 29) May 1801; and 7 June 1801.

42.   RB, 13 April 1805; 22–4 and 26 May 1805; and 1–2 April 1821.

43.   RB, 15–16, 19, and 22 March 1794; and 2–3 April 1794.

44.   The custom of having a particular tailor as a kind of shared servant persisted among the better-off classes in Calcutta until very recently, though of course it diminished with the spread of ready-made clothing.

45.   Stockings: RB, 10 and 12 August 1796; and 5 January 1797. On the buggy: RB, 16 May 1797.

46.   RB, 1 and 24 October 1796; 11 February 1797; 16 May 1797; 19–20 April 1797; 12 August 1797; and 2 November 1800. Earlier, Padre had been lent to Doncaster for the cost of his feed: RB, 17 March and 16 June 1797.

47.   RB, 4, 9, and 10 February 1795; 8 January 1800; 28 September 1800; and 1 December 1800.

48.   RB, 2 and 8 October 1795; 18 and 20–1 July 1796; 27 August 1796; 2 October 1796; 25 November 1796; 21 March 1797; and 4 August 1818. On Buddoo: RB, 8 April 1801.

49.   On Deenoo: RB, 30–1 October and 1 November 1800. On Teen Courie: RB, 22–4 February 1801; 5 and 23 March 1801. On Buxoo: 13, 15, 17, 20, and 27 March 1801; and 9 May 1801. The competing case concerned the durwan and the neighbours: Robb, *Sex and Sensibility*, chapter 6.

50.  RB, 29 October 1794 and 29 April 1796. On another occasion, hearing a woman from his service at the gardens was secretly in Calcutta, he wrote: 'I must have a traytor in my House': RB, 4 February 1795. The woman was Bucktar and the informant the town bibi: they feature in Robb, *Sex and Sensibility*, chapter 4.

51.  RB, 2–3 August 1796. 'Gool', maybe *gul* (flower), is possibly something to flavour the hookah smoke, as when a fruit shell or peel replaced the earthenware bowl (chillum); *gul* is also used for ash on a cigarette.

52.  RB, 2 September 1796 and 8 July 1817. A female sweeper, detected by the durwan trying to steal tumblers from the house, breaking one when discovered, and sent to the justices, was 'only punished with a few Slippers': RB, 12 and 15 September 1794.

53.  RB, 22, 23–4, and 26 May 1797.

54.  RB, 11 May 1799; 29 June 1799; and 16–17 July 1799. On Seeboo: RB, 8 July 1799. On Forbes and Andiram: RB, 28–9 September 1799. There are many mentions of 'Lilloo Sircar' again in 1800, for example: RB, 22 January 1800. For long periods, Blechynden employed both Lilloo and Jaggernaut.

55.  Teen Courie was repeatedly unreliable and a 'precious rascal', earlier imprisoned for debt. Then the cook, who initially disappeared with him, said on his return that he had been seized as he was surety for the three rupees Teen Courie owed to a bania. Blechynden refused to help, but wrote to Blaquiere to ask that the prisoner might be sent to him to give up the keys to his plate and table linen. This was done, and thirty towels and two tablecloths were said to be missing. Teen Courie seems to have been a locum tenens for Deenoo, who returned from Beerbhoom when summoned by Lilloo and reported four table cloths and thirty towels missing. Blechynden told him that *he* was responsible for them. RB, 5, 22–4 February, 20, 23, and 27 March 1801.

56.  RB, from January 1801; the fullest accounts on Lilloo (Nilmunny Ghose) are at 18, 20–4, 26, 28, and 30 April 1801; 5–6, 9, and 22–4 July 1801. Cassinaut: RB, 18 May 1801. Goyram: RB, 30 April 1801. For Jaggernaut and Lilloo's proceedings: RB 7 and 10–11 July 1802; 26 August 1802; and 1 September 1802. For Lilloo's return: RB, 8–9 March 1803; 27 October 1803; and 17 August 1805. On Cassinaut: RB, 16, 18, and 24–5 December 1801. Rammohun Chatterjee: RB, 8 April 1803; 18 October 1803; 30 November 1803; 1, 12, and 15 December 1803; 21, 23–6, and 30–1 July 1804; 3–4, 10–11, 13 August 1804; 13, 20–3, 25–7, and 29–30 March 1805; 1–3 and 8 April 1805; 3 and 23 May 1805; 4, 10, 16–17, 21–2, and 26 June 1805; 5 July 1805; 12 December 1807. On dustoory: RB, 29 August 1802. On the disgrace of being sworn in: 7 and 9–10 December 1807; 30 July 1810; and 4 August 1810. For some reason, Blechynden was making wage payments, acting as his own sircar, on 15–16 October 1806. Lilloo was being sued for debt again, by others, in 1809: RB, 5 April 1809. He was still employed by Blechynden in 1818, buying

screens for him, though ill at the end of December that year. Blechynden walked to his house, found he had pains in his chest and difficulty breathing, and told him to soak his legs, keep warm, and take castor oil. He survived, was working in April 1820, and died unexpectedly on 23 December 1821: RB, 7 July 1813; 1 August 1813; 5 and 30–1 December 1818; 2 April 1820; and 1 January 1822. On Davy Naug's shrine, see RB, 12 September 1813: the words used are 'Seek Takoor Bharree', lord's house, which could mean a grand mansion, but as it is described as being at his country house, is presumably a house for an image.

57. RB, 21 March 1799; 8 and 10 April 1799.

58. RB, 30 April 1798; 1–3, 13–14, and 22 May 1798; 19 October 1798; 5 November 1798; 14 September 1801; 9, 20–24, and 26 October 1801; 3 October 1803; 14 and 20 October 1804; 16, 18, and 30 May 1805; 17 June 1805; 8 and 23–5 October 1805; and 12 October 1809. Gopey sent home from work when ill 'with a flux': RB, 10 June 1799. A shorter Durga holiday for him: RB, 4 October 1800.

59. Frederick Cooper, 'Colonizing Time: Work Rhythms and Labor Conflict in Colonial Mombasa', in Nicholas B. Dirks (ed.), *Colonialism and Culture* (Ann Arbor 1992), p. 211.

60. RB, 28 February 1793 and 3 April 1795.

61. One by John Maclachlan was published by the Mirror Press in 1792; Shaw, *Bibliography*, p. 242. Blechynden also undertook such work.

62. RB, 26 October 1794 (but passim).

63. When Blechynden's neighbour Doncaster stayed with him, Blechynden could not fathom why, awaking at midnight, he would find Doncaster still up, chatting with friends. Earlier, when involved in building work for Doncaster, who was sending dinner from his kitchen, Blechynden was repeatedly irritated by its late arrival—Blechynden would call for it at 4.00 PM, a 'Christian-like time', but would have to wait until seven and fill in with bread and cheese. Doncaster was also keeping the workers until six, when their hours were eight to four, which was cheating them, said Blechynden, of a quarter of their labour. Doncaster was 'sulky' and 'glum' at these complaints, and Blechynden made himself appear 'merry to vex him': RB, 6–7 August 1796 and 21 May 1797.

64. Rachel Sturman, 'Marriage and the Morality of Exchanges: Defining the Terrain of Law in Late Nineteenth-century Western India', in Durba Ghosh and Dane Kennedy (eds), *Decentring Empire: Britain, India and the Transcolonial World* (London 2006), pp. 51–75.

65. RB, 29 April 1793.

66. RB, 23 and 27 February 1794; 16 and 18 May 1795; and 17 November 1795. When Mary ran away in May 1795, Blechynden had his sircar turn away the sweeper who failed to point her out to the peon; the sircar was to find two more attendants for the bibi. Later, Blechynden refused the bibi's wish that Mary be reinstated.

# NOTES TO CHAPTER 4

1.   Edmund Burke's comment on Fox's East India Bill, House of Commons, 1 December 1783.

2.   RB, 16 July 1799.

3.   Peter Robb, *Sex and Sensibility: Richard Blechynden's Calcutta Diaries, 1791–1822* (New Delhi 2011).

4.   The reference is to N.B. Halhed's translation via Persian of a Sanskrit compilation, published as *A Code of Gentoo Laws; or Ordinations of the Pundits* (1776). Blechynden might have referred to Exodus 21, 20–1.

5.   RB, 9 December 1796; 6–7, 12, 21, and 29 July 1800; 1 and 18 August 1800; 5–11 and 22 September 1800; 16, 17–18, 20–21, 23, 25, and 27–30 October 1800; 3–9 and 1–14 November 1800; and 6 December 1800. On Rothman: RB, 29 January 1801. Lloyd, an attorney's clerk, is recorded as a Calcutta resident in 1803. Blechynden consistently avoided involvement. Initially caught to serve on the coroner's jury, he pleaded his disagreement with Jones. Lloyd said that if such things mattered, they could never hold an inquest. Blechynden, insisting, was allowed to wait to see if twelve others could be found and was then excused. Lloyd, stinking of liquor, thanked him for his scruples. When Jones heard, he did not believe it, saying 'by Jazuz that rascal would be glad to see me hung'.

6.   For example, see Andre Wink, *Land and Sovereignty in India* (Cambridge 1986). See also K.N. Chaudhuri, 'From the Barbarian and the Civilised to the Dialectics of Colour: an Archaeology of Self-identities', in Peter Robb (ed.), *Society and Ideology: Essays in South Asian History presented to Professor K.A. Ballhatchet* (Delhi 1993), pp. 22–48.

7.   For one example, see RB, 17 January 1794. In a general discussion, with some Bengal examples (Chapter 4), Lauren Benton, *Law and Colonial Cultures: Legal Regimes in World History, 1400–1900* (Cambridge 2002), argues that a growing subordination of ethnic and religious communities to state law from the eighteenth century was qualified by 'state-centered legal pluralism' from the mid-nineteenth. Arguably, pluralism of a sort started earlier in Bengal; but there was, as Benton claims, both a sharpening of the division between 'modern' and 'traditional' realms *and* 'rampant border-crossing'. Also, given appeals to 'multiple legal authorities' and 'internally fragmented' colonial authorities asserting themselves within local power structures, rules of engagement were more important than institutions (pp. 6–11)—in India at least until the 1860s, with the introduction of High Courts and more local legislation.

8.   James Mill, *The History of British India* (ed.) H.H. Wilson (London 1858; 5th edn), book V, chapter VI, p. 228. A new version of this idea among so-called new imperial historians argues that 'English law and administrative regulations in British dominions ... aimed at maintaining the boundaries

between "home" and "abroad," ... keeping the less savory aspects of imperial rule ... from metropolitan view': Kathleen Wilson (ed.), *A New Imperial History: Culture, Identity and Modernity in Britain and the Empire, 1660–1840* (Cambridge 2004), p.16. Such an impulse is not denied, but nor are more powerful alternatives: rationalization of empire in terms of legal and other benefits bestowed; readiness of subject peoples to embrace or adapt some imported institutions and ideas; even implied or potential equality of subjecthood and rights under law. For economic aspects, linked inter alia to obsession with liberty, property, and legality (eighteenth-century parliaments, the American War of Independence), see Sudipta Sen, 'Liberal Empire and Illiberal Trade: The Political Economy of "Responsible Government" in Early British India', in Wilson (ed.), *A New Imperial History*, pp. 136–54. Also see Peter Robb, *Empire, Identity and India: Liberalism, Modernity and the Nation* (New Delhi 2007), pp. 13–20; Uday Mehta, *Liberalism and Empire: A Study in Nineteenth-Century British Liberal Thought* (Chicago 1999).

9.    RB, 13 September 1796. On 'Vigour beyond the Law': RB, 18 June 1799.

10.    On the bearer: RB, 16–17 February 1794. On the sircar: RB, 12 January 1795. On the mistri: RB, 24–5 June 1795. On Grant: RB, 1 and 3 February 1797. Addison is perhaps John, merchant, father of Henry Robert Addison, the Irish playwright. For Grant: see Chapter 1, n47.

11.    RB, 18 April 1788; 10 April 1799.

12.    RB, 1–4 September 1793. For another incident, see RB, 1 June 1794. Miller, born in 1720 in Virginia which he left in 1736, bore his age well; 13 October 1797. Wales was notoriously 'hot-headed', for example, when in dispute with the Marine Board; 14 August 1795.

13.    RB, 5–7 January 1793; 12 and 15 September 1794.

14.    On the incident featuring Smith: RB, 9, 10,12, 15–16, and 22 August 1794. Blechynden did not always prosecute absconders—for example, the absent durwan (RB, 12 August 1794) or bearers missing for five days (RB, 17 May 1794). On Smith's highhandedness, see RB, 3 March 1794. There are several possibilities for Shakespear.

15.    RB, 27 November 1794. The house was in Meer Jaun Gully.

16.    On Mahomed: RB, 6, 9, and 11 January 1798; on Martyn: RB, 22 June 1798, 9 October; prostitutes: 27 June 1799. Martyn also had a case before the Supreme Court, almost all the other justices being subpeonaed, 'about slippering a native months ago at the cutcherry': RB, 15 January 1799. 'Cutcherry' here is court house.

17.    RB, 9 December 1796; Robb, *Sex and Sensibility*, chapter 6.

18.    RB, 18 July 1799.

19.    Blechynden had two friends named Bishop: Captain Thomas Bishop of the *Maria*, and (RB, 15 November 1805) another mariner, James (1781–1818).

20.   RB, 15, 17–21, and 26–9 September 1799; 9, 11, 16, and 19–21 October 1799; 1–2, 5, 7, 13, and 16–19 November 1799. On the Circular Road: RB, 29 April 1800. On first meeting Reed, who had represented Doncaster in Chittagong, Blechynden described him as a 'young native' (7 March 1796). The attorneys were William Burroughs (or Burrows) and Robert Ledlie. Matthew Louis's evident partiality towards Doncaster's case was more than race solidarity or anti-Indian prejudice. Rammohun said that Louis and one Morris owed Doncaster a joint bond of Rs 5,000. Louis interfered in Doncaster's affair with the Brahman woman (Chapter1) and in complaints against Doncaster to Sir John Anstruther about a blanket maker's wife. Doncaster cancelled the joint bond, took one from Morris, and left Louis exposed for his own share, still a large sum. Some regularization of the justices began: Martyn, Blaquiere, Macklew, and Thorston were appointed, under new rules; Rothman, Jessup, Boileau, and Louis lost their posts and were given pensions, Boileau until he succeeded Jackson as Company Attorney and Louis for thirty months as coroner on a reduced salary. Blechynden thought Louis would not long retain that post: RB, 16 April and 13 June 1800. Doncaster, arrested on the plea of Indian merchants claiming fraud against them and the Company on salt contracts, spent many months in gaol: RB, 21–2, 24, and 26 February 1800; 19 March 1800; 26 June 1800; and 2 July 1800.

21.   RB, 28 December 1799; 11–12 and 27 June 1800; 8, 12, and 16 December 1805; and 26 November 1807.

22.   RB, 8 January and 11 February 1799.

23.   Dowdeswell: Secretary, Board of Revenue, 1794; Judical and Revenue Secretary, 1801; Superintendent-General of Police, 1805; Chief Secretary, 1812; resigned 1823. Charles Blunt was presumably the son of the late Postmaster-General.

24.   On Sultan: RB, 30–1 January 1801. Rumjohnny: RB, 16–18, 25, and 28 March 1804. Tilluck: RB, 1, 3–4, and 7 May 1808. MacArthur never apologized: AB, 25 May 1809.

25.   RB, 20 December 1796; 5, 7, and 21 February 1800; 10 April 1800; and 5 December 1805. A peon might have been heard by the court. When his durwan told him that a Portuguese woman had struck him and he had put her in the thana, Blechynden told him to go to the justices as he would not interfere: RB, 9 February 1797. Blechynden's attitude to insanity was relatively benign. He sat for half an hour with one Kissen Kunt Sein when he was insane, incoherent, but not violent, and thought he ought to be surrounded by his family, not isolated: RB, 5 June 1801.

26.   RB, 14 April 1805; 4, 5, 8, and 10–11 April 1806.

27.   For example, see Tanika Sarkar, 'Performing Power and Troubling Plays: Public Theatre in Colonial Bengal', paper presented at the School of Oriental and African Studies, 3 March 2008, on Bengali 'court-room' dramas

such as *Nil Darpan*. For elite Bengal's encounter with English law (redefining criminality and social discipline; the bhadralok as a law-abiding class): Anindita Mukhopadhyay, *Behind the Mask: the Cultural Definition of the Legal Subject in Colonial Bengal (1715–1911)*, (New Delhi 2006).

28.   RB, 28 March 1801.

29.   Nandini Bhattacharyya-Panda, *Appropriation and Invention of Tradition: The East India Company and Hindu Law in Early Colonial India* (New Delhi 2008), pp. 7–11, 243–53, questions continuities proposed by C.A. Bayly, Rosalind O'Hanlon, and David Washbrook. Robert Travers, *Ideology and Empire in Eighteenth-Century India: The British in Bengal* (Cambridge 2007) argues for the attempted *reconstruction* of 'ancient constitutions' and *reformulation* of European political ideas. Besides precolonial continuities and the empire's influence on the metropole, I trace connected processes leading to *varying* forms of modernization. On the generality of challenges and change: P.J. Marshall, *The Making and Unmaking of Empires: Britain, India, and America* (Oxford 2005). For corruption engendered in Europeans by experience of the East that a reformed empire would supposedly cure, in both ruler and ruled: Nicholas B. Dirks, *The Scandal of Empire: India and the Creation of Imperial Britain* (Cambridge, MA 2006).

## NOTES TO CHAPTER 5

1.   RB, 13 January 1813.

2.   Peter Laslett (ed.), *Household and Family in Past Time* (Cambridge 1972); Stone, *The Family*; Roy Porter (ed.), *Rewriting the Self: Histories from the Renaissance to the Present* (London and New York 1997). Bibis are the subject of *Sex and Sensibility*.

3.   RB, 9 and 11–12 March 1793; Stone, *The Family*, pp. 57, 58, 269–73. Sidney's grave: RB, 16 January 1799. Sidney's mother, distraught: Peter Robb, *Sex and Sensibility: Richard Blechynden's Calcutta Diaries, 1791–1822* (New Delhi 2011), chapter 4.

4.   Harriet: RB, 17 October 1807; 25 November 1807; and 1 July 1808. Arthur's and Sally's upbringing by their mother and concerns over their health: RB, 28 November 1793; 2 and 4 March 1794; 31 January 1795; 18–20 and 23 March 1795; and 27–8 April 1795. Language: RB, 7 April 1794. Hindustani (here the broad, eclectic lingua franca called Moors) was codified and taught to Company servants: Robb, *Sex and Sensibility*, chapter 1.

5.   For Blechynden's aunt, Jane Harriet Theobald; her husband, James; Blechynden's two sisters, Lydia Harriet and Charlotte. Richard was named for his father; Thomas Blechynden for his grandfather; but Arthur for Arthur Hesilrige. Arthur's first son was Richard (7 October 1814), his second Arthur Henry (23 October 1815). But Blechynden's mother was Mary (Brown).

6.   On teething: RB, 2 March 1794. On heights: RB, 17 May 1805. On illnesses of Harriet: RB, 24 and 26 September (Hare was called), 14 November 1810; Tom, Emma: RB, 5–6 January 1812 (Burlini).

7.   Inoculation: RB, 7, 9, 13, 16–17, and 21 February 1799. Baptism: RB, 6 February 1799; 19 and 21–3 March 1799. Arthur named his 'sponsors' as Sir Arthur Hesilrige; Captain John Wales (Bombay Marine); Miss C.F. Blechynden (his aunt), represented by Lieutenants Phillips and Roper (Bombay Marine); and Mrs Reeves: AB, undated (1809). (Jane) Harriet was christened by the Rev. Dr Buchanan, the sponsors including Mrs Theobald, represented by Mrs Macey, and James Dunbar; a grand dinner and puppet show followed: AB, 28 March 1807.

8.   RB, 29 and 31 July 1794; 27 February 1796; 12 May 1796; 28 June 1796; 5–8 August 1796; and 21–2 September 1796. On the hydrocele: 6 February 1797. Blechynden also arranged schooling for children, girls and boys, of friends stationed up-country, such as the illegitimate daughters of Henry Berkeley: 1 August 1794. If 'Mary' was the absconding slave who returned at the death of the older children's mother, there is no note that she was kept in employment. For more on her, Ramzanny, and Mary Anne, see Robb, *Sex and Sensibility*.

9.   RB, 3 January 1801; 7 October and 2 November 1802.

10.   RB, 6 July 1796; 9 September 1796; 28 October 1796; 1 and 7 November 1796. Mrs Mulder was married in Cochin, leaving her husband to come to Calcutta with Collins. Their relations were troubled. She was said to be always reproaching him about his bad teeth, saying 'she did not admit such people to touch her shoes in Cochin'. Collins had money problems resulting from the failure of his partnership, later staying in Blechynden's garden house, in a small downstairs room, leaving Mrs Mulder and a few possessions in town. When visiting, she had Blechynden's room with her daughter; he slept elsewhere, plagued by mosquitoes. Collins brought Rs 5,000 to his partnership with Callendar, dissolved in 1796 (RB, 12 and 16 September). Collins drew back Rs 3,000 the first month, and then another Rs 500 per month. Winding up the partnership, over the cost of refitting a ship, *Belfrey*, which, being already mortgaged, could not be sold when a banian's debt fell due, Barber made Collins a debtor to the business for Rs 14,000, saying each partner's account was fairly stated. Collins was later gaoled for debt. RB, 12 September, 19 October, 10 December 1796, and 24 February 1797.

11.   RB, 13, 16, and 27–8 April 1796; 5, 18–21, and 26–7 July 1796; 3 and 19 August 1796; 1 and 9 September 1796; 6 October 1796; and 23–5 December 1796.

12.   Discussed briefly in Robb, *Sex and Sensibility*. See Ann Laura Stoler, *Carnal Knowledge and Imperial Power: Race and the Intimate in Colonial Rule*

(Berkeley 2002), p. 49, on the Indies Civil Code, 1848, and a concubine's lack of rights over children born to a European man in the Dutch East Indies.

13. For Mary Wade, see Robb, *Sex and Sensibility*, chapter 6.

14. RB, 15, 29, and 31 May 1797; 21–2 and 24 July 1797; 7 August 1797; 4 January 1798; 2 February 1798; 29 March 1798; 21 and 23 May 1798; 27 and 29 June 1798.

15. It may have been the prospect of his sister Charlotte's marriage, to which he gave written consent in June: RB, 1 March and 11 June 1797.

16. RB, 1, 3 January 1796, 22, 25 March 1797. W.N. Farrer, on the Andamans station, had command of the *Bellona*, described by Blechynden as small, stinking, and quite unsuitable for his children (30 October 1795, 6 January 1796); presumably Lloyd was its owner. Farrer, an occasional guest of Blechynden's (again in 1800), commanded the Company's ship *Cumberland* in 1802.

17. RB, 12 June 1797; 3 April 1797; 8 May 1797; and 16 June 1797. Bishop was an 'old acquaintance' (12 February 1797).

18. RB, 7–8, 10–14, and 20 April 1797; 10, 12, 14, 17, and 29–30 June 1797; 1 and 19–20 July 1797. On the farriery text, see RB, 14 October 1795: Deletang wanted Blechynden to bring out a new edition with extra notes of a work Deletang had published in Madras; Sir John Shore had subscribed for 100 copies. The *Chronicle* stopped publishing on 27 March: RB, 24 March 1797.

19. RB, 4, 8, 14, 18, 20, and 26 April 1797; 14–15, 22, and 27 June 1797; 4 and 20–1 July 1797.

20. RB 9, 15–17, 19, 21, 23–4, 27, and 29 June 1797; 16 July 1797.

21. Unruly Jones: RB, 7 December 1795; 'dying' Jones child: 10–12 January. On the departure: RB, 24 June 1797; 16–17, 20, and 24–5 July 1797; 4 and 18 August 1797; 1 and 5 October 1797.

22. RB, 14 and 20 April 1798; 23 and 29–30 October 1798; AB, undated (Add. Mss. 45654). As Mary Anne Jones died in April 1797, her mother, the children's grandmother, would probably not have known before the arrival of the *Maria*.

23. RB, 20 and 22 December 1798; 3 September 1800. The ayah was for Trail's children.

24. Arthur: RB, 21 January 1795; stockings: 16 December 1800. On the *Bengal*: 25 and 30 July 1802; 16 September 1802. Richardson: RB, 12–15, 19–21, 23–4, 26–7, and 29 January 1803. Marmaduke decided to sell his cargo 'privilege' in Madras rather than Calcutta to get a better price, as there was less shipping available there.

25. RB, 4 February 1803; buggy: 18 December 1802.

26. Africa: RB, 14 May 1803; Powell: 15 August 1804; Theobald: 12 November 1804. Mrs Whitchurch became 'deranged' after the death of her

husband, a fact which (Blechynden thought) contributed to the death of their aunt, Mrs Theobald, along with the death of her own husband. On this and Blechynden's and Arthur's troubles with their employment in India: RB, 1 October 1816.

27.   RB, 2–3 January 1811; 7 August 1812; 1 October 1812; and 1 January 1813. A friend (3 January) called Rs 1,500 a 'shameful' price, saying four children, their mother, and a 'coffree girl' had been sent for only Rs 3,000. Emma and Harriet did not return to Calcutta until 1824, after Blechynden's death, when they were bond passengers with a security of £400 from Isaac Palmer Neale.

28.   RB, 17–18 January 1793; 21 February 1795.

29.   Alan Mcfarlane, *The Family Life of Ralph Josselin: A Seventeenth-Century Clergyman* (Cambridge 1970), especially part III.

30.   Stone, *The Family*, p. 80 and chapter 7, esp. pp. 190–1.

31.   French language: RB, 14 October 1803. Cummins: RB, 16 February 1805. Arthur: RB, 21 November 1809. On Rev. French: RB, 20 July 1809 (and AB). On Emma: RB, 2 May 1813. Bidon: RB, 9 October 1821.

32.   On skin colour: RB, 2 January 1822. On Arthur: 21 January 1795. On Sally: RB, 4 March 1795. Stone, *The Family*, p. 331.

## NOTES TO CHAPTER 6

1.   Epigraph to volume 70 of Blechynden's diaries. Following Virgil, *Georgics*, I.145.

2.   Arthur thought overcoming all the problems would give his father a great name, but the bridge cracked—a 'standing disgrace'—because of the poor materials provided by others for its construction: AB, 1 October 1809; 1 January 1810.

3.   RB, 31 August 1802; Peter Robb, *Sex and Sensibility: Richard Blechynden's Calcutta Diaries, 1791–1822* (New Delhi 2011), chapter 1, n23.

4.   RB, 25–7 October 1806. Ladd, mentioned as a creditor of Dowling, 12 April 1798, may possibly be Charles, a music teacher.

5.   The Committee initially comprised George Dowdeswell, Charles Buller, Captain Thomas Wood, Peter Moir, C.F. Martyn, W.C. Blaquiere, A. Stewart (see below), and Thomas Chartres, but not Blechynden. He pondered on why he was left out and concluded that it might have been Dowdeswell's way of ensuring he had the work, as he 'ought not to command' himself. See n6.

6.   This was puzzling. For twenty-four scavengers, many of them Portuguese, each paid Rs 15: see RB, 30 August 1808.

7.   RB, 25–7 October 1806; 1 July 1807; 14 and 22–4 October 1807.

8.   AB, 1 October 1810. Many houses—presumably forming Middleton Row in the grounds of a grand house, later Loreto House (once occupied by Frankland, Vansittart, and then Impey that Middleton bought in 1806)—were built speculatively, underfunded despite John Palmer's involvement, and let only slowly. One early tenant was Dowdeswell (much involved with Blechynden in 1807 over details of his house); all were taken by late 1808 (AB, 8 November 1808); and by the 1820s, occupied by leading Company and Calcutta dignitaries. Middleton, allegedly corrupt and brutal, was a judge at Jessore (RB, 18 and 28 July 1810) and temporarily without a post until 1810 (RB, 3 November 1810). His procrastination and obfuscation, despite arbitration and action in equity at the Court of Chancery, cost Blechynden his fee and many of his costs, ending his hope of a return to England: RB, 1 July 1810.

9.   RB, 27 and 31 October 1807; 2 November 1807; 6–7 January 1808; 1 April 1808; 4 August 1808; 10, 16, and 18 September 1808. Arthur helped with his father's report on the Town Hall construction: RB, 14 July 1810; then worked independently, including a very accurate survey at the salt lakes: RB, 8 April 1811. On learning Bengali: AB, 6–9, 13–14, and 17 October 1808.

10.   *Bheesti* was the name for any water carrier, whether for a household or an army. Here their work may have been sanitary disposal and drain clearance, or carrying water to keep down dust on roads or for use in repairs and construction.

11.   RB, 14–16 and 30 August 1808. On the arguments: RB, 3–7 and 11 October 1808. On Andrew: RB, 9 October 1809. On allowances: RB, 6 and 9 November 1809. On the bheestis: RB, 10 July 1810. Blechynden's Committee salary barely covered the interest on money he had to borrow (nearly Rs 10,000 by July 1813) for work he was asked to carry out by verbal orders, in advance of or even without authorization or funds from government: RB, 3 July 1813.

12.   Jones: RB, 4 April 1811. Canal: AB, 1 April and 1 July 1810 (original deadline, May).

13.   Ghulam: RB, 1 and 4 May 1813; AB, 2 and 5 March 1812; 10 April 1812. Competitors charged various amounts: 10 per cent of estimated value (not cost) plus travelling expenses; 15 per cent on the prime cost of materials and work; or even contract commission at 20 or 30 per cent. Commission on *what* was an issue: for repairing and painting a small house, where Davy Naug (advised by Blechynden) would charge Rs 4,000, a certain F. Rose—diamond cutter, indigo planter, and 'architect'—wanted over Rs 7,600, including Rs 1,793 for painting alone. Blechynden's real charge had been only Rs 968 for Dowdeswell's large, lofty three-storey house, gates, and outbuildings— meaning Rose's effective commission was at least 120 per cent: RB, 2 July 1813, and also 10 and 14 July 1813. The usual architect's commission in England

was 20 per cent, but rates were rising and enormous profits being made from a 'kind of architectural mania', as also in Calcutta: RB, 5 July 1813.

14.   Pay: AB, 15 February 1812. On animosity and zeal: RB, 1–2, 4, and 9 July 1814; 1 April 1815. On Theobald: RB, 1 October 1816. On his isolation: RB, 4 April 1815 and 1 September 1819.

15.   RB, 25–7 and 31 August 1813; 1 and 3 September 1813; and 10 October 1815. Richard Brittridge was then in Benares.

16.   RB, 3 and 6 July 1813; 1–9 July 1814; 1 April 1815 (Arthur not yet reinstated); 1, 3, 7, and 12–13 January 1816; 1 October 1818 (Arthur with the Committee for Improvement); 12 December 1818; 9 July 1819; 11 October 1821; and 11 November 1821. Arthur was Superintendent of Roads at his death in 1836.

17.   RB, 3 October and 4 December 1802. Another fever and prescription from Hare: RB, 15 August 1801; and again: RB, 18 March 1802.

18.   RB and AB, 12 July 1812. Arthur said that James was expelled for refusing to be flogged in front of the school (120 boys); the Theobald household thought that he was not in the wrong, but the victim of a 'spite' by the schoolmaster.

19.   RB, 4 April 1813; ., 14, 27, 29, and 30–1 July 1813; 1 and 7 August 1813; and 23 September 1813.

20.   RB, 3 September 1813. Relevant also, perhaps, is that Stewart seemed to have got himself into his uncle's firm ahead of one J. Hastie and may have informed on Hastie as not being licensed to be resident in Calcutta. At a dinner, Arthur told Stewart that he had acted badly, but he refused to see that he had done wrong. Arthur then put his views in a long letter to him; Stewart in turn claimed to have been insulted by Hastie: AB, 3–4 and 9 July 1812. For Alexander Stewart's appointment as a justice (not yet sworn in): RB, 28 May 1805.

21.   RB, 5 and 8 October 1815; 4, 6, 11, and 21 January 1816; 5 February 1816; 1–2 July 1816; and 1 January 1817.

22.   RB, 1 January 1817; 12 and 24 July 1817. On Roberts: RB, 13–15 July 1817. Price died in 1818 and Blechynden was executor of his will.

23.   This is probably Robert, a justice of the peace in 24 Parganas, despite other possibilities.

24.   Several members of the Betts family, indigo planters, were based at Chinsura and in Nadia district. The most likely candidate for Blechynden's closest acquaintance is Thomas Betts (d. 1834), whose son, also Thomas (b. 1801), appears in Blechynden's account (see Chapter 7). The younger Thomas married his cousin Charlotte Betts in 1820 and was serving as a Lieutenant in the Nizam's army in 1822. His mother, the elder Thomas's wife Gabriella, née Caton, of French extraction from Mauritius, died in 1809. The date of another marriage is unrecorded, but Thomas's second wife Sarah died in 1821, aged

thirty-six. Other Bettses, younger, included Robert Thomas William, who married Antoinette Herklots in 1817; Charles or 'Luckyn' (1800–1838), who does not seem to have married until 1831, when he was wedded to a sixteen-year-old (Mary) Sarah Deverell, who died the same year; and his older brother Lewis (see n27). Lewis married his first wife, née Elizabeth Manini (d. 1816), in 1814 and his second, née E.M. Herklots, in 1817.

25. On James's defection and return: RB, 1 October 1816; 23–4 July 1817; 12, 22, and 24–5 December 1818; 1, 5, 10–13, 15, and 18 January 1819; 8 and 10 February 1819; and 2 April 1819. The nephew was presumably Lewis Betts (c.1786–1837), an indigo planter when first married, but Superintendent of Embankments, 24 Parganas, by 1820, and Assistant in the Accountant-General's Office, 1825. John Betts, another planter, served as a Writer in the same office in the 1820s. Alfred Betts was a free merchant and indigo planter from the 1820s.

26. RB, 28 January 1821; 2 February 1821; and 2 May 1821. Arthur was told that Stewart, as a judge, was the best of the five, with the 'best head & heart', and unbiased: AB, 21 July 1812. (I assume this was Alexander Stewart, a justice of the peace, not James Stuart, one of five puisne judges of the Sudder Diwani and Nizamat Adalat.)

27. RB, 2–6 February 1819; 7–8 July 1819; 13 and 22 January 1819.

28. RB, 11 and 13 February 1819. The Lieutenant was probably Robert Wroughton (b.1797), later Deputy Surveyor-General of India.

29. Byron wrote the first five cantos between 1818 and 1820; the unfinished poem was published between 1819 and 1824. Blechynden quickly took up the first parts, perhaps finding it apt: the satire of English life; its unprincipled hero (James?); the prevalence of 'adultery…where the climate's sultry' (canto 1).

30. RB, 4–5 January 1820; 1 August 1820; December 1820; 2 January 1821; and notes for 3 January 1821. Sarah Thackeray (1804–1841) was the illegitimate daughter of Richmond Thackeray (d.1815) and his Eurasian mistress Charlotte Rudd. On Sarah's death, an annuity went to her half-brother, William Makepeace Thackeray (1811–1863). Her sister Jane married the surveyor Rennell. Of James and Sally's children, Augusta (b. 15 May 1823) married Charles Henry Salter, 1839, and Emily Harriet Catherine (b.17 July 1824) W.R. Langstaff, 1842. On Rudd: RB, 1 February 1822. On James's career, *Biographical Notes* (to Phillimore, *Survey of India*, vol.III), part 1, Oriental and India Office Collection, British Library. Blechynden explained his consent for James while trying to refuse approval to a marriage of twenty-year-old J. Roberts, who said he regarded Blechynden as a father. Blechynden thought that he was being used to mollify Roberts's parents: they should be consulted by letter. The girl, Miss Vincent, whose father was dead and mother had consented, was fifteen, French, and Catholic. Blechynden allowed himself to be persuaded in the end, 'finding all arguments useless'. Later, Roberts's

parental approval did come. Miss Vincent's brother's salary was doubled to Rs 200; Roberts made fifteen rupees: all would 'chum together' and 'make it out very well': RB, 3 January 1822.

## NOTES TO CHAPTER 7

1.   Jane Austen, *Pride and Prejudice* (1817), chapters 22 and 50.

2.   RB, 25 June 1812; 1, 12, and 27 July 1812; 7 and 15 August 1812; 1 October 1812; 1 January 1813; 1 and 3 May 1813; 14 and 20 July 1813; and 4 January 1816. Also AB, 15 February 1812 and 1 July 1812.

3.   RB, 3 and 21 August 1813. Arthur and Josephine must have been acquainted in England through the Theobalds, but he left when fifteen or just sixteen; she could have been twenty or more. Her mood on arrival suggests that her future was then uncertain: RB, 1 January 1813. Arthur's diary (ending 1812) does not mention his awaiting her.

4.   RB, 3 April 1815; 2 July 1815; 10 October 1815; and 1 January 1817. They were again with Blechynden in July 1817. Warner remained in Bengal, remarrying in 1835 after Charlotte's death on 2 October 1833, and dying in Rajshahi, aged seventy-seven.

5.   Her story is told in Peter Robb, *Sex and Sensibility: Richard Blechynden's Calcutta Diaries, 1791–1822* (New Delhi 2011), chapter 2.

6.   RB, 2–3 July 1814; 2 and 11 January 1815; 5–6 February 1816; 1 October 1816.

7.   On Thomas Betts, b.1801, see Chapter 6, n24.

8.   RB, 2 April 1814; 11 July 1814; 6 January 1816; 7 February 1816; notes for Sunday 4 April 1819; 2–3 July 1819; and 2 August 1821.

9.   RB, 1 July 1815; 4 October 1815; 10, 12, 14–15, and 19–20 July 1817; 1 October 1817; 1–3 January 1818; 2 July 1818; 6–7 October 1818; 20 January 1819. The identities of the eight are uncertain: presumably excluding James, they may been himself, Arthur, Fanny, the grandchildren Richard and Henry, Sarah, Harriet, and Emma. Though (apart from the two girls in England) these formed two households in Calcutta, they often dined together, and Richard's and Arthur's finances were managed jointly. However, Warner and Charlotte were in Calcutta at this time. It is not known if they received support from Blechynden other than hospitality.

10.   RB, 1 April 1817; 2, 9, 21, and 23–4 July 1817; 3 October 1818; 1–2, 7, and 9 December 1818.

11.   Foster Fyans (1790–1870) was an Irish Anglican born in Dublin who served in the Peninsular War and then, from 1817, in India, remaining there (except for a brief return to Britain after he bought his captaincy in 1827) until the 1830s. In 1833, he joined another regiment in Sydney, was captain of the guard at Norfolk Island, and a humane and successful commandant at

Moreton Bay. He sold his commission rather than return to India in 1837. He became one of the founders, a pioneering police magistrate, and the first mayor of Geelong, Victoria. Later he was to be Commissioner for Crown Lands in Portland Bay and a noted landowner, running a cattle station. See *Australian Dictionary of Biography*.

12.    RB, 15–21 December 1818. The objection to indigo planters was that they could lose everything in a season and did not seem to grow richer—witness Brittridge, no richer after twenty-five years: RB, 4 July 1820.

13.    RB, 23 December 1818. When Blechynden lost his tortoiseshell spectacles, the last articles sent to him by his uncle Theobald, he was so vexed that he wanted to dismiss all his servants. His *sircar* Ramnarain said that he was sure none of Blechynden's own servants was responsible, but the servants of others might be: the house was like a tavern, and everyone who could not secure a dinner elsewhere was sure to come to Blechynden's and then to introduce a friend, and so on. There was some truth in that, Blechynden thought: RB, 16 January 1819.

14.    RB, 26–8 December 1818 and 1–9 January 1819.

15.    No sister of young Thomas Betts has been identified as living at the time, nor any other girl of a likely age. Possibly Miss Betts was his cousin and future wife, Charlotte.

16.    RB, 12–13 January 1819. Tom also received a letter from Warner shortly after this and kept it to himself, which made Blechynden suspicious. When a second letter arrived, however, he found that the first had been to introduce himself to Tom and the second was to enclose two bank notes of Rs 100 each, which Tom was asked to deliver to Blechynden. He set Tom to reply in Latin, as it would appeal to Warner, a 'great Latinist': RB, 17–18 January 1819.

17.    Blechynden suspected contact with Fyans at the 'warehouse', presumably the bond store containing goods imported by commission agents. See Ian Woodfield, 'The Calcutta Piano Trade in the Late Eighteenth Century', in *Music of the Raj: A Social and Economic History of Music in Late Eighteenth-Century Anglo-Indian Society* (New York 2000), pp. 1–21, on the sale of pianos from commission warehouses, a mark of the town's changing culture. See Chapter 6, n26: work at the warehouse might suggest that Betts was one of the younger merchants or had responsibility for custom duties. The family had evidently moved to Calcutta at this time. Thomas (like his relatives) may have combined indigo and other occupations.

18.    RB, 13–16 and 30–1 January 1819; 1–2 February 1819; and 6 March 1819.

19.    RB, 7, 9, 11, and 14 February 1819; 1 July 1819; 4 October 1819; 1 November 1819; 1 January 1820; 4 July 1820; 1–2 January 1821; and 1 March 1821.

20.   RB, 4–8 and 10 October 1821; 1–2 November 1821; and 1 January 1822.

21.   See 'Introducing Richard Blechynden' in this book, and http://www. ukcensusonline.com.

## NOTES TO CHAPTER 8

1.   Locke, *An Essay Concerning Human Understanding* (1690), book 2, chapter 1, s. 15; book.4, chapter 19, s. 4.

2.   RB, 23 December 1800.

3.   It is my assumption Josephine/Fanny was European. Her father was French (or just possibly Italian), her mother unknown. Given current mores, it is improbable that the elderly Tiretta would have married her sister had she been of mixed race. Blechynden only infrequently referred to the mixed race of his friends, but did in some instances, especially if he disapproved of something on other grounds, as he did of Tiretta's marriage.

4.   RB, 14 July 1801; 4 July 1820; 1 and 3 March 1821. Blechynden warned Fanny against sending Arthur Henry round the Cape in winter in a 'crazy free trader', the *Timandra*, but he went despite his grandfather's 'melancholy forebodings', at the cheap enough cost of Rs 1,400, a friend having offered to provide his food for eight months.

5.   Lane was in the 37th Native Infantry; Rice was Supervisor, Custom's House, by 1825.

6.   AB, 22 April 1807; 6–9, 13, 14, and 17 October 1808. RB, 4 January 1815.

7.   AB, 1–2 and 16 November 1806; 18 and 23 December 1806; 1 and 12 January 1807; 5, 20, and 29 March 1807; 25 April 1807; 1 and 2 May 1808; and 22 July 1808.

8.   Stone, *The Family*, pp. 259–60. AB, 7 January 1809; 1 April 1809; and 18 June 1809.

9.   AB, 4–5 October 1808; Peter Robb, *Sex and Sensibility: Richard Blechynden's Calcutta Diaries, 1791–1822* (New Delhi 2011), chapter 9. Arthur was prevailed upon to join in this traditional ceremony despite repeated resistance, but became more stubborn as he grew older. On Blechynden's opposition: RB, 4 October 1808.

10.   AB, 1 January 1807; 11 April 1807; and 2 June 1811. In the hook-swinging ritual, devotees swung from a pole, suspended on ropes to which they were attached by metal hooks passed through the muscles of their backs.

11.   The insistence that identity could be *made* by individual endeavour does not deny that there are circumstances (such as slavery) in which this approach 'seriously misrepresents the ontology of identity as a coercive process': Kathleen Wilson (ed.), *A New Imperial History: Culture, Identity*

*and Modernity in Britain and the Empire, 1660–1840* (Cambridge 2004), p. 5. However, while agreeing that 'practices of empire and nation-state building…made possible the invention and representation of categories of collective identity' (p. 7), I consider these processes not to be abstractions. They had human faces. Individuals and groups, even colonized peoples, had some agency before and alongside the behemoth of 'modernity'.

12. A convenient summary of theoretical options is Stone, *The Family*, pp. 254–6.

13. It is not known what Blechynden was translating for Sonnerat, then in Calcutta. His celebrated *Journey to the East Indies and China* was published in 1782.

14. Blechynden spent a long time translating Bernard Forest de Belidor's *L'Architecture hydraulique* (1737–53), and in common with other architects of his day admired the neo-classical theories and works of Andrea Palladio (1518–1580); see also Chapter 1, n21. For George Louis de Buffon (1707–1788), see Chapter 1, n24.

15. See Chapter 5, n2, and also, on controversy about the social meanings of language that 'naturally engendered self-consciousness', Peter Burke, 'Language and Anti-language in Early Modern Italy', *History Workshop Journal*, vol. 11, no. 1, p. 24; for historiographical discussion, Melissa Calaresu, Filippo de Vivo and Jean-Paul Rubiés (eds.), *Exploring Cultural History: Essays in Honour of Peter Burke* (Farnham 2010); and on exploring relations between rhetorical codes and mental processes, ibid., p. 3.

16. David Riesman, *The Lonely Crowd* (New Haven 1961; abridged edn), p. 44; quoted by Mcfarlane, *Josselin*, p. 5, and Stone, *The Family*, p. 153. Mcfarlane, following Riesman, attributes the growth in diary writing from the late sixteenth century to religious introspection, household accounting, changes from oral to literary culture, and changes in education.

17. If this is part of their early history, such attitudes have a long subsequent career, such as in Foucault and those influenced by him, including sociologists. For example, Nikolas Rose, *Governing the Soul: the Shaping of the Private Self* (London 1990), takes up connections between psychology and politics: that is, between the creation of self (forms of subjectivity), self-regulation, and governability.

18. For related but different accounts of identity, nationality, and mixed race, see Ann Laura Stoler, 'Sexual Affronts and Racial Frontiers: European Identities and the Cultural Politics of Exclusion in Colonial Southeast Asia', in *Comparative Studies in Society and History*, vol. 34, no. 3 (1992), pp. 514–51, or Frederick Cooper and Stoler (eds), *Tensions of Empire: Colonial Cultures in a Bourgeois World* (Berkeley 1997). Stoler, *Carnal Knowledge*, discusses the education of children to resist 'degraded environments' (p. 120).

19.    RB, 15, 19–20, and 22 November 1804. On Brittridge: RB, 20 August 1805.

20.    Cf. Epigraph and n12 to Chapter 8.

21.    RB, 6 May 1797. Perhaps this was Dr Hugh Smith, inventor of the 'bubby pot' (1770), a device for feeding liquid to infants.

22.    Dorothy Fugueira, 'Civilization and the Problems of Race: Portuguese and Italian Travel Narratives of India', in Balachandra Rajan and Elizabeth Sauer, *Imperialism: Historical and Literary Investigations, 1500–1900* (New York and Basingstoke 2004).

23.    On Fanny: RB: 15, 19, and 23 October 1793. On Cleland: RB, 28 August 1793.

24.    On Ball: RB, 30 November 1798 and 16 August 1801. On Tiretta: RB, 4 and 9 February 1799; 19 March 1799; 11 May 1799; and 27 June 1800. Tiretta had the wing removed eventually: RB, 28 June 1800.

25.    RB, 1 and 11 August 1794. Arthur was withdrawn on 7 May 1795.

26.    Stone, *The Family*, pp. 274–5 and 279–80; Julie Peakman, *Mighty Lewd Books: The Development of Pornography in Eighteenth-century England* (Basingstoke 2003), chapters 6 and 7.

27.    On Charlotte: RB, 7 July 1797; on the schoolboys: RB, 1 June 1799; and on Harriet: RB, 6 July 1810.

28.    Mark Harrison, *Climates and Constitutions: Health, Race, Environment and British Imperialism in India, 1600–1850* (New Delhi 1999), especially pp. 11–18.

29.    See Robert Young, *Colonial Desire: Hybridity in Theory, Culture and Race* (London and New York 1995). Noting that extreme polygenicists predicted infertility and, when that was found to be obviously false, degeneration (pp. 6–19), Young argues that 'none was so demonized [in the nineteenth century] as those of mixed race' (p. 180). His examples include (chapter 3) Matthew Arnold's belief in the natural superiority of English ('Semitico-Saxon') culture, a concept Young regards as 'interwined' with race. However, evidence on 'demonization' is not conclusive. Gobineau (chapter 4) theorized on the decline of civilizations but also their mutual incommunicability, and therefore thought 'miscegenation' could be beneficial for the 'lower' party: Peter Robb (ed.), *The Concept of Race in South Asia* (New Delhi 1995), introduction. Young says little about India, but quotes (p. 143) a similar suggestion from W.J. Moore, *Health in the Tropics* (1862): as English settlement was ruled out, the mixed races might take over instead. At the personal level (Blechynden's family and friends), reality was more complex than theory, but there *were* very disadvantageous changes for those unable to 'escape' their mixed race as the Blechyndens did. Eurasians were found special niches in colonial employment (secretariats, railways), often at the cost of being stereo-

typed and derided. Change came as identities were redefined by racist theory and practice in India and worldwide.

30.   RB, 12 February 1795.

31.   Robert to James Kyd, 28 February 1773, in Kyd, *A Short Account of Colonel Kyd, the founder of the Royal Botanic Garden, Calcutta* (Calcutta 1893).

32.   RB, 30 January 1801; 24 February 1801; 15 January 1802; 17 and 26 February 1802; and 5 March 1802.

33.   Captain J.G. Stedman, *Narrative of a Five Years' Expedition against the Revolted Negroes of Surinam ... 1772, to 1777* (London 1796), vol.1, pp. 99–105; vol. 2, pp. 70–1, 81–4, 364, 371–9, and 395.

34.   Mrs Craik [Dinah Maria Mulock], *John Halifax, Gentleman* [1857] (London and Glasgow, nd), pp. 16–17 and 513.

35.   David Ricardo, *On the Principles of Political Economy and Taxation* (1817), argued that agrarian rents represented the natural excess in production from 'the original and indestructible powers' (ch. 2) of (superior) soils and conditions, over and above prevailing returns on labour and capital. For an account of the anti-aristocratic stance among Utilitarians, see Javed Majeed, *Ungoverned Imaginings: James Mill's The History of British India and Orientalism* (Oxford 1992).

36.   I relied on Joe Lockard (http://soc.berkeley.edu/~lockard), citing George P. Davies, Catherine Porter, and Thackeray's letters. Some earlier commentators found Thackeray not to be racially biased, citing the character of Gumbo in *The Virginians*: see George Saintsbury's introduction, Oxford Thackeray edition, n.d.

37.   Stone, *The Family*, chapter 6 , p. 151 (the growth of affective individualism and its broader intellectual and social context).

38.   Christopher Hawes, *Poor Relations: The Making of a Eurasian Community in British India, 1773–1833* (Richmond, Surrey 1996), pp. 142–6.

## NOTES TO CHAPTER 9

1.   Jane Austen, *Sense and Sensibility* (1811), vol. 2, chapter 12.

2.   See http://www.blechynden.co.uk.

3.   Nirad C. Chaudhuri, *Autobiography of an Unknown Indian* (London 1951).

4.   Roger Smith, 'Self-reflection and the Self' in Roy Porter (ed.), *Rewriting the Self: Histories from the Renaissance to the Present*, p. 56.

5.   This list partly defines the range of what I mean by 'everyday'—not quite as in Harry Harootunian, *History's Disquiet: Modernity, Cultural Practice, and the Question of Everyday Life* (New York 2000), related to industrialized cities and capitalism and to 'a unified experience of modernity', though I share

his disquiet at the one-time over-confidence of quantitative social history and at adapting (imitating or familiarizing) Euro-American concepts to analyse Asian societies (pp. 4–19).

6.   See Sylvana Tomaselli, 'Death and Rebirth in the Eighteenth Century', in Porter (ed.), *Rewriting the Self*, pp. 91–2.

7.   The suggestion is that Descartes separated mind and soul; John Locke explained the mind as being formed by remembered experience constituting the person; David Hume, while claiming memory did not create so much as discover human nature (that is, 'natural' passions and mutual sympathy, or morality), laid stress upon human development or rational improvement, concerned lest personality be thought a mere sum of impressions. Kathleen Wilson in *The Island Race: Englishness, Empire and Gender in the Eighteenth Century* (London and New York 2003) emphasizes Hume's assertion of the invariability of human nature in the *Treatise* and the *subsequent* questioning of this idea. Arguably, the influence of experience, imagination, and thought upon actions and beliefs was already central to the *Treatise*. By the same token, common experiences produced national identity. Wilson also asserts that Georgians tended not to assess themselves internally but through 'behavior, social position and reputation', though anachronistic psychological interpretation might be useful nonetheless (p. 2). Not sure of this distinction between internal and external identities, I seek instead (also in Robb, *Sex and Sensibility*) to disentangle and relate the internals of feeling and morality to the externals of reputation, conduct, and professional or social standing. Wilson says that 'identities were, and are, inextricably bound to a historical social order and both concretized and challenged through practices of everyday life'; but that though 'performative' to that extent, they could nevertheless pose 'as both universal and irreducible, an essence of the individual or national character' (p. 3). This chapter, recognizing that definitions were in flux, seeks aspects of the colonial experience that shaped Britishness.

8.   Notably in *An Introduction to the Principle of Morals and Legislation* (1780–9), Jeremy Bentham dismissed natural law and emphasized human actions, and treated concepts such as 'rights' as meaningful fictions that could be understood by 'paraphrasis' (in explanatory sentences rather than abstract words), by sense not 'sounds', and reason not 'caprice', and that were justified not by morality but by consequences, his Utilitarian principle of maximizing pleasure and minimizing pain.

9.   John Mullan, *Sentiment and Sociability: The Language of Feeling in the Eighteenth Century* (Oxford, 1988); Ann Jessie Van Sant, *Eighteenth-Century Sensibility and the Novel: The Senses in Social Context* (Cambridge 1993), p. xii; G.J. Barker-Benfield, *The Culture of Sensibility: Sex and Society in Eighteenth-century Britain* (Chicago 1992), p. xvii. See also above, n7.

10.   John Ruskin, *Unto this Last* (1862), essay 3.

11.   Smith, 'Self-reflection', p. 56.

12.   Stuart B. Schwartz (ed.), *Implicit Understandings: Observing, Report-ing and Reflecting on Encounters between Europeans and Other Peoples in the Early Modern Era* (Cambridge 1995). I use this phrase rather than insisting only on misunderstanding between cultures.

13.   Greg Dening, *Islands and Beaches: Discourse on a Silent Land* (Honolulu 1980); see also Schwartz (ed.), *Implicit Understanding*, pp. 2 and 169. Maya Jasanoff, *Edge of Empire: Conquests and Collecting in the East 1750–1850* (London 2005), p. 7, concludes from 'stories of imperial collectors' that 'the process of cultural encounter involved crossing and mixing, as well as separation and division'.

14.   Richard Helgerson, 'Camões, Hakluyt and the Voyages of Two Nations', in Nicholas B. Dirks (ed.), *Colonialism and Culture* (Ann Arbor 1992), pp. 27–63.

15.   See Schwartz (ed.), *Implicit Understanding*, chapters 1 and 2: Seymour Phillips, 'The Outer World of the European Middle Ages', and John B. Friedman, 'Cultural Conflicts in Medieval World Maps'. The Castilian conquest of the Canaries in the late fifteenth century is sometimes taken as the model for this process.

16.   Journal (1780). On British attitudes to Europeans and Catholicism: Linda Colley, *Britons: Forging the Nation, 1707–1837* (New Haven & London 1992).

17.   *The Travels of Dean Mahomet: An Eighteenth-Century Journey through India* (ed.) Michael H. Fisher (Berkeley 1997), p. 58, referring to 1772.

18.   On Corbett: RB, 14 December 1793. C.A. Bayly, *Empire and Information: Intelligence Gathering and Social Communication in India, 1780–1870* (Cambridge 1996); Charles Moore, *The Sheriffs of Fort William from 1775 to 1920* (Calcutta 1921), pp. 9–10; *Guidebook for the Indian Science Congress* (Calcutta 1928); Mukherjee, 'Forever England'.

19.   RB, 2 February 1795. Helgerson, 'Camões, Hakluyt', pp. 45–6 and 62.

20.   John L. and Jean Comaroff, *Of Revelation and Revolution, Vol. 2: The Dialectics of Modernity on a South African Frontier* (Chicago 1997), p. 6.

21.   See Sudipta Sen, 'Passages of Authority: Rulers, Traders and Market-places in Bengal and Banaras, 1700–1750', *Calcutta Historical Journal*, vol. 7, no. 1 (1995), on the plurality and dispersed control of precolonial markets and market taxes. He adopts the term 'heterotopia' (in a somewhat variant sense), implying that alternative modes of classification applied more broadly than in the spheres of market, polity, and myth with which he is concerned. But he sees Company rule as a watershed. It was, eventually, in hindsight; but with con-tinuities, as many stress: in my case here, in Robb, *Ancient Rights and Future*

*Comfort* (Richmond 1996) and *The Evolution of British Policy towards Indian Politics* (New Delhi 1992), especially chapter 5.

22.   Edward Said, *Culture and Imperialism* (New York 1993). This is also the epigraph to *The Travels of Dean Mahomet: An Eighteenth-Century Journey through India*, ed. Michael H. Fisher (Berkeley 1997).

23.   Reginald Heber, *Narrative of a Journey through the Upper Provinces of India, from Calcutta to Bombay, 1824–1825* ... (2nd edn; London 1828), p. 4.

24.   Marchioness of Dufferin and Ava, *Our Viceregal Life in India* ... *1884–1888* (1889; London 1890), pp. 10 and 34–8.

25.   For example, S.N. Mukherjee, *Citizen Historian: Explorations in Historiography* (Delhi 1996), pp. 143–5.

26.   On a version of the following in *Modern Asian Studies*, see Acknowledgments.

27.   Tom Tomlinson reminded me that this caveat was necessary.

28.   P.J. Marshall, *East Indian Fortunes* (Oxford 1976).

29.   Huw Bowen claims members of the Company's permanent staff in London followed set procedures and, by drafting despatches and repeating certain key words of good governance, set an agenda for the Company even in faraway India: 'C.H. Philips and the East India Company', lecture at the Royal Asiatic Society, London, 16 April 2009. The same institutional trajectory was followed in India despite manifest corruption and ad hoc vagaries of bureaucratic structures, practice, and finance. For a longer perspective on the rule of law as a liberal foil to temptations and practices of despotism, see Thomas R. Metcalf, *Ideologies of the Raj* (*New Cambridge History of India*, III. 4, Cambridge 1995), especially ch. 2; and Peter Robb, *Liberalism, Modernity, and the Nation* (New Delhi 2007). Metcalf describes a later nineteenth-century creation and ordering of 'difference' despite legal and intellectual pretensions to universalism, all clearly having considerable prehistory as well, as argued in this book and Robb, *Sex and Sensibility*.

30.   It was linked to the separation of Crown and Parliament and to the slow growth of civil government, with milestones in the sixteenth and seventeenth centuries, and before, as well as in the eighteenth. Pepys's diary and career illustrate the point. In India, a notion of service was not unique to European administration, but could not advance far until power was objectified in the state as opposed to the ruler's person, whether Company satrap, nawab, or zamindar.

31.   This will seem the direct opposite of Dirks, *Scandal of Empire*, claiming that scandal not only (as is true) became 'attached to Indian customs rather than British activities', but also 'normalized in the assumptions and categories of modernity itself'. It is not obvious what the latter means in practice. Dirks goes on: 'Scandals do often lead to reforms', usually to protect scandal's agents rather than its victims, permit the normalizing of excesses, and transform the

venality of private individuals into the national interest (pp. 23–31). My disagreement, if there is one, is only over the extent to which colonial attempts to create a sense of public duty and to 'do good' were *merely* a camouflage of imperial greed, or (while being that) also a restraint and an influence upon policy.

32. AB, 30 May 1809. Laws and officials existed to maintain roads: Wellesley, on 16 June 1803, had called for investigations and measures to improve Calcutta's drainage and public hygiene; the Lottery Committee was set up to effect improvements; but 'no bold and comprehensive plan was carried out', so that in Calcutta (as in London, before remedies were found), there were 'closely built, ill-ventilated dens', 'accumulated deposits of filth and rubbish', 'tainted pools and putrid drains', 'a remarkable complication of prejudicial influences', a 'greater and more appalling array of fatal causes' than in any other city, and an 'unparalleled extent of general sickness': 'Sanitary Condition of Calcutta', *Calcutta Review*, vol. V (January–June 1846) (Calcutta 1846), pp. 373–95, quoting 'Report of the Committee … for the establishment of a Fever Hospital and for inquiring into Local Management and Taxation in Calcutta' (1839), J.R. Martin's 'Notes on the Medical Topography of Calcutta', and Rev. Dr Duff's sermon at the Free Church of Scotland, Calcutta (1844).

33. AB, 22 April 1807. This account is based on Arthur's diary, but the topics are also very fully covered in Blechynden's otherwise more fragmentary diary. Blechynden details the problems and corruption, and what he felt was undeserved criticism of him for the resultant shocking state of the town, against a backdrop of his long experience and awareness of how procedures should work and be improved. Arthur gives more immediate impressions of principled indignation in both father and son.

34. AB, 16 July 1811 and 7 July 1812. His later reputation, less than deserved, was as a reformer of the city's infrastructure and governance.

35. AB, 8 October 1808; 22 April 1809; 1 and 19 May 1809; 1 December 1809; 14 July 1810; 3 April 1811; 11 and 26 May 1811; 1 and 15–18 July 1811; 2 January 1812; 6, 9, and 18 July 1812.

36. AB, 7–9 July 1812; Long, *Calcutta*, p. 209.

37. AB, 19 May 1809; 14 July 1810; 2 January 1812; and 6 July 1812. Blaquiere's allegedly corrupt friendship, not always obvious in practice, was with his former schoolfellow, Dowdeswell.

38. AB, 22 July 1813. RB, 18 and 23 June 1811; 1 October 1811; 13 December 1811; 16–17 January 1812; 2 and 7 May 1812. On the 24 Parganas incidents: RB, 29 March 1813 and 25 September 1813. Strictly speaking, Calcutta's roads were now under the jurisdiction of the Commissioners of Police, not the justices or magistrates. (Eliot, expecting to have the general superintendence of the Police Office, decided that he had better be a Commissioner too in that case: RB, 13 June 1811). Much business was conducted

informally, without written orders; different offices were held by the same people. Eliot was very active before officially appointed: RB, 7, 11, and 13 June 1811; 6 and 11–12 July 1811.

39.   RB, 4–5 July 1810 and 18 September 1810. AB, 4 July 1810.

40.   For example, Colley, *Briton*, pp. 169–70, and the Cambridge prize essays of 1804, with topics on 'civilizing' Indians or the divine purpose of empire.

41.   John Malcolm, *Sketch of the Political History of India* … (2nd edn, London, 1811). For the following discussion, see pp. 4, 9, 458–62, 468–75, 478, and 512–30.

42.   Balachandra Rajan and Elizabeth Sauer, *Imperialism: Historical and Literary Investigations, 1500–1900* (New York and Basingstoke 2004), p. 262. This differs from earlier suggestions. Kate Teltscher, *India Inscribed: European and British Writing on India, 1600–1800* (New Delhi 1995), p. 62, suggests the gaining of colonial power produced a 'more precarious sense of self'. I propose a different trajectory and explanation. A second idea is that India 'played no central part in fashioning the distinctive qualities of English civilization': E.T. Stokes, *The English Utilitarians and India* (Oxford 1959), introduction. But Sudipta Sen, *Distant Sovereignty: National Imperialism and the Origins of British India* (New York 2002) (pp. xxv–xxvii on Stokes), notes the link between character and duty in the ideal imperial official (pp. 44–9); provides a rich, wide-ranging account of patriarchy and its effects (chapter 4); and reviews the concept of just rule and the European fear of degeneracy (mainly in chapter 5). It ends on gaps in historiography rather than wider origins for a developing British identity (pp. 151–5). Also see Ann Laura Stoler, *Race and the Education of Desire: Foucault's History of Sexuality, and the Colonial Order of Things* (Durham 1995), p. 79: 'Colonialism was not a secure bourgeois project. It was not only about the importation of middle-class sensibilities to the colonies, but about the *making* of them.' For a later period, Jose Harris, *Private Lives, Public Spirit: Britain 1870–1914* (Oxford 1993; London 1994), p. 6, sees empire's impact as favouring 'hierarchy, militarism, "frontier mentality", administrative rationality, masculine civic virtue …', contrary to domestic influences, including egalitarianism and consumerism.

43.   Joseph Conrad, *Heart of Darkness* [1902], in *Heart of Darkness and Typhoon* (London 1976), pp. 12–13.

44.   B.S. Cohn, 'The British in Benares: A Nineteenth Century Colonial Society', *Comparative Studies in Society and History*, vol. IV, no. 2 (January 1962), p. 199.

45.   'Poem by Thomson': RB, 23 December 1801, an extract from James Thomson (1700–48), *The Seasons* (1730), 'Winter: Hardship and Benevolence'. See above, on 'sentiment'.

# Frequently Cited Works

*For Blechynden papers, including the diaries of Richard and Arthur Blechynden, cited as 'RB' and 'AB', see the Preface.*

Banerjee, Sumanta, *The Parlour and the Streets: Elite and Popular Culture in Nineteenth Century Calcutta* (Calcutta 1989).

Blechynden, Richard, 'Journal of the Capture of the Ship *Godfrey* and the Sufferings of One of Her Unfortunate Young Officers, Written by Himself', Add. Mss. 45578, British Library (cited as Journal 1780).

————, 'Journal of a Voyage from England towards Madras and Bengal in the Ship Deptford...', 1781–2, Add. Mss. 45578, British Library (cited as Journal 1781).

Busteed, H.E., *Echoes from Old Calcutta, being Chiefly Reminiscences of the Days of Warren Hastings, Francis and Impey* (Calcutta 1888; 2nd edn).

Chatterjee, Partha (ed.), *Texts of Power: Emerging Disciplines in Colonial Bengal* (New Delhi 1995).

Chattopadhyay, Swati, *Representing Calcutta: Modernity, Nationalism and the Colonial Uncanny* (London 2005).

Chaudhuri, Sukanta (ed.), *Calcutta, the Living City—Vol. 1: The Past* (New Delhi 1990).

Colley, Linda, *Britons: Forging the Nation, 1707–1837* (New Haven and London 1992).

Dirks, Nicholas B., *The Scandal of Empire: India and the Creation of Imperial Britain* (Cambridge, MA 2006).

———— (ed.), *Colonialism and Culture* (Ann Arbor 1992).

Finn, Margot, 'Slaves out of Context: Domestic Slavery and the Anglo-Indian Family', *Transactions of the Royal Historical Society* (Sixth Series), vol. 19, 2009.

Ghosh, Suresh Chandra, *The Social Condition of the British Community in Bengal, 1757–1800* (Leiden 1970).

Harootunian, Harry, *History's Disquiet: Modernity, Cultural Practice, and the Question of Everyday Life* (New York 2000).

Kyd, *A Short Account of Colonel Kyd, the founder of the Royal Botanic Garden, Calcutta* (Calcutta 1893), reprinted from vol. IV of the *Annals of the Garden.*

Long, James, *Calcutta and its Neighbourhood: History of Calcutta and its People from 1690–1857* (ed.) Sankar Sen Gupta (Calcutta 1974).

Mcfarlane, Alan, *The Family Life of Ralph Josselin: A Seventeenth-Century Clergyman* (Cambridge 1970).

Moore, Charles, *The Sheriffs of Fort William from 1775 to 1920* (Calcutta 1921).

Mukherjee, Rudrangshu, '"Forever England": British Life in Old Calcutta', in Chaudhuri (ed.), *Calcutta.*

Phillimore, R.H., *Historical Records of the Survey of India, Vol. III: 1815–1830* (Dehra Dun 1954).

Porter, Roy (ed.), *Rewriting the Self: Histories from the Renaissance to the Present* (London and New York 1997).

Ray, A.K., *A Short History of Calcutta Town and Suburbs* (reprint from *Census of India 1901*, vol.VII, pt. I [ed.] N.R. Ray [Calcutta 1982]).

Schwartz, Stuart B. (ed.), *Implicit Understandings: Observing, Reporting and Reflecting on Encounters between Europeans and Other Peoples in the Early Modern Era* (Cambridge 1995).

Shaw, Graham, *The South Asia and Burma Retrospective Bibliography* (London 1987).

Smith, Roger, 'Self-reflection and the Self' in Porter (ed.), *Rewriting the Self.*

Sreemani, Sumitra, *Anatomy of a Colonial Town: Calcutta, 1756–1794* (Calcutta 1994).

Stoler, Ann Laura, *Carnal Knowledge and Imperial Power: Race and the Intimate in Colonial Rule* (Berkeley 2002).

Stone, Lawrence, *The Family, Sex and Marriage in England, 1500–1800* (London: 1976; abridged edn, 1979).

Taylor, Stephen, *The Caliban Shore: The Fate of the Grosvenor Castaways* (London 2004).

Webster, Anthony, *The Richest East India Merchant: The Life and Business of John Palmer of Calcutta, 1767–1836* (Woodbridge 2007).

Wilson, Kathleen, *The Island Race: Englishness, Empire and Gender in the Eighteenth Century* (London and New York 2003).

———— (ed.), *A New Imperial History: Culture, Identity and Modernity in Britain and the Empire, 1660–1840* (Cambridge 2004).

Yule, Henry, and A.C. Burrell, *Hobson-Jobson: The Anglo Indian Dictionary* (1886, 1902; Ware 1996).

# Index